M000304792

Fire and Water

Fire and Water

Awakening the Dragon Within

by

Hydee Tehana

Trinity Rose Productions, LLC

Kealakekua, Hawaii

Fire and Water

Awakening the Dragon Within

Copyright © 2020 Hydee Tehana

All rights reserved. No part of this book may be used or reproduced by any means, graphic, electronic, or mechanical, including photocopying, recording, taping or by any information storage retrieval system without the written permission of the publisher except in the case of brief quotations embodied in critical articles and reviews.

Hydee Tehana's books may be ordered through booksellers or Amazon.com.

Trinity Rose Productions, LLC
PO Box 1041
Kealakekua, HI 96750 USA

HydeeTehana.com
Hhtehana888@protonmail.com
ISBN: 978-1-7341995-7-4 (pbk)
ISBN: 978-1-7341995-2-9 (eBook)
ISBN: 978-1-7341995-9-8 (hbk)

Front cover design by Jean-Luc Bozzoli

Eyewithin.com

Back cover image by Lisa Denning

Lisadenning.com

This book is dedicated...

To all firefighters and first responders everywhere. Thank you for your service.

To all the guys I worked with on the fire department both past, present, and future. Thanks for all the fun and making me feel like one of the guys.

To Joe for all the support and love you showed me throughout my life.

To my parents for teaching me so many soul life lessons.

To Tommy and Alex for waking me up when my soul was asleep.

To Lisa, my friend, partner, playmate, lover, soul sister, and wife, who continues to awaken my soul on a daily basis as we navigate this river of life.

Thank you.
I love you all deeply.

ACKNOWLEDGMENTS

I have great appreciation for the forces of nature which include Earth, fire, water, air, and ether. I am the embodiment of every one of you. Thank you for teaching and reawakening me once again to your presence within the stillness. I was so connected to you as a child and spoke with you until somehow, as modern life happens, I lost my connection with you. This is really my connection to Source and all the great secrets of the universe. I will never be disconnected from you again. Thank you for awakening the dragon within.

AUTHOR'S NOTE

This book is an autobiographical work and all stories are true. To honor their privacy, some names of individuals and a few identifying details have been changed as with emergency calls, too. The name of the fire department, city, and other identifying details have been changed to a fictious name of Sparrow City and department. Conversations that were had and quoted are close as many were taken from my journals. They are not always exact as memory does fade, yet the intention is true. The grammar and writing is unique to my style and may not always follow the rules...

Listen to the wind, it talks.

Listen to the silence, it speaks.

Listen to your heart, it knows.

~Native American proverb

CONTENTS

Introduction

PART ONE:

INTRODUCTION

I have always loved to write and as I told my stories over the years, many people would comment telling me that I should write a book. I realized that I really wrote this book for me and for expanding my own consciousness, yet I feel that I would like to share it with the world. Please enjoy the journey of awakening the dragon within!

This book can be read as a whole or as a few chapters at a time…it's really up to you. The chapters attempt to go in order of how things happened, but some reflect back upon an early time in my life especially when I describe emergency calls I responded on. I went on thousands of emergency calls, and in this book, I often tell stories of calls that made me open myself to a bigger part of life, but I also talk about calls that made me laugh or were just different. I don't go into much blood and gore as that is not what this book is about.

There may be some crudeness, but you will find that I evolve through much of that in the second half of the book, as my consciousness evolves, which is why there is a part one and part two of this book. Part one talks about my life in the fire department and stories of how I grew up. There are many lessons that I learned through profound experiences including the exploration of death and dying. In the second part of the book, I explore experiences that most of society doesn't talk about like extraterrestrials, behind the veil, sexuality, past lives, Mother Nature, and lots of other fascinating stuff.

I take you through my journey…my transformation, really, of how I went from being unconscious in this life to becoming conscious to the real meaning and purpose (in my view) of what life is about. This is my reflection of what I learned working as a firefighter in the fire department for over twenty years and how my questioning of life expanded even more during these years as it just didn't make sense to me.

My dad told me when I was young that I needed to be successful and be the boss at whatever job I chose. Somehow, I interpreted that if I did this, then I would "be happy." I went beyond that and got the husband, two kids, a big house, money, and became a fire captain. Yet, something huge was missing in my life and I just couldn't put my finger on it. It was the elephant in the room and I began to have my own spiritual crisis!

In the fire department, I saw things that most people never see or have to deal with in their lives. I witnessed the chaos of the human condition in many forms as well as witnessing lots of death and dying. I explore death and dying deeply in this book as it brought up many questions for me. I would sometimes feel, see, or hear the dead as they crossed over. This, in itself, made me reflect and question life often about what we are REALLY doing here and what happens when we die.

My life has been one of questioning this reality and rebelling against the system in place. I questioned anything that didn't make sense to me and wondered "why" we did things the way we did. Who decided this is the way life is? The fire department was great for questioning everything as most firefighters don't like change much. Well, most people don't like change either! So, in comes me…a rebel at heart and system buster (but even these are just labels).

There have been so many lessons that I have learned in this lifetime that it feels like I have lived at least twenty lifetimes in this one life. My memories as a child and what I knew of the bigger picture were shut down from about the age of seven until I had children at the age of thirty-two. Having children re-awakened me to the deeper meaning of life and I began to question everything that I had built around me. Seeing life through their eyes reminded me of all I had forgotten. You may even feel a difference in the book after I had children.

In the fire department, we worked twenty-four hour shifts and I had "downtime" when we weren't running calls or training. I chose to read in the evenings instead of watching television or movies. This "downtime" allowed me to relax and reflect where I would often journal as well. Going through EMDR (Eye Movement Desensitization and Reprocessing) therapy helped release my need for adrenaline rushes and allowed me to be more open to exploring consciousness, wondering what else is out there.

As I learned more about the brain, I found that our brains go through cycles every two hours. We have frequencies going from beta to alpha to theta to delta and back to beta where the whole cycle starts over again. Typically, in our Western civilization, we stay in beta most of our day as most of us are working eight or more hours a day. Beta is an externally focused consciousness, so if we don't go into the other frequencies during the day, we pass out in our beds at night and have to "catch up" in alpha, theta, and delta all night.

I bring this up as in the alpha state, we reflect and relax. In theta, we daydream, imagine, and create. In delta, we nap or sleep and this is where we repair our bodies and cells. If we only get to do this on the weekends, our consciousness often stays stuck in beta to only look out at the external reality which we all created together. We don't daydream and imagine what we want anymore. How do we expand consciousness if we are always working? Who designed this system?

I am grateful for the fire department for when we had downtime, I relaxed and reflected often. I daydreamed a lot. We also took naps, which I remember thinking was absurd when I saw this my first year on the fire department, but I came to embrace naptime just like when we were little. Many times though, we had emergency calls which interrupted this brain wave cycle. When I moved to a slightly slower station, I had more time to go through this cycle instead of having twelve to fifteen calls a shift at the busier stations.

In this book, I reflect on the other side of the veil as I realized that I was always guided and protected. Every one of us has an inner teacher, spirit guide, angels, or whatever you want to call them that are guiding us. Always. Reminding me that I am not alone in this universe or even on this planet expanded my perspective of life. I was going through a huge transformation almost daily and Mother Nature was showing me the way to awakening the dragon within myself. To me, the dragon represents a reconnecting to my inner power.

There are so many ways to expand our consciousness if we are ready to, but many of us don't want to change. It can be frightening to change, as it takes a strong person to move through this fear of change into the unknown. When we heal, we expand our consciousness. We can heal and explore consciousness through breath, sound, shamanism, therapy, dolphins, whales, sexuality, psychedelics, past lives, energy healing, extraterrestrials, near death experiences, Mother Nature, having children, etc...

If we look at the relationships around us and our roles in them, we can learn so much. We are not victims and really, we are all playing out roles in each other's movies. Some of the people we have the hardest time with are really those that chose a hard role to play when we were on the other side. We can change the costumes and script anytime we aren't having fun. We are the STARS of our own movies and creating them whether we are consciously or unconsciously creating them. It is up to YOU as to how you want to play this game of life. What are you creating?

If you want to dive in and read this book, GO FOR IT as there is much deeper meaning behind all the stories. It is really a multidimensional book depending on your perspective. The stories may bring stuff up for you as you read them, but just know, that is for you to look at, transform, grow, and expand your consciousness if you chose.. It takes a strong person to look inside themselves and to "know thyself!"

Take what resonates and discard the rest. It is my deep honor to share my story. May you enjoy this amazing journey and remember!

PART ONE

CHAPTER 1
INFERNO TO WATERFALL

I am not afraid. I was born to do this.
~Joan of Arc

I can't see anything.
It's pitch black and extremely hot.

I put my hand in front of my face and I can't see my hand. It sounds like a roaring jet engine all around me and I feel as if I am in a giant oven being cooked at over 1000 degrees Fahrenheit.

I grasp the firehose tighter knowing that this is my lifeline out of this burning building. My engineer, Nick, is in front of me and he has the nozzle. We have gone up two flights of stairs and around a corner. We are now stopped as we had been crawling on our hands and knees and I have been pulling hose for Nick.

I wonder why we stopped. Neither of us can see anything and we are trying to get to the seat of the fire to put it out. I am listening, feeling, and my mind begins to chatter.

I realize that my ears are burning.
Really burning.
Shit.
Did I forget to put my hood on?

I check to make sure my hood is on and covering my ears.
It is on and is covering my ears!

Oh damn.
That means it is really, really fucking hot in here.

This is what the old time firefighters said was a telltale sign for them to get out of a burning building…right before a flashover. They used to not wear hoods because their burning ears would tell them when to leave a dangerous situation.

I remember from the fire academy…a flashover occurs when the contents of a building are heated to ignition temperature and everything spontaneously ignites. Basically, everything implodes with fire.

I am in this building and being heated to ignition temperature!

Suddenly, my captain, Adam, grabs my shoulder and he is next to me. He yells in my ear, "It's too fucking hot in here! My ears are burning! We need to get out of here!"

He tells Nick the same thing and we turn around leaving the firehose there. We attempt to follow the hoseline outside to safety. I am following the hoseline and Nick out. I keep going on my hands and knees and something all of a sudden doesn't feel right.

I think I took a wrong turn.
I still can't see anything.
Where did they go?

Somehow, I missed the stairs we came up on, lost the firehose, and lost Nick and Adam.

Damn.
Where am I?

I realize that I was crawling for too long and the stairs should have been on my right. I now have another wall on my right.

Something instinctively tells me to turn around and feel with my left hand. I feel like something is guiding me. I crawl and feel. Suddenly, the wall stops and there is an opening.

Stairs!
Fuck yes!
What a relief.

I crawl down the first flight of stairs and I see firehoses. I stand up and continue to walk down the stairs.

Just then, Adam and Nick are coming back up.

"Oh, thank God," says Adam. "We thought we lost you. We were just coming back up to find you."

So, let me back up a bit and fill you in on this story before I continue on…because the fire is still raging!

It's 1997, I am new on the job and fresh out of the fire academy by about four months. I am just so excited to be a firefighter/paramedic and to do a good job during my probationary year. This is my dream job.

I work with Sparrow City Fire Department which is in Southern California and has a population of around 100,000 people. It is on the west coast and also sprawled east into the flatlands and mountains. It is an old city started in the 1800's with both old and new buildings. It has the threat of brush fires since it is in the hills as well.

I am eager for my first big fire and just emergency calls in general. I am also a paramedic and a rookie firefighter as well as a woman in this traditional job of male firefighters. This is a "man's" job according to most of the world.

And I know this is exactly where I am supposed to be in this world as it is the perfect job for me.

I am twenty-six years old and feeling on top of the world.

So, this particular winter morning, we have rescue training where we are blacking out our masks in our full turnout gear and searching for other firefighters to rescue. We work as a crew of three to rescue one firefighter.

Just as my crew and I finish our rescue of another firefighter, an emergency radio dispatch goes out stating a large fire in the downtown area. We aren't far away and we can see the header of smoke coming from a building.

Big, black smoke...

I am so excited that I can hardly contain myself!
I am such an adrenaline junkie.

"I wanna go to the fire!" I think to myself.
"Come on...dispatch us, please!"

We are in training, so even though we would be the closest engine to get there, we are training. Being in training, we are the last engine to be called for emergencies, usually.

Damn!

The smoke is getting bigger and bigger.
It's a big, fucking fire.
Big!

Dispatch is upgrading from a first alarm fire to a second alarm fire and then, to a third alarm fire. More and more fire engines and trucks! Our training captain sees how big this fire is and puts all three engines that were in training there available to be called into the fire.

YES!!!

Dispatch picks us up quickly and dispatches us to the fire.
We are on our way!

Woohoo!

We get dressed in our turnout gear quickly as everyone is excited to go to the fire. I am dressed and ready really fast, but then, I notice my captain. He has seen lots of fire and is taking his time putting on his turnouts.

I am thinking in my head, "Hurry up! Let's go! I wanna go put out the fire!"

He's finally ready. We head to the fire and there are two engines already there. The fire is in the old district of town with buildings over one hundred years old.

It is a two story building where all the businesses are connected to each other along the block. The fire looks like it started on the first floor in a restaurant and moved to the upstairs into a hair salon. It is pumping thick, black smoke out of the buildings.

The first engine company is trying to get into the building when we arrive and we see them head upstairs. We get assigned to back up fire attack which is to back up the first crew that just went into the building.

Sweet!

I jump out of the engine as soon as my engineer pulls the parking brake. I go and open the cabinet on the fire engine that has our SCBA's. I pull one down and put the bottle on my back, so I can breathe inside the building that is on fire.

I meet up with my engineer, Nick, and we head towards the building on fire. Adam, my captain, says that he will meet up with us as he is busy on the radio talking to the incident commander. Nick and I walk up to the first engine that was on scene and pull a firehose off of it. The engineer from that engine charges it with water and we begin walking upstairs into the fire. We will back up the other crew.

Just then, the first crew comes down the stairs. They say that they tried to find the fire, but are unable to. They are out of air and need new air bottles. We continue up the next flight of stairs into the fire.

It's getting hotter and blacker by the second!

We have our hoseline in hand and Nick and I are crawling around in the building on our hands and knees. From the top of the stairs on, we can't see a thing. It is just thick, black smoke from floor to ceiling and it's really hot. We are both breathing air from inside our masks off our SCBA's. If we didn't have the SCBA on, we would breathe superheated air and die.

We move in deeper and deeper into the building towards where we feel the fire is. Nick is in front of me with the nozzle in his hand and stops.

This is my first big fire and I am wondering what he is doing.

This is what happened before I began telling the story at the beginning of this chapter.

So now, I will continue with my story as I reunited with Nick and Adam coming down the stairs…

The three of us head downstairs and outside the building. Thick, black smoke is coming from the windows and the roof. This fire is getting really big, but it hasn't come through the roof yet. We have our truck company on the roof attempting to cut a hole in the roof to ventilate the fire because it is too hot to get crews inside to find the fire.

The captains regroup with the incident commander and figure out our tactics to get a handle on this fire. They decide since it is too hot and the truck company is having a hard time getting a hole cut in the roof, we should break out all the windows to get rid of some of the smoke and heat.

A couple firefighters do this as Nick and I are getting new air bottles. The smoke is now pouring heavily out the windows. I am high on adrenaline and there are firefighters everywhere. Everyone has a job and is doing it. We are told to go back into the building and find the fire since hopefully, there is less smoke and heat in there.

So, Nick and I along with Gary and John (another captain and firefighter) all go back up the stairs, putting on our masks and gloves, heading into the fire.

We had no idea what we were in for.

Gary is in the front leading the way. He is an old, crusty captain with red hair and over twenty-five years of experience. This feisty Irishman can kick anyone's ass even though he is only about 5'6" tall.

Nick is behind him and he is English. He has over twenty years of experience on the fire department and a dry sense of humor. I am behind Nick and John is behind me. John is a new firefighter like me, but has been on the department a year longer than me.

None of us have a hoseline with us as we all left them inside the building. Gary leads the way following the hoses in. I find a nozzle and hoseline right at the top of the stairs and I grab it.

I think to myself, "Never pass this up…it's my lifeline!"

Never a good idea to be inside a fire with no water.

We continue on our hands and knees and Gary and Nick are ahead of me. I can't see them, but I know they are there. I am pulling this hoseline with me and John is behind me. He knows I have the nozzle and is pulling hose with me.

I run into the back of Nick as he is stopped. I wonder if he and Gary need the nozzle that I have. I yell to Nick to see if he needs the nozzle when literally everything turns to light...

Yes, seriously.
Everything is totally light.

I can't figure out what is happening.
I realize from floor to ceiling, everything is on fire!
I'm confused.
Pure fire everywhere I look.

Am I in hell?
Is this what people call "hell?"
Did I die and I am in hell?!
Well, I wouldn't doubt it given my past history!

I think all of this in a split second and something tells me to lie on my back while opening up the nozzle. Fire is everywhere and I am spraying water straight up to the ceiling. I am having a hard time still trying to wrap my brain around this. This is nothing like any of the fires we trained on in the fire academy.

I am fully engulfed in flames!

I have always felt my whole life that I am protected by something bigger than me. This "something" is like my sixth sense. It is screaming at me to get out and back down the stairs.

Letting go of the nozzle, I begin to scramble back the way I came. I can see now and I find the stairs launching myself down them on my belly. I land on top of Nick and John at the bottom of the stairs. We all start laughing as we are in a dog pile!

We get up and our turnouts are not yellow anymore. They are black and steaming. We start to go back down the other flight of stairs when we suddenly realize...

Gary!?

Shit.
Where is he?
He hasn't come out yet.
He was the furthest one in the fire.

The three of us turn and head up the stairs to find him. Just then, Gary comes down the stairs with this pissed off look on his face and his turnout coat still on fire. We put the fire out on his coat.

He rips off his mask and a slur of obscenities come out of his mouth. Gary never likes fire to win. He stomps down the stairs towards the incident commander.

Then it hits me…
We all just survived a flashover!

Holy shit.
We all could have died.
And I am just getting started in this career!

Most firefighters don't survive flashovers. If you get caught in one, you are usually goners.

Maybe we all survived because we weren't that far in the building yet. Breaking out the windows and not having a hole cut in the roof yet, actually gave the fire more air and allowed the conditions of flashover to happen.

As we come down the stairs, we see other firefighters staring at us in amazement. They help us take our gear off and we are told to take a break.

We've, literally, just been through hell.

Well, this is what I was always told hell was like from my parents and the church I went to as a kid.

Burning for eternity?
This never made sense to me.
For real?
Why?
A threat to keeping us in line?
Power trip?

I always wondered if hell was even real or just a made up place to scare people into doing the right thing and believing in God.

Maybe it's just a state of being on Earth as to how you are living?
You are living in either heaven or hell?
An inner state of being?

Anyways, the fire is now coming out of every window and flames shoot out the rooftop!

We go defensive now with this fire as the building is now destroyed by fire. We have hoselines shooting water into the building from every side and above. There are about twenty engine crews and four truck company crews here fighting this fire which adds up to about seventy people or more. Police have the streets shut down and there are people everywhere watching.

Fire crews are also working to keep the businesses on each side of the building on fire from catching fire since they share a common wall. My crew and I get another assignment. We are to keep the businesses from having water damage from all the water we are now spraying into building on fire.

My crew and I are tired.

Our adrenaline rush is gone and Nick and I are spent. We go into an old business that sells office equipment and we are going to cover up what we can to keep it from getting water damage.

We have salvage covers which are really large tarps and we place them over as much as possible in the business. We cover their file cabinets and computers and we are trying to figure out how to shuttle out some of this water coming down from the ceilings. Adam, Nick, and I use ladders and tarps to do this. One of them comes loose and all the water comes straight at me.

I am now soaked and standing under a manmade waterfall!

Well, this seems fitting...

Engulfed in flames to immersed by water all in the same day!
Perhaps some type of transformation took place?!
Something sure wants me here on this planet!
My exploration of what life is all about continues...

CHAPTER 2
WHO I CAME IN AS

Most people consider life a battle, but it's not a battle, it's a game.
~Florence Scovel Shinn

It's funny to think back to how I got here and why I picked the parents that I did. I would have never said that I picked my mother and yet, I have been shown that I fully did.

Crazy.
And I am grateful.

Here is a quick overview of how I grew up…

I was born in Los Angeles, California in the early seventies to two physically and emotionally young people. Beth and Pedro met in Iowa in high school after Castro was sending Cubans to America. They were kinda like Ricky and Lucy from the *I Love Lucy Show* in the fifties.

Except, my mother was not Lucy.
She was evil.
I call her "the devil" based on all my dealings with her.

I know this sounds harsh, but this is my story and feelings.
I wrote this book with integrity speaking my truth from my heart.

Anyways, other than my father being Cuban and my mother being very white, there was no funny episodes going on in my house. I know they were doing the best they knew how. I feel that my mother was trying to play out Lucy and Ricky in her own life, yet she had so much unresolved trauma.

I grew up for the first seven or so years in southern California as it was growing rapidly. We lived in San Diego when the homes were about $20,000. My father was a teacher and my mother stayed home to be with my brother and I.

Now, I shouldn't say my mother was all bad. I do remember her trying to do a good job when I was little. Yet, I had a great love for my father and always wanted to be with him. I felt like my mother never really liked me, but loved my brother. From what I know now is that she is really just traumatized from her childhood.

Issues?
Nah…

As a teenager, I found out that there were lots of issues going on between my parents. They divorced when I was six years old. My father was having an affair and my mother was crazy. She was into a cult church and thought everyone was having orgies and sleeping with each other.

I don't know…maybe they were!

My parents were into spreading the word of Christ to everyone. All good and yet, something was way off. They were listening to tapes from a church (I call it a cult) in Houston, Texas called Blessings Church. The pastor was from the military, Colonel Ryan Stern. He ran his church like you were in a military inspection line up. Kids there sang military songs of war and with a God slant.

Yeh, no.
No thanks.
Really, I'm good.
I will pass on church forever!

Anyways, apparently when my dad asked for a divorce, she came at him with three knives. He still shows me the scars on his hand where he grabbed the knives before she sank them into his belly. I was just five at the time.

Oh the fun of relationships!

I do remember some good times growing up. Playing with my dad and brother was fun as we played baseball, swam, and had great imagination time together. Christmas was also fun and we got lots of gifts. One time, I remember catching my parents putting presents around the tree at Christmas time and being so upset realizing that there was no Santa.

But, maybe there was Santa?
Santa is Satan…
Just rearrange the letters.
I was already living with the devil aka Satan.
I tended to like Santa better.

I love reflecting on how my perception is constantly changing as I have new insights and a deeper understanding to my experiences. As I relate my mother to this being called "Satan," I realize that in ancient times, the "Great Satan" was really an immersing of yourself into this material world of money, fame, and power. It was something to overcome as you come back into your power seeing the illusion of the world we live in.

Did I need to overcome my mother's attacks and she was going to teach me great lessons?

Was she there to get me to forget who I truly was?
Did we plan this before we incarnated?

Anyways, let's dive deeper into this funny thing that we call "life."

We were the nice family in a big house with two dogs and now, my parents were divorcing. My dad stopped coming around as much because my mother was so caustic and attacking. So, instead of her taking her anger out on him, she took it out on me. Constant emotional mind fuck which I now understand is worse than physical abuse because it is so subtle and chronic.

So pervasive.
So hard to "put your finger on" the issue.

Just before my seventh birthday, I was looking forward to my dad picking up my brother and I for the weekend. Instead, I was awoken in the middle of the night by the devil, told to get dressed, and into the car. It was all packed up and my brother was in the back seat. My mother looked crazy with this wild look in her eyes.

Where were we going? I knew better than to ask when she was in her devil persona and I was scared.

Dad?
Help!
Where are you?

We got on a plane and flew to Houston, Texas.

Yep.
We did.
We moved there and didn't tell my dad who was still in California.

Remember that cult church I talked about earlier?
Well, looks like "hell" just came to my doorstep.
And the devil delivered me.
Damn!

We landed and my mother was still in her crazy. She already had a car which I found out later that she had already come to Houston, gotten an apartment, a car, and even a job. After landing, we got in a car accident on the freeway on our way to our apartment and all the luggage came crashing down on my brother and I. We were crying and upset. My mother was yelling at us and so angry.

Welcome to Houston!

I didn't know when I was going to see my dad again and my mother wasn't telling us anything about him. She was mad so we stopped asking. I felt so out of sorts and scared. She didn't know what she was doing.

I knew that I had to take care of myself and my brother and on some level, her as well.

We went to this cult church six times a week and twice on Sundays. Every evening, we went to Bible school and learned about Jesus and the cross. We sang Bible type military songs while the parents were in the "big" church listening to their Colonel indoctrinate them.

Aka…brainwashing.

I say this, yet looking back at this church experience, there was something that I have never gotten out of my mind. One day while sitting in the "big" church with my mom, I heard the Colonel say that God is omnipresent, omnipotent, and omniscient. This means that God is all present, all powerful, and is everywhere.

Does the Colonel realize what he is saying?
If God is these things then we are God because God is everywhere.
How did this little detail slip past most people?
We are God?!

I sat with this concept for years and it wasn't until I was in my late thirties that I began to understand the deeper meaning of those three words. This would mean that we are the creators of our realities and not victims of our circumstances. We created this world?

We are Gods?!
There is more to explore on this later…
Meanwhile, back to my parents…

I found out later that my dad was very upset that we were in Texas. The devil had told him to send money to a PO Box. He refused and said that she (my mother) needed to tell him where we were.

Years later, he told me that she wanted to tell my brother and I that our dad had died. He fought with her about this and won.

She finally called him a month or two later after we moved to Houston and told him that she was having sex with some guy there to make him jealous. He told her that she needed to put his kids on a plane back to California. She did and we spent the summer there with my dad.

It was Heaven.
I felt safe with him and we had so much fun together.
I never wanted to leave him.

Then, back to Houston and into "hell."

I could go on and on with all kinds of verbal abuse stories and some physical abuse from my mother as well from her boyfriend. Really, I was my mother's dumping ground for anything she couldn't deal with and her punching bag as I reminded her of my father.

Stories like her blaming me at the age of seven for our house being robbed. Being whipped with a belt bare butt by her boyfriend, Max, for not buttoning up my coat when I was hot. She killed my cat and my pet rat. I was beaten with a belt many times by her. Never hugged or told that she loved me. I could go on and on…

Never being hugged and feeling unloved is truly the worst.

And yet, she was the victim. My mother played it well and people felt sorry for her. She acted like she was sweet and innocent but, behind closed doors, the devil showed up again and again.

I waited for my dad to rescue me and take me home with him. He never did. We would spend the summers in California with him and the school year with her. It was always brutal leaving him and I would cry and cry for days, sobbing my heart out.

I wondered why life was so horrible sometimes, yet I made the best of it.
Why was I with the wicked witch of the South?

School was a vacation for me as I could get away from her and feel good. I had lots of friends and I was good at sports. Volleyball was my favorite and I excelled. We didn't escape much in the religion department as we went to an Episcopalian church/school. We had good ole' uniforms and prayer every day.

So much indoctrination from religion.
What was that about?
This cycle with my mother went on and on till I was a teenager.
But guess what?

I couldn't take anymore and my rebel nature came out.
More on that later.

CHAPTER 3
SHE'S ALIVE

The key to growth is the introduction of higher dimensions of consciousness into our awareness.
~Lao Tzu

Paramedic school was one of the most stressful things I ever did. It was much harder than college and I studied every night for tests the next day as you had to get above an eighty-five percent or you could get kicked out of the program. It lasted nine months and included classroom for four months, hospital internship for two months, and a three month field internship with the fire department or ambulance company.

It's really a crash course in becoming an emergency room doctor in less than a year knowing drug dosages, putting tubes down people's throats to breathe, and starting IVs plus all types of other life saving techniques.

And I love it.
For me, it is the perfect rush of adrenaline and helping people.

I passed the classroom portion and finished my hospital internship. All of this was done in Los Angeles. I actually went to the very first paramedic school, Daniel Freeman, in Inglewood where the show *Emergency* came from. Anyone remember Johnny and Roy?

I loved this show.

Working as a paramedic intern with a fire department in the Los Angeles area, I have three months to get the emergency calls I need for my paramedic license. I could possibly be done in two months if I do well on calls and get the number of calls I need.

David and Rich are my paramedic preceptors who have been paramedics for over twenty years each and are really good teachers. At the station, there is an ambulance and a fire engine. We are on the ambulance and there are four guys on the fire engine.

When a call comes in, we all go, but sometimes the ambulance goes alone.

The guys are great and funny. Lots of jokes are played especially on me. Things like flipping my bed upside down, so I sleep on the box spring instead of the mattress when I get back from a call to putting grease under my door handle on my car to seeing who sits in a water puddle at dinner.

You know that you are accepted when they play jokes on you.
We have a really good time.

One time after dinner, we are playing cards to see who does the dishes. The tones go off for a call. It's a traffic accident a few streets over from us. Someone was ejected from the car. I am still pretty new with this being my fifth shift, but I am ready to go.

We all head out with the fire engine leading the way. I am in the back of the ambulance. Other fire engines and ambulances are on their way, too.

We arrive on scene and there are three cars involved. One is a convertible and it is upside down on its roof. I see a pickup truck that has major front-end damage and another car smashed up. Another person is lying face down on the street not moving.

I am supposed to tell David and Rich what to do and I tell them to start assessing the patients to see who needs help the most. Luis, from the fire engine, checks the woman ejected from the car for a pulse.

No pulse and there is brain matter on the ground.
He goes to get a sheet to cover her.
She's dead.

Other engines and ambulances arrive. David and Rich are talking to other patients as am I. We direct the other paramedics to take care of certain patients. David asks me if I have looked to see if anyone is still in the convertible that is on its roof.

I haven't.
He says that we should head over there.

We do and I get on my belly and look in the car. The driver is not there and I am guessing that is who is lying in the street. I see that there is a woman passenger who is upside down in the front seat. I go to the other side and I see her eyes are closed. The top of her head looks like it scraped the asphalt and it's a mess. I am guessing that she is dead. David looks on too.

I put my hand on her neck to check her pulse and yell, "Hello, can you hear me?"

Just then, she opens her eyes wide…
She's alive!

It actually kinda freaked me out as I really thought she was dead especially with her head looking like spaghetti.

David and I immediately get the truck company to cut her out of the car as it is severely damaged. This takes about twenty minutes. While they are doing this, I crawled in and started an IV on her. Once she is free from the car, we get her on the gurney and on the way to the hospital.

She is breathing fast and shallow.
Not good.
Her heart is beating rapidly.

We get her on oxygen and fill her with fluids. The hospital is just around the corner. We pull into the emergency room and there is a team of nurses and doctors waiting for us. We tell them what we have and they take it from here.

I take a breath.
I wonder if she will be okay and if that was her friend that died on scene.

No time to think about that anymore as David tells me we have another call to go to…

CHAPTER 4
TOMBOY

Please be responsible for the energy you bring into this space.
~Dr. Jill Bolte Taylor

I am a tomboy and always felt like I liked the more masculine things in life. As a girl growing up, I wanted to be like my dad and do everything he did. Not wanting anything to do with dresses or dolls, I wanted my brother's toys. I even tried to pee like a boy as a kid and I remember that my dad walked in saying that girls don't pee like that.

Whuuuutttt?!
I was devastated.
I must have been three years old.

My dad loved to tell a story of when my grandmother gave me a doll for my fifth birthday. He says that I looked at it and threw it against a wall saying that I wanted a gun like my brother got.

He always got a kick out of this story.

I loved sports and being active. It always seemed boring to play with dolls and act like a mommy. I didn't want to be like my mom and didn't care about makeup or dressing up. Boys were way more fun to play with.

What is that?
Why do some girls act like tomboys and gravitate more towards being like a boy?
Was I born into the wrong body?
Was I male in many lifetimes and now chose to be a female?
Was this just not wanting to be like my mom as I saw my dad as strong and fun?
Do men have more power?

So many questions…

My mom had the idea that girls were "less than" and that boys were better. Men were to be in charge of the family and women sat in the back of the car not to be heard. I knew all this early on as a kid.

So, I aligned with my dad.
Why be seen and not heard?

I can remember freaking out that someday my boobs would get big and my period would start. So, I decided that if I pushed on my boobs then they wouldn't grow. I did this a lot before puberty in hopes that I wouldn't turn into a woman.

Just so you know, it backfired.
I ended up with big boobs.
My guides must have thought this to be hilarious!

Wearing a bra was so embarrassing. The boys loved to snap our bras at school and that pissed me off. My period didn't start till I was in eighth grade and most of my friends had already started it. Somehow, I couldn't stop this puberty thing and realized that I was going to become a woman.

I can remember telling my best friend in seventh grade that I wished that I was a boy, so I didn't have to deal with period stuff. She said that she loved being a girl and looked forward to becoming a woman.

Hmmm…
Really?
What's wrong with me?
Why can't I just be okay with girl stuff and being a woman?

I began to settle in more and more into being a woman as the estrogen flowed into my developing body. I surrendered to what was inevitable. I still loved being physical and sports. Being a woman became kinda fun and yet, there was still a part of me that wished I was either all male or all female.

Why was I drawn into being in the fire department?
Why couldn't I just be happy getting married and staying at home?
How about being a nurse or teacher?
Was something wrong with me?

As life continued, it was sometime in my thirties that I began to see that women were amazing. My women friends were strong and went through divorces and painful things. They bonded together and were stronger after it. They were open and vulnerable and I realized that I had pigeonholed women into being weak.

I was really in awe of my women friends.
I wanted to be strong like them.

It was much different than the men I was around in the fire department who I found were more loners in the emotional realm. Sure, they got together and drank beer, but they didn't have deep conversations. Men are physically strong, but they seemed to be scared of the emotional realm and their female side due to society's programming. And men are amazing in so many ways.

Most of the guys I was around wouldn't go to those deep places that women would with each other. I did find that the guys would open up and talk to me though if I was by myself.

Every day, I became more in love with being a woman.
I know women are strong and powerful.
It was time for me to embrace my femininity.

What I have come to realize is that we have both male and female energies coursing through our veins. It doesn't matter what body we are in, but how we balance those energies within. It's not about gender. Both male and female energies are powerful and to balance these within one's self would be amazing. Some days, my masculine side comes out more and other days, my feminine side rules. Other times, it's a perfect balance.

I am nearing fifty years old and life is just really getting good!

CHAPTER 5
I CAN'T WAIT TO DIE

Fantasy is a necessary ingredient in living. It's a way of looking at life through the wrong end of a telescope, and that enables you to laugh at life's realities.
~Dr. Seuss

All my life I have looked forward to the day I die. I never really knew why, but I just did. I was never scared of death and never understood why people got so upset about it.

Shouldn't we should be celebrating people that died. They are so happy. We are the ones we should be having the funeral for. We are the ones still left here on this crazy planet!

I remember in fifth grade, I was at a new school in Houston, Texas and I was walking to the bathroom. As I walked up the hallway, I looked to my left and on the wall, a vision appeared and opened up. It became animated and I could see it with my physical eyes. There on the wall was pictures and videos of my life that had happened so far and many future events as well.

Stopping, I could see that each was a scene that had happened or was going to happen. A hologram that I could go into and see and feel everything from that memory or future coming attraction.

I thought to myself, "I can't wait to die."

I somehow knew that once I died, I could watch everything that had happened to me in this body known as "Hydee." I knew it was fun and I did it there with everyone watching too. I even felt like we ate popcorn while laughing and crying during my movie of my life. I was a great actress.

How did I know this?
I don't know.
I just knew that it was so peaceful on the other side.

Years later, in my thirties, I was listening to a spiritual talk about death and dying. They were talking about what it was like on the other side when you die. They began to talk about when you die that you do a life review with your guides. They look at your life, lessons you learned, and decide where you want to go next. It is all studied in great detail of every decision you made feeling it all.

Suddenly, I remembered what happened to me in fifth grade. I could see the whole thing. I never knew what it meant and now I did.

A life review.
No need to fear death.
It's all just a game.

Many years later in my early forties, I awoke from a nap and as I was waking up, I was swiping my hand across a wall next to my bed. In my sleep/wake state, I could see that I was scrolling through different reality systems and stopping them when I wanted to go into one and explore it. It was very similar to what I saw in fifth grade, but I was actually going into them and it wasn't scenes from the life I was currently in.

Is this what we do when we sleep?
Do our multi-dimensional selves have lives in other realities?
Are we tending to these lives as we sleep?
Some of these lives aren't human lives.
Are we time travelers?

According to Penny Kelly in some of her YouTube videos, she shares what she knows from the other side and says that once we die, we immediately begin creating another body within three to four hours of dying. We are just in another dimension. She says that the goal of life is to evolve our consciousness and to keep our energy together "in a pile" when we die. Penny says that when you see the light calling you back into it that you should talk to it first and ask questions on what is next for you.

This is fascinating and I realize that there is so much that has been distorted about death.

How can I die before I die?
Die to what I have been taught before I die physically?
How can I know the secrets of this reality?
I want to know everything!

CHAPTER 6
FLYING RATS

Love and a good sense of humor strengthen the entire body; remember your cells respond to your input.
~Barbara Marciniak

Disclaimer: This is all in good fun...

So, one night coming back late from an emergency call, we see a rat scurry across the apparatus floor. We don't think much of it and I think to myself, "There is no way a rat can squeeze under the door to get into our dorms."

Right?
Guess I was wrong.

Maybe an hour later, I hear yelling coming from the room next to mine. It's Andy and things are crashing and flying inside his room. Expletives are flying out of his mouth!

It's loud and I get up out of bed. I open my door and find the other guys doing the same when out runs Andy chasing a rat!

He is pissed and the rat is scared running for its life.

I watch the show and I am there in my t-shirt and boxers while the other guys are all in their tighty whiteys. The rat runs for the front closet and Andy grabs a box fan smashing the rat. He keeps smashing it and I lean in through the door to look.

This was a mistake.

I say outloud, "Ooohhhh, nasty!" "Yuck."

Right then, I look up and meet eyes with my Captain Jay.
Somehow, I know exactly what he is thinking.
I begin to run down the hall as he grabs a shovel.

Now, you may wonder why there is a shovel in the dorm closet?
I have no idea.
But, he scoops up the dead rat!

I just turn the corner to go out the dorms and I hear a smack!
The dead rat just missed me and hit the wall instead.
I knew better than to say outloud how I feel about a dead rat!

This is really all fun and games, but a lacrosse game at 1am in the morning?

I am in full sprint across the apparatus floor as the other guys come out the doors. Jay quickly follows and chucks the rat again in my direction just missing me. It is truly amazing how quickly our brains and bodies work when a full adrenaline rush is coursing through our veins. I have already analyzed my options in less than a second to get out of this situation.

My options…

I can lock myself in the ambulance inside the station.
I can get to the other side of the station and lock myself in the bathroom.
I can open the apparatus door and get completely outside the whole station!

I opt for the third option and hit the button on the wall to open the apparatus door as I run by with them chasing me. I know I can swing back around and get out of the station.

It's about halfway up and one of them runs over and pushes the button to close it!

Damn!

I sprint fast around and pull an "Indiana Jones" with about three feet left before the door closes. I throw my body on the ground and roll out under the door just as it closes.

I made it!
Woohoo!
Suckers!

I run across the street in case they come after me. I am totally laughing as I beat them at their game.

Yes!!!

"In your face!" I yell to them.

The four of them are all laughing and Jay chucks the rat across into some bushes.

Now, I would never ever say that I was being harassed in any way. This could have happened to any firefighter who commented on a dead rat the way I did. This was an initiation to their "boy's club."

And I'm sorry beautiful rat for your loss of life.
I never like to see anything being killed.
All of life is precious.

CHAPTER 7
DECIDING WHO LIVES OR DIES

Whatever life takes away from you, let it go. When you surrender and let go of the past, you allow yourself to be fully alive in the moment. Letting go of the past means you can enjoy the dream that is happening right now.
~Don Miguel Ruiz

Finally, I am off of probation as a firefighter/paramedic after a stressful year of passing tests (physically and mentally), running emergency calls, having tons of training, staying busy cleaning the fire station, and learning the culture of being a firefighter.

I now have what is known as "bid rights" where you can pick what station you want to work at and with a particular crew. Being new, there aren't lots of choices, but I decide to stay on the Avenue.

I get my bid.

The crew that is available is great. It is with Adam and Bob who are older and wiser. Both served in the military during Vietnam and both were hippies. I find them incredibly smart, but others would say they are lazy.

No one bids to work with them because they just go about their day doing what they do. They don't have a fire lit up underneath them anymore. In fact, my new captain, Adam, tells me one day, "Don't be surprised if I tell you we aren't going inside to fight that fire."

I ask, "Why?"

And I am thinking to myself, "Are you kidding me!?! This is what I live for. The adrenaline rush and going into a house on fire. The possibility of saving someone!"

He continues, "Well, you see, if you watch how we risk our lives and go in to try to put a fire out, the whole house usually gets torn down and rebuilt. So, we put our lives at risk for a building. Doesn't make sense, does it? And it happens in ninety percent of our fires that they tear down the building."

I take it all in and it takes me years later to realize how right he is.
And right now, I want to go on every fire call I can and fight fire!
That is what I was trained to do.

There are many wild calls that I go on with this crew. We have so much fun working together and are always laughing. Bob is especially amusing. He is learning to speak Spanish at the age of fifty-five.

So great.
We are never too old to learn new things!

One call that haunted me for a long time was this traffic accident on the freeway. It was midday and we got our turnouts on hearing multiple cars involved in a head on collision. We arrive and since I am also a paramedic, I am in charge of the patients.

We see one car flipped upside down with two people hanging in it. One is in and one is part out. Another car is smashed with people in it. Two other people are walking around holding their heads and say they got out of another car that was hit.

Cars on both sides of the freeway are completely stopped with some people out of their cars trying to help. In total, I find I have six patients and there is only three of us to help on our engine. More help is coming, but at least ten minutes away.

This means that I have to triage and decide who is the most critical. I need to decide who needs help now and who has the best chance of living based on their symptoms.

It is like being on a battlefield.

My captain is busy keeping the scene secure and giving orders. He is ordering more fire engines and ambulances. The police are not on scene yet either. My engineer, Bob, is busy cutting battery cables and making sure no fires break out.

So, here I am...
Deciding who is going to be helped first.

I see immediately that the most critical are the ones in the upside down car. It appears to be a husband and wife. Witnesses are saying to me that they came across the freeway into oncoming traffic and hit the other cars.

The wife is hanging out the window. She has a head injury and keeps repeating things. I check her husband. He is hanging upside down and is a very large man. I go to him and witnesses say he just took his last breath.

I check.
He's not breathing and I can't find a pulse.

He also needs to be extricated out of the car.
I pronounce him dead.

My decisions are all based on our triage guidelines that we train on.

I move on. The two people walking around need help too, but aren't as critical. One has a broken arm. I go to the other car and the driver is having chest pain. The other person in the passenger's seat says that he can't feel his legs.

So, after a quick triage of all my patients, I have two that need immediate attention. Three that need to be treated after them. And one dead.

Another engine and an ambulance arrive as we are getting the wife out of the car. She is going to the hospital first. She has no memory of what happened and keeps repeating things. She has trauma to her abdomen as well and may be bleeding out internally.

More help arrives and we attend to the man with chest pain next. Other firefighters go to the man who has a back injury with no feeling in his legs. The walking wounded are taken care of as well.

Our truck arrives with extrication equipment to cut the husband out of the car who is dead.

On the way back to the fire station, I have a sinking feeling in my body. A woman has just lost her husband and I am the one who had to decide if he lived or died. I wonder if it had just been those two patients and we could have gotten him out, would he have lived? We could have done CPR on him and maybe given him a chance.

Damn.

This call stays with me and I wonder if I did the right thing. I know I did and yet, I wish it had a different outcome. I wondered what happened for them to cross the freeway. Did he fall asleep? Did he have a heart attack and that is what caused him to cross the freeway? Would he have died no matter what? Was this his destiny?

Talking to Captain Jay about it later one day, I ask him how he deals with all that he has seen on calls.

He tells me, "Hydee, we didn't cause the problem. We are there to help and do our best. It's never our fault."

Those words of wisdom followed me for the rest of my twenty year career.

CHAPTER 8
RIDING FOR MY LIFE

The ultimate tyranny in a society is not control by martial law. It is control by the psychological manipulation of consciousness, through which reality is defined so that those who exist within it do not even realize that they are in prison. They do not even realize that there is something outside of where they exist.
~Barbara Marciniak

I grew up in the seventies and eighties. Life seemed simpler then and I know we all think this as we get older. I have heard older people say this about their generation. They say, "It was simpler growing up in the fifties" or whatever generation they lived in.

Really though…life was simpler.

I wonder if life is simpler when we are kids. We are still connected to the formless realms and don't usually have to worry about money or jobs.

Although today, kids seem more stressed.

Why is that?
It feels like it's tough to be a kid today.
So much pressure to grow up and compete in school.
There is so much that they are exposed to with social media and such.

I remember growing up and playing till dark. We would be with our friends and playing was so important. After school and on the weekends, we would be running around, on our bikes, playing games, climbing trees, and just being physical.

What happened to this type of freedom and safety? Most parents don't let their kids run around and play outside until dark anymore. Parents set up playdates for kids to play with other kids.

Some would say it is the screen time affecting kids with iPhones, television, video games, and social media.

Perhaps it is something bigger?

Kidnapping has grown rampant in this world. It is something like 800,000 kids go missing all over the world and many in the United States every year. Parents don't feel safe letting their kids be outside without someone watching them.

So, what happened?

Thinking about all this reminds me when I was nine or ten years old. It was 1980 or 1981. I was living in Houston, Texas with my mom and brother. He and I would ride our bikes all over, usually within a radius of about four or five blocks.

One of our favorite things to do was to ride down to the local 7/11 store and use the money we made from chores to buy candy and baseball cards. Inside the baseball cards was gum and we collected the cards to show our dad when we would go back to California. This was about a five minute bicycle ride to the store.

One time, we rode down and got our candy. My brother was done sooner and told me that he would see me back at the house. I was still looking for what else to buy.

I got what I wanted and left. I rode back slowly and was daydreaming as kids do.

As I rode down the long street back home, I noticed a white van following me slowly and wasn't going around me. I sped up and something inside me lit up as if every cell was awake. I started to ride really fast and the van sped up. It began to get alongside me and I could see the side door was open. I heard a voice tell me to pedal fast and turn into the bank on the corner.

I did.

I pedaled so fast and turned right into a bank parking lot.
I knew it well and it was a short cut back home.
Not looking back, I'm sure that I was riding faster than those on the Tour de France!

I came across and through the parking lot out the other side onto my street. We lived only a few houses away. Seeing my house, I drove up the driveway and braked right by the garage throwing my bike down. I ran inside my house.

Safe.
I'm safe!
I realized now that I have always been protected.
Always guided and watched over.

A part of me still doesn't want to believe this would have happened to me.
Why are they stealing children?
Who is doing this?

I write about this as so much is coming out in 2020 about all the kids being kidnapped all over America and the world. Apparently, there is an underground ring stealing kids for the elite, bankers, politicians, movie/music industry, religious leaders, etc…

This is insane.
Is this true?

Articles are coming out about pedophilia and satanic ritual abuse/sacrifice. This is tied to our legal system, foster care system, and our child protective system as a front for taking children. Law enforcement and judges are being bought off. They have been stealing our world's children for their energy and life force?

What?
Adrenochrome.
Say again?!

I know this sounds crazy, but apparently, those in power drink the blood of children or infuse it intravenously to get a high like no other. They torture children and sometimes kill them to make the child's adrenaline pump through their veins siphoning it from them. Apparently, they believe it makes them powerful, stronger, and younger to drink this.

Was the movie *Monster's Inc* or *Tangled* created by coincidence or to tell us what they are really up to? Scaring children to harvest their "screams" for energy? Stealing a child and keeping her locked up in a tower because her healing energy can keep you young?

These people are sick!
Is there evidence of this?
Is this just a made up conspiracy theory?!

Apparently, there are underground networks all over the world shipping adrenochrome and children to these people. There is a shadow hiding in the wings of every facet of our society running this world. And if that information isn't hard enough to believe, now stories tying in dark extraterrestrials races and trading humans off planet are coming out.

Is this true?!
Truth is stranger than fiction.
Sometimes, it's just too much to wrap your head around.
Just makes you wonder what is real.

It reminds me of some of the *Star Wars* movies and the slave trading going on in those movies. Lately, I am realizing that everything you see in the movies is real somewhere out there.

It's just a different reality.

Are "they" telling us what they are doing through the movies?

Now, I know that I may sound nuts and just for clarification, I am! Honestly though, there is much going on that we, the ninety-nine percent, don't know or want to acknowledge.

How can we discern truth?

For me, I feel truth in my whole body. I can feel it from the vibration that someone is putting out or when they are speaking. When I have my hand on my heart and come from my heart, discerning truth is a no-brainer. When I am in my head, it is much more difficult.

I do know this...

The one percent have controlled us for a long time.
Those in power have all the money and power.

What kind of world have we created?
Why are there so many secrets?
Do we live on a prison planet?
Why do so many struggle in this world?
Is it necessary?

There is much that we truly don't know.
So, what is really going on?
Ever see the movie called *They live*?

Perhaps many of us don't want to know the truth because it would be just too difficult to take and it would shatter our view of the world? What if we were a telepathic society and we did know everything? There would be no secrets. Is this how a more evolved civilization lives?

It is time for us to awaken and live in harmony.
It is time for us to be free.
It is time for us to know the truth.
Let's evolve our consciousness.
It's time, people!

CHAPTER 9
FUN BUMP

You are Perfection and Imperfection's Love Child.
~Sera Beak

I was a total rebel in high school and junior high, as well. I had enough of being told what to do and to follow the rules. Trying to be a "good girl," I found that was not honoring my truth.

I just couldn't contain who I really was any longer.

Not wanting to totally disappoint my mother, I was getting into trouble and acting out within limits, yet she was a big reason that I was acting out. Smoking cigarettes with my friends in seventh grade and drinking beer in eighth was things I experimented with. I was a good kid, but looking back, I had so much pain inside. I was trying to numb the pain somehow.

I found no matter what I did through these teenage years, I was always protected. Always.
Someone or something was always looking after me.

Believe me, unconsciously, I was trying in many ways to kill myself and just consciously didn't realize it. I wanted out of this hell called "my life." Living on the edge and doing dangerous things were fun for me as I enjoyed adrenaline rushes. I did things just on the edge of getting in trouble with the police. In fact, sometimes I thought that I would end up in jail or in a psychiatric ward.

I was always having fun with my friends though. They helped keep me sane and they had their own issues, too.

One day, not too long after I got my driver's license, we had a half day at school. A few of my friends decided to all go hangout at Linda's house because her mom was cool and they had a pool. We all played in the pool and while we were there, we found a hurt bird. We didn't know what to do with it and someone suggested we take it down to the animal hospital.

So, my friend Pam and I drove the bird down there in our bathing suits. I drove and I usually drove fast and wild. On our way back, I decided we would go over the "fun" bumps. These were dips in the road where you could catch air if you went fast. There was two of them on the residential street.

Pam dared me to see how fast I could go to see how much air we could catch.
I took that dare.

The windows were down, the sunroof was open, and the music was blaring. Neither of us had our seat belts on. I sped up the hill and reached the top hitting the first "fun" bump. We launched a bit and then I sped up faster for the second "fun" bump.

I hit that "fun" bump so fast probably going about sixty mph and it launched us so high that when we came down for a landing, it was too late. There was a curve coming up quick that I needed to make a hard left turn before I ran into a brick wall.

When we landed, my car began skidding as I tried to hit the brakes and turn to the left. It was one of those times where everything starts going in slow motion...

I knew we were going to hit the wall hard and I tried to hold the turn. I was just going way too fast and my car wasn't a race car.

It was a Nissan Pulsar.
Yep.
That's right.

Anyways, so we skidded right into the wall on the right side of my car and ended up spinning in circles in the middle of the street. Luckily, it was a residential street that wasn't very busy.

My car was totaled.

Pam and I got out of the car without a scratch on us except for my pride. Pam did see later that she had a bruise on her knee. We were in shock. We were down the street from Linda's house and they heard the crash. They ran down to see what happened. They were so happy that we were okay.

Of course, the neighbors came outside and the police were called. A tow truck came and towed my car away. I had to call my dad. He was just happy that I was okay. To this day, when I think about this accident, I am amazed that neither of us were hurt or killed. We weren't ejected from the car. We didn't have our seatbelts on and somehow, we stayed in our seats.

How is that even possible?

I know I have always been protected and watched over.
I know I have made my guardian angel work overtime for sure.

I wonder if she knew what she was getting herself into or maybe she likes all the action!?

Also, looking back, I realize how my thoughts created this reality. I had hit a taxicab two weeks prior to this and it dented my bumper, but causing no damage to taxi. I was so upset by this. My perfect car now had a dent and I began wishing that I would have totaled my car instead of having a dent in it.

I said this out loud and in my thoughts over and over again with feeling.

Careful what you wish for.
Our thoughts and words are powerful.
They create our reality.
What do you want to create?

CHAPTER 10
THE LOOK

Part of this experience involves your being able to say to a person who is dying, "You are loved. You are beautiful. You are like a newborn babe, going into another realm. Release now anyone, and everything, that is a burden to you. Release everything and know that you have lived your life to the fullest. There is no judgment on you. Go in peace, put a smile on your face, and release any judgments you hold. Relax, and allow your life to have meaning as you embark on the next phase of your identity."
~Barbara Marciniak

There is a look that I will never forget when someone knows they are dying.

They just know and you can see it in their eyes.
There is nothing you can do either.
Sometimes, they tell you that they are going to die.

I can remember the first time I saw "the look." I had been a paramedic for about six months and we got dispatched to a man who couldn't breathe. It was only a few minutes away from our fire station. I was not a firefighter/paramedic yet. I was with the fire department, but a paramedic on the ambulance.

So, off we went, the five of us…three on the fire engine and two on the ambulance.

The house was close to city hall and up a steep hillside. We climbed up some near vertical stairs to get to the patient. We were all thinking on our way up the stairs how it was not going to be fun to carry someone down to the ambulance if they are critical.

We walked in and a woman greeted us at the door hurriedly. She is panicked and tells us her husband just got out of the hospital from leg surgery. He has been home for a couple days and just got out of the jacuzzi.

She says he has been doing good with no issues. She goes on saying, "Then, suddenly, he said that he couldn't breathe and I called '911.'"

My partner and I who are both paramedics can feel the urgency as do the firefighters

41

who we are with. They are EMTs and have been on the fire department for anywhere from ten to twenty years. Immediately, they are putting oxygen on the patient. We begin asking more questions and the patient can hardly speak. Telling him to focus on breathing, we ask him to just nod as we ask yes or no questions. We get more information from his wife.

He is young and about thirty-five years old.
We can see the panic in his eyes.
We know that we need to move quick.

My partner and I decide to get him into the ambulance as soon as possible. We can do the rest of what we need to do in the back of the ambulance on the way to the hospital as he is going downhill fast. He needs surgery quick!

It takes all of us to get him out of his house and down the steep stairs. He is getting worse and breathing faster. He is looking more and more pale.

My partner and I know what is going on, or so we think.
Pulmonary embolism.

This is pretty much one of the worst things to happen when you aren't near a hospital as the patient needs immediate surgery. It is common for someone after surgery to throw blood clots especially after going into the jacuzzi. Unfortunately, sometimes these blood clots go straight into the lungs and cause a blockage. So, the patient can breathe, but the patient can't actually get the oxygen their body needs. They are literally suffocating.

We get him in the back of the ambulance and I look at him as I get in.
He's got this look that gives me the chills.
He says to me with gasps, "I'm going to die."

I am not willing to give up yet and I say to him, "No, you aren't. We are doing everything we can. Hang in there. We are about five minutes from the hospital."

He is on high flow oxygen and has an IV in his arm that I started. His oxygen saturation is in the eighties and continuing to spiral downward. Normal oxygen saturation is ninety-eight to one hundred percent.

Not good.
Fuck!

I call into the hospital and let them know what we have so they can prepare. I don't want him to die. My partner is driving lights and sirens to the hospital. We pull into the hospital and quickly unload him. The emergency room staff is ready and waiting.

Just as we move him over from our gurney to their bed, he codes.

Damn!

He stopped breathing and his heart stopped. They begin CPR and give him lifesaving drugs. The doctor is running the code and we stand there watching.

He was alive just minutes before.

My partner and I walk away wishing there was more that we could have done. We hope that the emergency room staff can save him. We have to do paperwork and get ready for the next call.

About twenty minutes later, we come back through the ER on our way to the ambulance as we have another call. We walk by the room where they were working on him.

There is no more action.
It is quiet in there.
We peak our head in through the curtain.
He is covered in a white sheet.
He's dead.

I'm shocked and sad at the same time. "Only twenty minutes and they pronounced him dead?" I think to myself. "Why didn't they spend more time on him?"

Just then, we hear a nurse bringing back his wife to see him. My partner and I don't want to be around when she sees him, so we head out.

It's too late though.
We are still in the emergency room, but around the corner now.

We hear the wife say. "Oh honey! No!?" in the saddest and most grief stricken way. She begins to sob loudly.

I can't get out of there quick enough.
I begin crying myself.
I can feel her pain and her grief.
It's just too much.
I look at my partner, he's crying too.

It is some things that just stick with you. You just don't forget. This look that a patient gives you when they know they are going to die.

The death look.

I saw it many times over the years in the fire department and I learned to not tell a patient that they weren't going to die when they said that they were.

It just didn't feel right to lie to them in hopes that we were going to "do something" to save them. They already knew deep down that their time was up. I just needed to do everything that I could and be there with them. I just needed to be present with them as they crossed over into another dimension.

I began to get comfortable with death and dying, but I always felt sad for those who were left behind. The ones who died were free of their bodies. They were free of this place. I could feel their spirits soar! They were just so happy!

Another call sticks out in my memory...

I was a firefighter/paramedic and we got called for a woman run over by a bus. We arrived and a city bus had run over an elderly woman. She was still alive.

A crowd was around her and we moved them out of our way. Two people were holding pressure on her legs. One bystander told us that she was crossing the street in the crosswalk and hadn't gotten up on the sidewalk yet, when the bus turned. She was hit by the back tires and it rolled over her legs.

We looked at her legs.
They were mush.

I looked at her face and tried to reassure her that she will be okay even though I knew she wasn't.

She had "the look."

We scooped her up quickly as we knew if she had any chance, it would be in surgery at the hospital. I got in the back of the ambulance with her, another paramedic, and a firefighter. She is pale and her breathing slowing. She looks at me, "I'm dying."

"We are doing everything we can for you. Hang in there. We got you," I say.

We are moving fast in the ambulance on the way to the hospital. Her breathing stops and I see her heart rate is slowing quickly. She is bleeding out due to this major trauma.

Her heart slows to less than twenty beats per minute and we begin CPR. We continue as we pull into the ambulance bay. As we enter the emergency room, we give the doctors and nurses a report. They take over and end up pronouncing her dead within ten minutes.

They know there is nothing left for them to do.
She's gone.
Gone to the great beyond.
Life is truly precious.
You are here one moment and gone the next.

CHAPTER 11
MISSED OPPORTUNITY

Your life is the manifestation of your dream; it is an art. You can change your life anytime if you aren't enjoying the dream.
~Don Miguel Ruiz

I love volleyball. It was one of my favorite sports while growing up. I played the game from sixth grade on and I was pretty good at it. In my sophomore year of high school, I had scouts from colleges watching me and told me that if I kept up what I was doing, I could get a scholarship to college to play volleyball.

I was excited about that, but I didn't really know what it meant.

My team wasn't very good, but we tried. Our coach wasn't the best coach either and parents complained about her.

I was good, but I had an attitude.
Imagine that.
A teenager with an attitude.

One day in a game, I got frustrated that we were losing and our team was giving up. The other team served the ball and instead of lobbing the ball to my setter, I kicked the ball as hard as I could straight up in the air.

My coach yanked me out immediately.

I didn't care and I knew she needed me. She talked to me and ended up putting me back in later. After the game was over, I told her that I was quitting and I walked off towards my car.

She came after me and asked me not to quit. She said that she needed me. I told her that I had better things to do.

Do you ever regret things you did in your life?
I regret that I left volleyball.

I had a deep love for that game.

In college, I was close friends with some of the volleyball players and I wondered if I hadn't quit, would I be playing with them? I look back sometimes and wonder how my life would have been different if I chose to stay on the team in high school and that I played volleyball in college.

On some other multidimensional timeline, I did go back and played volleyball in high school and college. I pursued beach volleyball and was good at it. I was professional volleyball player and I never became a firefighter. I travelled the world playing volleyball and having fun. I ended up coaching later on and, and, and…

Isn't it wild to think that for every decision we make, another part of you goes off and creates that reality that you didn't chose in this reality? Another timeline is created and off you go.

So, really, there are NO REGRETS and there are ten thousand yous playing out all kinds of realities that you didn't do in this reality!

Wowza!
Mind-blowing, really.
So much we don't know about.

CHAPTER 12
REBEL WITH A CAUSE

If people don't like what you're creating, just smile at them sweetly and tell them to Go Make Their Own Fucking Art.
~Elizabeth Gilbert

We all have some rebel nature within us. I feel like this is true because of watching two and three year olds stand up against their parents. There is something within us all that wants to follow our own hearts and not do what we are told to do. We want to follow our own inner guidance.

And really, we are told what to do by so many people like our parents, teachers, bosses, pastors, society, etc…

I'm over it.
Done.

How about this…
How about we follow our hearts and let this be our guide?
How about we stand up for what we know is true?
Who is running this fucking world anyways?

What I mean is…

Question the world and why it is the way it is. Question the rules and why they are the way they are. Question who made them and why? Question those in power and how they got there.

Tap into your inner rebel.

We are told to sit and listen. We are told to behave or we will be spanked. Kids shut down their imagination early on in their lives and told that it is not real. We are told to stop talking to our imaginary friends.

Well, I have news for you.

Imagination is real.
It is how we create what we want in this world.
It's powerful.

Kids are still in touch with the other realms and beings from the other realms.
They don't need to take drugs to remember.
They STILL remember.

Now, I was one of those strong-willed kids, but I was also a pleaser. I rebelled in my twos and threes against the establishment which was my parents. These years should really be named the "terrific twos and terrific threes" instead of the "terrible twos and threes." It should be celebrated because children are learning that they have an opinion apart from mom and dad. Of course, keeping them safe while they explore this is important.

Think about it for a minute.

How could we honor the opinions of our little people and give them enough room to explore while keeping them safe? Let them choose the clothes to wear or how to comb their hair. Give them some type of victory every day where they decide things for themselves. Perhaps then, in their teenage years, rebelling would be less?

I was not given freedom to express who I was at those ages. I was beaten to conform to what my parents wanted and what society told them. The belt was my mother's favorite although her judgmental nature towards everything I did, kept me in line while making me hate her deep inside myself.

I needed her to survive, yet my whole being hated her.

So, I boiled in my anger and resentment for her being in charge of my life. I was her whipping child for her unexplored traumas from her own life. In fact, I hoped she would die, so I could go and live with my father.

Why would I have chosen a mother like this?
What bigger lessons was I learning on a soul level?
Is this a karmic relationship?
Oh, for sure.

The church stuff was over the top for me.
Six days a week and twice on Sundays was fucked.
I quit going after I was given the choice at the age of twelve.

I think I had enough brain washing.

So, I got older as kids do. I stopped being so afraid of her and began to act out. I began to rebel against everything. I began to stand up for myself and talk back to her. I got into trouble at school and began to get detention. I toyed with smoking and drinking. I snuck out of my house at night to be with my friends and had a boyfriend.

I pushed my mother to her limits.
I had enough of being a prisoner in her home.
I wanted some freedom.

I got caught one night after I snuck out when my mother realized I wasn't in my bed. She found me at my friend's house and she was upset. She was scared and angry at the same time. I didn't care that she was upset. I was going to do everything I could to cause her pain.

She knew by the look in my eyes that she had no control over me any longer. The next day, she called my dad and told him that she couldn't handle me anymore. My brother and I were on a plane to California within a week. I was fourteen.

Within my heart, I got exactly what I wanted.
I got to be with my dad.
I was so fucking happy.

We stayed with my dad and he wanted my brother and I to move in with him and his wife. The strange thing about brain washing is that I felt bad leaving my captor aka my mother. I actually felt like I was being disloyal to her.

Talk about a mind fuck.

Thank goddess, my stepmom, Priscilla was a therapist and began to talk some sense into me. She knew the trauma I had been going through with my mother. So, I lived my high school years with my dad and Priscilla. She had three kids of her own and the youngest was my age.

I can't say that I was less of a rebel moving in with my dad as I put him through hell, too. I still rebelled against the system...him, teachers, society, etc...

Yet, I respected my dad.
I loved him and tried to listen.
My soul just wanted to destroy the system.
Deep down, I was still mad at him for leaving me with the devil all those years.

I still did good at school and was a good student. My dad represented the system in a different way. I didn't like that my dad told me to look good, so that I could get a boyfriend.

Huh?

I didn't care about that. I was pretty and I didn't need to dress up as I got lots of attention from boys. If anything, I needed to not dress up, so I would get less attention. I went from wearing nice clothes and dresses to wearing sweatpants and t-shirts.

I rebelled against the unspoken rules of the system.

My dad called me a farm worker and tried to get me to dress nice.
This made me want to never dress up and to show him that people loved me no matter how I dressed.

Yep.
Total rebel at heart.

I questioned everything I could that didn't make sense. I caused trouble and even got voted "Class Rebel" my senior year.

Now, that was an honor that I was proud of.
Finally, they see who I truly am.
A system buster.

My rebel nature is still deeply imbedded within me and comes out as she needs to.

As I near being on this planet for almost half a century, I feel like the next phase of my life is becoming clearer. It feels like I am one of those visionaries who knows we can make this place amazing by dreaming it into being. My rebellions have been one of destroying the old systems in place and to make people question it.

How about this…

Let's create this new world the way we want it to be, not the way the one percent that have been in control of this world has wanted it to be. Let's all work together and create something amazing!

What do we want our world to look like? Are we developing our consciousness? What do schools teach our young? Do we have cars or do we have teleportation technology? Have we become a telepathic society and don't need phones? Have we let go of judgment? Do we need money or debt? Do we have to work? Do we have a president or do we have a council of Elders? Can we instantly manifest what we need? Are we in contact with the nature beings and galactic beings? Are we working together with all of them?

So many questions involved in making a new reality system.
Question everything and change what isn't working.
Have the courage to listen to your heart and trust your truth.
Be humble.

Remember, opinions are like assholes…everybody has one!
May the rebel be with you.

CHAPTER 13
BODY PARTS ON FIRE

Never mind what is. Imagine it the way you want it to be, so that your vibration is a match to your desire. When your vibration is a match to your desire, all things in your experience will gravitate to meet that match...Every time.
~Abraham-Hicks

I went on lots of strange calls over the years. Let me tell you about one of the strangest calls I ever went on...

And yes...truth is stranger than fiction.

Well, I had about a year and a half on with the fire department, so I am a pretty seasoned firefighter by now...

Ha!
Yeh, right.
I crack myself up!
Anyways...

I was on my new crew with Adam and Bob. They were both thirty years older than me and had lots of experience. We were coming back from dinner when our dispatch spoke over the fire engine radio.

"Engine 1, respond to body parts on fire across from the freeway on Main Street."

We all looked at each other.
Did we hear that right?
Body parts on fire?

Adam asks for clarification, "Dispatch, clarifying that you said, body parts on fire?"

"Affirmative." Dispatch replies.

We head in the direction of the call as we are not far away.

We arrive and are met by a security guard. He goes up to my captain and says, "I was approached by a homeless man and he told me there were some body parts on fire in the drainage ditch. I grabbed a fire extinguisher and tried to put them out. Then, I called you guys for help."

Captain Adam tells me to grab a fire extinguisher and go see if anything else still need to be extinguished. He continues talking to the security guard.

I grab a fire extinguisher and head to the area, seeing some smoke coming from the drainage pipe underneath the road. It is dark out, so I use my flashlight to see. I shine it into the drainage pipe wondering what I am going to find.

I look and I am perplexed as to what I am seeing. It feels like something out of a haunted house or horror movie.

It doesn't look real.

I see a human torso, two arms, and two legs smoldering and burned with a burned bag underneath them.

I see no head.
It's all pretty burnt
And it smells of burning flesh.

It's strange to me how these body parts seem fake or maybe it's because of seeing pretend ones in Halloween shops. Staring at it longer, I wonder if I need to spray it more with the fire extinguisher. I know this will be a crime scene, so I don't want to mess up the evidence more, yet I don't want the body parts to keep burning.

I douse the body parts with more water and I don't move them. Bob comes up behind me and looks to see if this is for real. He jokes and says, "Well, this guy must have lost his head! I wonder if that is why he fell to pieces!"

I laugh.
We were always making light of what we saw with sick humor.
It kept us sane.
Bob was especially amusing and was always joking.

I am satisfied that the body parts aren't going to keep burning and now, Adam comes over to investigate. He tells me that the police are on their way and to just make sure no one comes to disturb the scene.

The police arrive minutes later and I show them the body parts. They take over the scene from there. I head back over to the engine where Adam is telling a police officer that a homeless man saw everything.

He leads the cop to the homeless man. I overhear the cop ask the homeless man what he saw and the homeless man replies,

"I was just sitting here in these bushes when a car pulls off the road. A woman gets out and it is right at dusk. She looks around and seems upset. She opens the trunk and begins take these plastic bags out of her car. She puts them in the drainage pipe. She stands there for a while with her hands on her hips and says, 'Good riddens!' She then lights the bags on fire and watches them. Then, she turns and leaves in her car."

"Yikes!" I think to myself. "She must have not liked this person."

He goes on, "I then went to see as the fire was going pretty good. I ran over to the store and found the security guard. He came with a fire extinguisher and called you guys."

We end up leaving the call and head back to the station wondering what really happened.

Humans are really interesting…the things we do.

Two days later, we find out that the cops arrested a woman just down the street from our fire station. She was the one that burned the body parts.

More of the story comes out as time goes on. Turns out that these body parts were her husband. She had suffered from years of abuse from him both physically and emotionally. They had four kids together. At night, he would go out drinking and womanize. He would then come home, beat her, and rape her.

One day, she had enough.
He came home one night after all this and she found his gun.
She shot him in the head and killed him.

She then spent the rest of the night cutting up his body. She cut off each limb and his head. She stored them in her washer and dryer for a day before she could dispose of him. She then drove him down to the drainage ditch and lit him on fire. The crazy thing is that the police said that if she would have cut off his fingertips, he would have never been identified. His fingerprints linked him back to her.

I feel for all of involved in this.
She went to jail.
The kids lost both their mother and father.

I ponder all of this. So, what do we do? How can we help these types of situations before they get to this? How can we help abused women before they feel that there is no way out? How can we help men to get support to stop the physical abuse?

I know there are others out there like this.
So much help is needed to un-traumatize us.

CHAPTER 14
DISNEYLAND AND ECSTASY

The left hemisphere is very interested in language; it communicates in words, it has a past, a present, and a future; it has a time component and it's all about details. The right hemisphere is more about the right now-right here experience where everything is an enormous collage of all the sensory systems flooding into our brains.
~Dr. Jill Bolte Taylor

Disneyland.
Happiest place on Earth, right?
Or this is what they want you to believe.
Funny place, really.

I grew up going to Disneyland once every year from about the age of four to my teenage years. It was close to my dad's house, so we would spend the day there having fun as kids do. Riding rides, laughing, crowds, eating cotton candy, and adrenaline rushes.

What more could a kid ask for.
It holds a special place in my heart.
A place where magic still exists.

After years of going to Disneyland, my stepsister, Susan, decided to take me with our boyfriends to Disneyland. This time though, we would do a drug called Ecstasy.

She was twenty and I was sixteen. We got along great, but she usually got me into trouble. She took me to parties and got me drunk. Now, apparently, we were all going to "drop" Ecstasy in the parking lot of Disneyland.

What a great idea?!
Who thinks of this stuff, anyways?
Ever look back at your younger years and wonder what you were thinking?
Yep, I sure do.

Anyways, Susan and I with our boyfriends, Dan and Bruce, all took "E" outside of

Disneyland. It takes about thirty minutes to take effect. We walk around and decide to go into Tomorrowland. It is just hitting all of us and I want a lemonade. We all get lemonades and I end up drinking another two or three more as they do, too. I am just so thirsty.

It's wild. The colors are so vibrant and I feel so much love for everyone. Bruce and I are hugging each other and don't want to let each other go. Everything just feels so good.

Susan and Dan are doing the same thing. We are all just over the moon for each other and all of humanity. I have never felt like this before. Bruce and I just continue looking into each other's eyes and saying sweet nothings to each other. We are so in love.

What is this drug?
A love drug?
Is there really such a thing?
Is this what cupid shoots out of his arrows?
Maybe all of humanity should be shot up with this!
The world would be a much better place.

Now, I am not saying for people to go out and "do" Ecstasy. I have no idea what it is called these days or if it is laced with anything.

I am merely just telling my story, people.
Get a hold of yourself.

Anyways, here we are at Disneyland at nighttime and Bruce and I don't ever want to let go of each other. It's not like we want to go a make love somewhere either. It is just an overall feeling of deep love for him and everyone.

We hold onto each other in line for the Matterhorn and even try to go together through the turnstiles. The people who work there get a kick out of this. We continue to ride this same ride over and over until the night is over. The effects lasted about six hours before eventually wearing off. Turns out that citrus drinks intensify the effects, so the lemonade made us feel even more love for all.

This is fascinating that this drug is illegal.
Can you imagine a world where everyone deeply loved each other?
What if drinking alcohol was replaced with Ecstasy?
A whole new world…

CHAPTER 15
MY FIRST DRIVING LESSON

Learn to get in touch with the silence within yourself, and know that everything in life has purpose. There are no mistakes, no coincidences, all events are blessings given to us to learn from.
~Elisabeth Kubler-Ross

I knew I could drive even though I was only fifteen and had never taken driver's education.

How hard is it?
Can't be that hard as millions of people do it every day.
I watched my parents do it all the time.
Move the wheel, don't hit anything...
Got it!

My dad and stepmom worked a lot when I was in high school and we were left alone often. Every teenage kid's dream. One day, my stepmom left her keys to her car and the car was in the garage. It was a newer Mercedes. My stepbrother (who was also fifteen) and I decided that we should drive it.

Great idea!
They will never know.
We would be back in a flash.
So into the car we went!

Jonah, my stepbrother, backed it out of the garage. It was a stick shift and he kept stalling it. This should have been our first clue as to not go driving, but he kept trying. We rolled out of the garage in neutral and he pulled the emergency brake. He tried again and started it, but he didn't have the finesse to keep making it move. It kept stalling and jerking.

Now, we thought we had this all figured out and would have the car back all safe and sound before they got home in a few hours. We just had one problem...neither of us knew how to drive!

57

The even bigger problem was that we needed to get it back into the garage and put the keys back.

I know!
I will drive it.
Move over Jonah.
Let me do this.

I got into the driver's seat and pushed in the clutch. My other foot was on the brake.

"Okay...so, take my foot off the brake and put it on the gas pedal," I say to myself.

I do this and I am revving the engine. Jonah is outside and watching one side of the garage because it is close. The last thing we want to hit is the garage!

I continue with my victory speech to myself, "Come on, Hydee. You got this. Okay, let off the clutch slowly, give it gas, and…"

I do it!
Yes!

Oh, I did it alright. I let off the clutch, but I am giving the car a little too much gas. I go careening into the side of the garage and smack the left bumper of the car. Some of the wood is broken on the house. The car stalls again.

Shit!
Shit! Shit! Shit!!!

I think, "Oh, I'm dead. What am I going to do now? I just moved here from Texas. Are they gonna make me move back in with my mother?! Fuck!"

Jonah comes over and he is as shocked as I am.

He says, "I will take the blame. It was my idea and I don't want them to send you back to Texas."

Wow. That sure takes the pressure off, but I can't let him take the fall for something I did.

I say, "Thanks, but I will take the blame since I did it."

We decide to put the car in neutral and back it away from the house somewhat. Maybe they won't notice anything and think that they forgot to put the car away.

We try to close the garage.
Damn!
The garage won't close.

Double screwed.

We go inside and watch a movie as we have a few hours to wait till they are home. This is the longest few hours ever.

It's dark and my dad comes in and says, "Hey, why did you guys leave the garage up?"

Ummm...
Yeh.
About that...

We came clean on all of it and our parts in it except for the part about us wanting to take it "joy riding."

They were pissed, but understanding.
We were gonna have to pay for part of it.
The best part was that I didn't get shipped back to Texas!
Thank, goddess!

FIRE AND WATER

CHAPTER 16
SUCKER PUNCHED

Fear is the path to the dark side. Fear leads to anger. Anger leads to hate. Hate leads to suffering.
~Yoda

There were certain places in the sector (area) that we covered on Engine 1 where we would go to all the time. One of these places was a seven story hotel that was converted into residential apartments.

It was in downtown Sparrow and was known for having lots of drug and alcohol issues there. We would run calls there quite often.

One shift early in my career, I was working as a firefighter/paramedic and we had a call for a person not breathing. We got there and found that the woman had stopped breathing and had no pulse. We began CPR, started IVs, and gave her life saving drugs. My captain and I rode into the hospital with the ambulance as we tried everything to save her life.

While we were on our way to the hospital, I heard another call go out in our sector for a seizure in the seven story residential apartments. Dispatch sent the next closest engine and I knew exactly who they were going on. My captain and I smiled that it wasn't us going on this call as the patient often had seizures and was a handful!

Some time went by and we were still cleaning up at the hospital. We were doing paperwork and putting our gear back together. The doctor had pronounced the woman that we brought in to be dead. She was eighty-five.

Another ambulance came in and brought in Frank, the seizure patient from our sector. He was strapped down and speaking in Vietnamese.

We knew him well. He had PTSD from the Vietnam war. He would drink, do drugs, and then have seizures from time to time. When he would begin to come out of the seizures, he was violent and aggressive. He would think that he was back in Vietnam when he was a POW and he thought we were his captors.

We all knew to stay away from him until he came back around a little more. Today though, a different engine company went on him and didn't know him at all.

Just then, the engine crew from that call came into the hospital. The captain, Jason, was holding an ice pack against his jaw. Staci came in next and looked disheveled. Tom followed after both of them.

Jason went in to be seen by the doctor. My captain, Jay, and I went over to talk to Tom and Staci.

We asked them what happened on the call.
Tom began to tell the story.
He was always a great storyteller.

Tom began, "Well, we got the call for a seizure in your area because you guys were on another call. We arrived and found this guy in his room unconscious from a seizure and his girlfriend with him. We began helping him by putting oxygen on him."

Staci jumped in, "So, I was starting an IV on his right arm when he started coming out of the seizure. Frank began speaking Vietnamese and his girlfriend says that sometimes he gets violent."

Tom continues, "So, Frank tries to get up and begins to grab Staci by her long braid and starts swinging her around and around. Jason goes to jump on him and he clocks Jason right in the jaw, knocking him out on the ground. So, I jump on top of him along with Staci and we wrestle him to the floor. Frank is still speaking Vietnamese the whole time."

"Luckily, the police came through the door just in time and helped us with him," Staci says.

Tom states, "And then, there is Jason grabbing his jaw wondering what happened?!"

They are both laughing hysterically at the whole situation as are we.
Just another day at the fire department!

CHAPTER 17
EMOTIONS FLOW

Feelings are your guide. Trust your feelings and learn to express them, and do not blame anyone for how you feel. Be yourself, observe yourself. Look to understand any crisis you have been in or will be in.
~Barbara Marciniak

I grew up in a house where it really wasn't okay to cry. My mom was Irish/English/German and my dad was Cuban/Spanish. I don't know if it was because of these cultures that taught you to hide your tears, but I watched my parents be stoic when it came to crying. My dad taught me that instead of crying, you should cuss instead. I remember being in first grade and teaching the other kids not to cry when they get hurt. I told them to say "damn" or "shit" instead.

Different, huh?

My mom just wasn't there emotionally when I cried, so I decided one day when I was about seven to never let her see me cry again.

It really is amazing what kids decide and how they feel.
Kids feel so much and can be happy one second and sad the next.
It's normal.
I didn't realize this until I had kids.

I began letting tears flow again when I was in high school. My dad had remarried a psychotherapist and I was learning about emotions. It was still hard for me to cry in front of someone as I felt like I was weak.

When I was doing my paramedic internship in the hospital in Los Angeles, I realized that other families deal with emotions differently. I would work ten hour shifts in the emergency room practicing my skills like starting IV's, doing assessments, and intubating patients.

Let me tell you about one shift that I will never forget…

It was about 3 pm in the afternoon and the ambulance was on their way Code 3 with a traffic accident victim in full arrest. This is also known as, not breathing and no heartbeat. They are dead. The paramedics and firefighters on the ambulance were doing CPR and trying to get her heart started again by giving fluids and lifesaving medications.

They pulled into the ambulance bay and came into the hospital doing CPR with a crew of four people. The crews were breathing for her and thumping on her chest. As they came into the emergency room, we were all waiting to take over. They moved her onto the hospital bed and we continued the CPR.

The paramedic gave a rundown to the doctor about the patient. He says, "She was the passenger in a vehicle and was broadsided by another car doing about fifty mph. It took us thirty minutes just to cut her out of the vehicle. She stopped breathing on the way to the hospital." He goes on to talk about the medications they have given her to start her heart again.

The doctor had the nurse push more medications and there is a rhythm on the heart monitor, but still no pulse. The doctor is having them give her fluids and blood as he says she has bled out. Her heart still works, but there is no blood in her system to feed her body.

We work on her for about another twenty to thirty minutes.
Nothing.
She's gone.
The doctor pronounces her dead.

The paramedics also tell us that her twenty-five year old son was driving the car when they were hit. He turned into oncoming traffic right in front of a car. He was transported to another hospital.

That really sucks.
I wonder if he knows what happened.
If he knows that his mom is dead.

His mom is now laying on a gurney in the middle of a room with a sheet over her.

All of us in the hospital are pretty somber and quiet. I go about my day with my duties in the emergency room.

Maybe an hour goes by and I hear this sound.
This sound of grief and pain.

Being twenty-three years old and growing up in an emotionally cut off family, this sound is unknown to me.

It is loud.

Wailing.
Pure heartfelt grief.

One of the family members is in there with the body of the mother. The rest of the family is showing up. They are gathered in the waiting room and in the hallways.

I go out there as I am curious as to what is happening.
So much sound.
They are crying hysterically and wailing.
I have never heard this before and it makes me cry.

I am amazed that this whole Armenian family is crying hysterically in front of each other and everyone else. The men are crying too.

This is so foreign to me, yet this is also so refreshing.
I am honored to witness such a raw level of emotion.
So deep, so profound…so utterly human.
I have a long way to go to get back in touch with my emotions…

CHAPTER 18
CRASH

You're picky about the car you drive. You're picky about what you wear. You're picky about what you put in your mouth, be pickier about what you think.
~Abraham-Hicks

In high school, I ended up with the name "Crash." My family felt given some things that happened to me in my life that I deserved this nickname.

I won't disagree.

As you have read in some of the other chapters, I crashed a few cars. So yes, the name "Crash" was quite fitting. I wonder why I was crashing so much? Looking back at those days, it was almost as if I wasn't in my body.

Maybe I didn't want to be fully in this reality and part of my consciousness was somewhere else?

Perhaps.
Let me tell you of a couple more funny stories involving yours truly, Crash.

One time, I was riding bikes with my stepsister, Susan. We were having fun and decided to just go out and ride. We went down a busy street and she was in front of me. We were cruising fast.

Somehow, I ended up on a bumpy part of the street. My front tire caught a hole flipping me up and over the handle bars. I went flying and landed on my forehead instead of my hands to brace my fall. I ended up with a huge scape. Susan stops her bike and runs back to me. She is laughing her head off and worried at the same time.

You know those times where you know someone is hurt, but you can't stop laughing?

This was one of those times.
She saw the whole thing happen as she had just looked back.
She thought it was the funniest thing ever.

My pride was hurt, but I was okay.
Another reason for the name "Crash!"

This story reminds me of the many emergency calls I went on especially traffic and biking accidents. Sometimes people were really injured and other times, they were just fine. I have always wondered why this happens and I have heard that many people "leave the body" at the time of an accident to keep their "soul" intact. Perhaps our guardian angels protect us?

I heard a story about a woman who got in a bicycle accident and she stayed in her body the whole time. While she was flying through the air, she kept breathing in and in until the air was equalized on the inside and outside of her body. When she landed and bounced, she hit a car and went unconscious. At the hospital, she was totally fine with no broken bones or issues.

So many things we have yet to understand.
Get a load of this next story…

When I went to live with my dad in high school, I really wanted to play softball. The girl's high school team was good and I would be coming in as a sophomore. I needed to practice and get my own bat, so I could go to the batting cages.

I grew up loving baseball as my dad had taught me all about it. I watched professional baseball with him and knew most of the professional players. One of my favorite things was to go to the Angels' games with my dad.

Anyways, my dad took me to a sporting goods store (not the giant sporting goods stores that we have now, but one of the old mom and pop stores) to get a bat and batting glove. We looked at all kinds of bats and settled on a couple.

"Okay, Hydee. I want you to really feel into the bat. Get into your stance and take a swing," my dad says.

So, I get into position and become one with my bat.
I feel it and take a big swing with a follow through.

Wham!
A huge display of sunglasses goes flying across the store!
Home run!

Little did I know that when I came around, the sunglasses' display was in the perfect position. I was totally embarrassed. It was a good hit though! My dad laughed out loud and helped pick up the sunglasses offering to pay for the broken ones.

He didn't shame me one bit. I got my new bat and glove, but I have to say, this was one of my most embarrassing moments! It also helped solidify my nickname as "Crash!"

CHAPTER 19
GOOD OLE' PRANKS

Play is the highest form of research.
~Albert Einstein

One of the best things about working in the fire department was that we were always joking with each other whether it was a prank, giving each other shit, or just telling funny stories. It was comic relief at its best and much needed for releasing some of the stress from responding on life and death emergencies.

Fireworks are illegal in California, so the police used to drop them off at the fire stations whenever they confiscated them from the public. Sometimes, however, they would end up being used as pranks.

You never quite knew when they would show up. One time, when I was in the shower and a brick of firecrackers went off for about twenty seconds in the bathroom. It's like feeling you are being shot at, but you know they are firecrackers. Still, for that split second, you wonder if you should hit the floor.

Nonetheless, I got them back when they were on the toilet...

Another time, before I was hired and fireworks were legal, one firefighter put an M80 firecracker in a sink to scare a new firefighter. It actually blew up the sink and they had to go buy a new one before the next crew noticed!

One of my favorite pranks was a fake spider that was rigged with fishing line up on the ceiling. If you sat in the chair below while watching television, the spider would land on you. It was all controlled by someone else in the kitchen.

It was good for unsuspecting overtimers who came to work not knowing of this.

Staci was the next victim and she had her feet up and chair back. She was "locked and loaded" as we called it and was watching television. Ted was in the kitchen and he began lowering the spider slowly. It was so good as the other five of us watched and waited giggling to ourselves. The spider just entered her field of vision when Ted lost control of the fishing line and it landed on her leg!

This was a tarantula looking spider, mind you.

Staci screamed and fell over backwards in a feat that you didn't know she was capable of.

It was hilarious and I wish we had a video of it.
She was so pissed and then realized the humor in it all.
You know she is gonna get Ted back!

We only did pranks to people we liked, so you knew you were accepted if they started happening to you. It wasn't to be mean.

Another favorite was scaring people with a gorilla mask. This was Paul's favorite pastime and you never knew where or when he would jump out. He would even wait in the dumpster just to get you and watch you scream.

One time, it was late at night and Paul waited outside Chris's room. He tapped on the glass window and Chris went over to see what it was. He saw nothing. Paul did this again and Chris went to check again looking out the window for longer.

Suddenly, Paul jumped out with his gorilla mask on and was growling! Chris grabs his chest and falls back on the bed! Paul was freaked out because he thought Chris was now having a heart attack. He didn't, but Paul didn't do this prank to the older firemen anymore.

We liked to have fun and joke with each other all the time. One time, a huge box of frisbees showed up at the fire station that we were to give out to encourage people to vote. We ended up having a giant war throwing frisbees at each other in the station laughing our asses off the whole time.

Nerf guns were also common to attack each other with. Some crews stepped it up a notch and used paintball guns instead!

Another good prank was to take a rubber band and wrap it around the sprayer on the kitchen sink, so when you turn on the faucet, it soaks that person. Usually, they are so confused, they end up soaked before turning it off.

Some of these pranks were pretty amusing.

There was a crew who watched the show *Jeopardy* every night to see who could get the most answers. Denny decided he would tape the previous day's show (since they weren't at work), bring it in, and then play it as if it was the current day's show. He and Chris memorized the answers.

They sat down, played the video, and Vern had no idea. Denny and Chris went back and forth answering all the questions perfectly. They both tried to keep a straight face.

By the second round, Vern was on to them. He couldn't figure out how they knew, but something was up. He finally got up and saw the VCR was on!

The gig was up!

Of course, there was always the water fights with our hoses and the buckets of water dropped on those below. There was also greasing your door handle or putting water on your seat, so it looked like you wet yourself.

So good!

It was always in good fun and it was never a dull moment around the fire station!

CHAPTER 20
COLLEGE DAYS

True freedom has to do with the human spirit. It is the freedom to be who we really are.
~Don Miguel Ruiz

Freedom!
Free from parents and their rules.
And everything is still paid for.
Thank goddess, because I am still a mess!

This is how I felt in college.
Free!

My parents paid for me to go to school for another four years. I hoped that I could figure out what to do in life within these four years before I ended up having to support myself. This stressed me out, so I chose not to worry about it.

It was a fun time for me in school. I made lots of friends and had fun in the sorority even though I really wasn't the sorority type. I was the athletic type, so this is where I excelled in helping the sororities with intermural sports.

I worked part time in college to make spending money and took a job as a valet. This was interesting because the company that I worked for often did celebrity events. It was amusing for me because I got to meet some of these people and drive their expensive cars around Los Angeles. Most of them tipped well.

A weekly gig that I sometimes worked was up at the "Playboy" mansion. They had big parties all the time and on Tuesdays, it was their movie night. We had specific rules to not look around or you would be fired. There were cameras everywhere. They fed us well and I always wondered what really went on inside.

Anyways, I was bored in college, but I loved that I could make my own schedule for classes. I learned to make my classes after 10 am because I slept in all the time. If I made them before, I usually missed the class. Somehow though, I was able to keep my grades to B averages. I was a biology major with the intent to go to medical school. I thought being a doctor would be a good idea as I loved helping people and it would make my dad happy. Chemistry was pretty boring though.

Being pre-med, I volunteered in the hospital to get hours for applying to medical school. I took an internship and worked in the emergency room as well as other floors in the hospital shadowing doctors. Working in the emergency room was when I found that I loved the adrenaline rush when critical patients would come through the door.

Such an adrenaline junkie.

I especially remember when we had a grandmother come into the emergency room who had been shot in a drive-by shooting. She was in full arrest (not breathing and no pulse) and I did CPR on her. The doctors ended up cutting her chest open to massage her heart as nothing was working. She had bled out.

She ended up dying, but my life was forever impacted by trying to save another's life. I was hooked.

After this internship ended, I volunteered at another hospital where I worked in the pathology department. Here, I worked with the doctors as they did autopsies. I was to cut open the intestines and clean them out with water. It was really disgusting as it was their shit.

Literally.

The pathologist's assistant was a sweet black man named Roy who basically did all the work in the autopsy. He would cut the body open and then cut the organs out for the doctors to look at and weigh. We talked often and he was always so encouraging to me telling me that I would make a great doctor. Roy had wanted to be a doctor, but blacks hadn't been allowed into most medical schools at the time when he was young. He was now in his late sixties and told me to never give up my dreams.

I learned so much from this internship about how the body systems work. Seeing diseased livers and other diseased organs made me want to take care of my body. Yet, here I was young and ignorant still abusing my body.

Once the autopsy was done, I was left to sew up the dead bodies for the funeral home. They would pick them up unless they were to be cremated. The job as a pathologist seemed lonely and I wanted people around to talk to. So, I knew becoming a pathologist was not for me. In fact, I felt I was done working in the morgue and needed to figure out what I was going to do in this world as I decided to not become a doctor.

During my junior year, I changed my major to psychology as I found that I really loved learning about the brain and human behavior. It fascinated me, but I didn't want to be a therapist like my stepmom. Listening to people and their problems sounded boring, plus I was a mess myself.

I was still trying to run from my pain of childhood and all my hurts, so I continued to drink and party as much as possible. The human body is truly amazing as I put mine through hell and tested it to its limits.

We all had fake IDs, so we could all get into bars and drink. Most of us had Oregon fake IDs as it was an easy one to fake. At USC, lots of us would go to the football games and have fun there. Then, we would take to the streets afterwards and drink at the fraternity houses or bars.

Drugs were always accessible and many people I knew were doing cocaine. Heroin was popular as well. This never interested me as cocaine amped people up and I didn't want to stick myself with needles to get high.

No thanks.
Really.
I'm good.

Some kids died from heroin overdoses in college. This really hit home as to how dangerous illicit drugs really are.

However, I was a magnet for hallucinating type drugs.
Something about these called to me.
Mushrooms and LSD.

They showed me a different reality and got me out of this one. It expanded my mind and my senses became acute. Colors were intense and everything became alive. It was like living in a Dr. Seuss reality.

I lived with roommates who sold LSD, but I was afraid of it until a bunch of my friends all decided to try it with me. It was a powerful experience and we rode our bikes all over downtown Los Angeles. I couldn't get over the colors...especially yellow. I wanted everything yellow, from a yellow Felix the cat to yellow lights on the stop lights to the yellow bag of Fig Newtons.

We even tried to ride our bikes into the grocery store.
That didn't go so well, so we walked around instead.
My senses were so alive.
I was just in awe.

This experience changed me and yet, I wouldn't totally understand the extent of it until years later.

I dated in college somewhat, but I was always getting back together with my high school sweetheart, Bruce. Something kept drawing us back together and he moved down to Los Angeles his junior year to get his bachelor's degree at CSULA. We decided to move in together.

It was good timing as I was panicked over trying to figure out how to take care of myself as I had less than two years left of college. I knew being a doctor was out for me as I didn't want to be stuck inside all day.

One day while having lunch with Bruce, I said to him that I had no idea what I was going to pursue as a career after college.

He says to me, "Well, what do you love to do?"

I respond saying, "I love being outdoors, working together as a team, doing something different every day, and being physical."

Bruce was working towards becoming a firefighter and says that I described the job of being a firefighter. He continues saying that I should go to the fire academy after college and become a firefighter.

Really?
Women can do that?

This hadn't entered my mind as I thought this was just a job for men. He tells me all about what firefighters do and that I would fit right in being that I am athletic and strong. This feels so right on. So, I decided that after college, I would go to the fire academy and paramedic school. I know my dad is going to freak out though because he doesn't like "blue collar" work.

Why do we need college anyways?
Is it to grow up more for those of us who are immature?
Is it an ego thing?
Is it a society thing?

My parents always told me that I was going to college, so I never questioned it. Yet, I didn't really need four years of college to become a firefighter.

Honestly, it seems some people need degrees and some don't. Why do people sometimes look down on others who don't have a college degree? These days, it just seems like a way to make people have big loans with lots of debt by the time you are twenty-two years old.

I learned so much more after college studying on my own than I ever learned in college. However, maybe for me, it helped me to mature in this wild world. Just maybe though, it was for my parents?

I wonder.
Who makes up this world anyways?

CHAPTER 21
RIOTS IN LA

Insanity is doing the same thing over and over again and expecting different results.
~Albert Einstein

It is always interesting to wonder how you ended up in certain places at certain times.

Is it an energy that draws you to be there?
An agreement on a soul level?

I don't know, but somehow, I ended up in the middle of the Los Angeles riots in 1992.

It was finals week at USC and it was the day before we started them. It was a free day to study and rest. I was with friends on campus in their apartment building studying when I received a phone call from my boyfriend who said to turn on the television NOW!

We did and on the television was rioting in the streets of Los Angeles. The area they showed was only a few streets over from USC.

Oh damn.

This was all due to a court decision where white policemen were proven innocent for beating the shit out of a black man named Rodney King who was on methamphetamines. The police used excessive brutal force for what went on for what seemed like hours. It was captured by a bystander using a video camera.

Today was the day to find out if they were guilty or innocent.

So, now there is rioting in the streets and all around the campus of USC. The news is showing a white man being pulled out of his semi-truck and being beaten senseless. People are looting stores and throwing Molotov cocktails into the looted stores where they start to catch fire.

It isn't a good day to be a white person.

What is it about color of our skin that we need to fight one another? Who decided these things anyways? Who decided that black people are inferior? Perhaps it is the white person who stripped away all their dignity and tried to control a very powerful race? What were they really after?

Maybe they were threatened by how powerful black people are?
Maybe they want to divide and conquer?
Who are "they" anyways?

Hmmm....

I still wonder why it is in schools that in kindergarten and on up we are taught to find the differences in things. We get school papers that say, "Circle the one that is different." We are taught from a very early age to look for things that are different. Why not teach all the similarities that there are?

Just that simple way of teaching could shift our perception.

Who decides what we are taught in schools anyways?
Why is it that they want us to be a certain way and believe a certain way?
Who is molding our perception?
Sounds like brain washing to me.

Kids would begin to see how similar we all are and grow up with a new way of thinking if we focused on the similarities. I mean, really, you could look at a black, white, Asian, and Hispanic person and ask, "What are the similarities?"

There are hundreds!
Can you imagine all the details?

Well, they all are human. They all have hands and feet. They all have eyes and noses. They all have arms and legs. They all have hearts and brains. On and on and on go the similarities. We would not be trained to look for differences in our world.

I mean really...

To fight over the color of our skin?
Or to fight over the shape of our eyes?
Or to fight over nationalities or what football team you support?

Really, people?!
Total insanity.

Is anyone paying attention that the people in power are keeping us from being united?

Why is this?!

It is because we are powerful when we are united.
"They" can't control the masses when we are all on the same page.
"They" need to keep us divided and fighting, so we never see what is really going on.

War is big business.

Okay, so I will get off my soapbox now and get back to being in the middle of the fucking riots in Los Angeles!

I am with four other college women in the apartment and we can't believe what we are seeing. We all question what we should do.

Should we get in our cars and leave now?
What if we get pulled out of our cars?
Are they going to burn down buildings on our campus?
Is it safe?

We call campus security and they tell us the campus is on lockdown. No one is going anywhere, not in or out. After a couple hours of watching the television with things getting worse, we decide to go up to the roof. We are in a twenty story building in my friend's apartment.

It's night now and we all get to the roof.
You can see everything from up here.
We see fires everywhere.

We look from every side of the building and there are fires all over the streets of Los Angeles.

All of us are nervous and scared.
Will we get out alive?
What's happening?

We find out that all finals are cancelled. This is good because no one is going to show up anyways!

For most of us, our parents live about an hour or two away from campus. We all check in with our families to let them know we are okay.

The night is restless and we all stay up late.
We all hunker down in the apartment for the night.
More looting.
More fires.

In the morning, we go up to the roof again. Lots of smoke and things seem to have calmed a bit. We have an idea. We all decide to try to get in our cars, drive fast without stopping through the streets, and attempt to make it home.

Sounds like a good plan?
Sure!

So, we all say goodbye and go for our cars. I get in my car and drive like a maniac towards the freeway. I have a bat in my car just in case.

I see some people still out looting stores.
Hardly anyone in the streets.
I don't stop at any red lights.

I make it to the freeway and drive north to my parent's house. No one is on the freeway. It is like a ghost town. It takes me about an hour to get home and I am so relieved as are my parents. I turn on the television and they are showing the exact stores I saw getting looted, but are now on fire.

Yikes!

These riots last for about five days.
The National Guard shows up.
When is this type of insanity going to stop?
Can't we just all get along?

CHAPTER 22
WATERMELON

There are only two emotions: love and fear. All positive emotions come from love, all negative emotions from fear. From love flows happiness, contentment, peace, and joy. From fear comes anger, hate, anxiety, and guilt. It's true that there are only two primary emotions, love and fear. But it's more accurate to say that there is only love or fear, for we cannot feel these two emotions together, at exactly the same time. They're opposites. If we're in fear, we are not in a place of love. When we're in a place of love, we cannot be in a place of fear.
~ Elisabeth Kubler-Ross

I was still pretty new on the fire department and getting to know this whole game. We were busy and I liked the excitement and adrenaline rush. Every call was so different and I knew that this was the perfect job for me.

I loved being a firefighter.

One night, we were all sitting at the table eating dinner and laughing when the tones went off.

Jumper.
A man threatening to jump off the overpass on the freeway.

We head to the scene with lights and sirens blaring. I love this part. Watching us weave in and out of cars as the captain hits the air horn. Just surreal. It still makes me smile.

We get to the call and the police shutdown the whole northbound traffic on the freeway. A man is super irritated and pacing back and forth near the edge. He is yelling for us all to stay back or he will jump!

It's at least twenty feet down.
Not good.

This goes on for some time with the cops trying to talk to him. It is decided that the real threat is down below if he jumps, so we load up in the ambulance and head to the area under the overpass. The fire engine stays above. We wait down below for another forty-five minutes or so and are close to where he would land.

Suddenly, we hear a lot of commotion and he jumps off the overpass.

Damn.

Most of my crew looks away as we don't want this etched in our minds forever. I don't look, but my engineer watches the whole thing. When he hits, it sounds like a watermelon hitting the ground hard.

Shit.
Not good.

We get to him and he is a lifeless, bloody mess. He is barely breathing and we all know it is a few minutes before he is totally gone. He has massive head trauma with blood coming out of his ears and broken bones everywhere.

We scoop him up as best as possible and get him on the gurney to go to the hospital. I ride in the back of the ambulance starting IVs. There are three of us in the back helping him as best as possible. We know it is futile.

I watch his heartbeat slow more and more. We are assisting his breathing as it has stopped and begin chest compressions as we don't feel a pulse anymore. We get to the hospital and they work on him for a while. He has bled out and died. He has succeeded in what he wanted.

The cops come to the hospital while we are still there. One of them tells us what happened from above. One of their cops tried to get close to him while trying to talk him down. He offered him a cigarette and the man took it. While he went to light it for him, he tried to tackle the guy to the ground. The man got away, took off in a full run, and launched himself off the freeway overpass.

We heard the rest.

My engineer watched the whole thing and is pretty upset. He can't get it to stop replaying in his mind. He wished he would have looked away.

This goes on for weeks and he can't sleep. He doesn't want to talk about it. Finally, he gives up and asks for help. He goes to one of our therapists who does EMDR. This helps him a ton and he can sleep again.

I think about this call on and off and wonder what was so bad in this guy's life that he had to jump off and kill himself in front of so many. I was there to witness as he crossed over and perhaps held space for him.

I wonder if he has any regrets or if this is exactly what he wanted to experience. I wonder if he knew when he took a body that this is how he would leave. I wonder if he felt it as he landed or if his spirit took him out of his body. It makes me think of the movie, *Groundhog Day* and how the actor kept reliving the day over and over again even if he killed himself.

It isn't until later in my career that I finally answer some of my questions around all this. I realize that death isn't the end and it is a doorway to many doorways.

Life is just an experience we choose to have.
What a wild fucking ride.
Enjoy it!

CHAPTER 23
WHAT IF

Imagination is everything. It is the preview of life's coming attractions.
~Albert Einstein

I always wanted to take the water from the oceans straight up and have it hover above with all the ocean beings in it as I explored all that was in and under the ocean.

I wanted to do this all through my childhood and even today.

I fantasized about all I would find.
Shipwrecks.
Gold.
Caves to other worlds.

What is really in the ocean? Are there underwater civilizations where the merpeople and ETs live? I believe there is and even have a faint memory of this.

When I was a kid, my dad, brother, and I would pretend that we were merpeople when we were in the ocean and in the pool. It felt so real to me.

My dad was Aquaman.
My brother was Aqui (for the son of Aquaman).
I was Aqualon (for the goddess of the sea).

Perhaps Aqualon was for the alone journey of me being away from my ocean family and on two feet here on land pretending to be human.

Ha!
That makes me giggle.

Just imagine, a whole world under the ocean and many worlds all over. Many portals to off planet places where extraterrestrials come and go as needed.

What a fascinating world we live in.

I have never quite bought into this reality. I have always longed to remember the other dimensions and what I knew. I know I am remembering more every day. It is time for those who keep information from us to allow us to move into a new dimension with our extraterrestrial friends.

One day at the fire station, I saw a snowboarding magazine and I flipped through it as I love snowboarding. There was an article in there that I read over and over. It was about these guys that went on a snowboarding trip on Mt. Shasta in California and were looking for the inner Earth beings!

Something in me just knew they existed.

The article went on to describe how they met a man there who told them all about the inner Earth beings from Telos who lived inside Mt. Shasta and were connected to many other inner Earth civilizations and galactic beings. It said how when Lemuria sunk below the ocean thousands of years ago, some Lemurians moved into the inner Earth. Apparently, these inner Earth beings also want to have contact with us.

Who are these beings?
Is this true?

Anyways, this makes me wonder…what if we had a civilization that didn't have any kings, queens, or presidents running the world? What if we worked together as one civilization for the betterment of all and didn't need people in power? We could step up and offer our gifts as was needed at the time and then meld back in with everyone else. It would be like different parts of the oneself stepping forward at different times.

It is like the dolphins where they are of "pod mind" and not of individualistic mentality.

So many ways to create!

Another thought…

What if it was all reversed?
Land was water and water was land?
Oh the fun!

Never forget to dream and dream big.
Imagination is everything!
It creates reality!

CHAPTER 24
I MARRIED AN ALCOHOLIC

Real love is accepting other people the way they are without trying to change them. If we try to change them, this means we don't really like them.
~Don Miguel Ruiz

Life is fascinating really, right?
I mean how things line up and the twists and turns.
Ups and downs and all arounds.
Then, years later, when you look back, sometimes it makes sense?

I met Bruce in high school apparently when I was playing volleyball. I was all sweaty and my stepbrother, Jonah, called me to come meet his friend, Bruce, at the door of the gym. I ran over quickly and said "hi" and ran back to play volleyball. I was fifteen.

I didn't think anything of it and didn't see him again until I ended up sitting next to him in Driver's Ed. He was funny and I liked that. The class was amusing too, but it was way too early in the morning with a bunch of teenagers who would rather be sleeping. The instructor would get upset with us if we were all too tired to answer questions.

In fact, one morning, he was late and we were all talking. When he came in, we all kept talking and didn't listen for him to tell us to stop. Next thing we knew, he was screaming at all of us and called us all a "bunch of barn animals." We all were laughing at his comment, but he wasn't.

Then, he kicked us all out of his classroom.
We thought this was the best thing ever.

I got to know Bruce better after all of this when we were sophomores in high school. He turned out to be a good friend of Jonah, so I saw him sometimes at our house. He always made me laugh and we both had friends in common, so we hung out a lot. We became good friends and he always wanted to go with my girlfriends and I to places.

It would be all girls and Bruce.
He loved it.
He fit right in as he seemed to get girls.

He wanted me to be his girlfriend, but I didn't want a boyfriend, so we just were good friends. I wanted to be free and to never have a boyfriend.

Well, that all changed over the summer before my junior year. Bruce was persistent and I finally gave in. It was actually a good thing, but I still wanted my freedom. He wanted me to come over to his house or do things together. I just wanted to play and be with my friends.

I had told myself at an early age, I am never getting married.

So, to have a boyfriend meant that was way too close to getting married. I also told myself that I was never having kids!

Vows to myself.
Freedom. Fun. Friends.
Party and play were really my mottos.

I got my driver's license at sixteen and that gave me lots of freedom from my parents and society. I so badly wanted my freedom to make my own choices and do my own thing. You would think I grew up in a communist house or something.

Nope.
Just an overly protective, crazy, Christian mother!

As I mentioned before, in high school I moved in with my dad and stepmother, Priscilla, in California. It was the total opposite from what I had grown up with in Texas during elementary school and middle school. They were always working and never home, so I got even more freedom. There were few rules as well which I loved and they had a pool which was awesome.

So, Bruce and I dated on and off through high school as I didn't want a boyfriend or he would get tired of my antics of wanting to be with my friends and not him. We also dated other people during this time, but we kept getting back together.

Lots of our friends including myself loved to party and we would go to someone's house whose parents were out of town. Word would get out and whoever could come over, would come over. There was lots of underage drinking there, some "pot" smoking, and sex.

Bruce was fun and loved to party, but he loved to get sloppy drunk. He would drink about a six pack of beer, throw that up, and drink about another twelve pack. In the days of partying in high school, everyone was drinking, but not everyone was drinking like this. Some of the guys drank like he did at parties though.

Really though, I had no idea what an alcoholic was.
I had no idea that he started drinking beer at age eight.
His mom thought it would be fun to get him drunk at this age.

Really?!
WTF?!

She was an alcoholic, as well as her father.

Bruce and I went away to different colleges and we continued to date and break up. We dated other people and yet, we kept getting drawn back together. We were connected emotionally in ways of our unresolved emotional traumas of growing up in divorced, dysfunctional homes with parents who had not dealt with their issues.

Our parents would trash talk the other parent and want us to take sides. Neither of us wanted to do this as we loved both our parents with all their flaws. Bruce and I connected together on this deeply and vowed to never get divorced if we ever married.

Bruce told me one day, "Remember when I met you in the gym and you were all sweaty from volleyball?"

"No," I say.

"Really? Well, I remember. And I knew that day that I would marry you," he replied.

I was blown away.

I don't even remember meeting him until the Driver's Ed class.
And how would he know that he wants to marry me on a day we first met?

Bruce ended up moving to Los Angeles where I was going to college to continue his degree as his college in Northern California was only a two year college. We moved in together and we had fun. We continued to play and party and Bruce would still get really drunk. I would get annoyed at his drinking and he would stop for a while. Eventually, he would start again while partying with his buddies.

After college, we decided to get married and began planning a big wedding.
I'm already breaking one of my "vows" to myself!
Getting married?!

Our parents were really excited. Although, I don't think his mom really was as she didn't like me much. She called me "the girlfriend from hell." She also had this weird relationship with Bruce. It was almost as if Bruce was her husband.

Past life perhaps?

They had a deep love for each other, but she didn't want to let him go.
This should have been a big red flag.
Well, the drinking should have been even a bigger red flag.

Anyways, we shifted all this as the wedding planning seemed to get really complicated, so we got married with friends in Las Vegas one weekend at a drive thru wedding chapel.

I remember sitting in the back of the Chevy Cavalier with the roof down as the woman minister was reciting the wedding ceremony. I was having cold feet and something inside me was telling me that I was making a big mistake.

I kept pushing those feelings down.
"It's just cold feet," I told myself.

As she continued with the ceremony, a drunk, homeless man crashed into a building across the street making a really loud noise.

We all laugh.
Maybe this was an omen of what was to come of our marriage?
Perhaps I should be listening to these signs?
Hmmm....

The next thing I find that I am saying out of my mouth is, "I do."

Yep. That's right.
I do.

I am excited and scared all at the same time. I wonder what I just did and I try to not think of the feelings that came up. I am good at shutting off my emotions or at least, I think so.

Bruce and I are good companions. We have fun together and yet we get into huge fights sometimes, typically when we are drinking.

A close friend of mine tells me one day as we are talking about the ups and downs of our relationships, "You and Bruce are either fighting or fucking! This is always how you guys have been since I have known you from high school."

I am actually kinda taken back when she says this.
It's the truth and I know it.
Truth sometimes hurts when it is in your face like that.

Life goes on and Bruce and I are committed to staying married as neither of us want to get divorced like our parents did. It also means "failure" to me and neither of us want that.

Funny, the agreements that you decide for yourself.

I need Bruce and Bruce needs me. This is really the premise of our relationship. We like to have fun, play, party, and have sex. We were kids when we met and we are really raising each other. He is there for me and I for him. We like to travel and be with friends.

We both get jobs as firefighters in different fire departments within a year of each other and now, we are both making good money. It allows us to buy a house and travel more. Bruce is really good at remodeling houses, so we buy, fix up, and sell a few homes making a good profit.

So many fun places that we traveled to during these times before kids. We took a trip to Greece, Italy, Switzerland, and France for a few weeks one time with friends. It was so much fun. For some reason, I had always wanted to go to Greece and Italy. It called to me.

I loved the gods and goddesses in each of these cultures and I knew quite a lot about them. Something kept calling me to the Oracle of Delphi and we made a special trip there. It was a beautiful ride through the mountains to get there. Apparently, there was a priestess or many priestess that were oracles here who told the future to those who came to seek it.

I saw an inscription there at the Oracle of Delphi that read, "Know Thyself." This stuck with me and it would be many years before I really understood the deeper meaning of this. It felt powerful.

I still wondered why I had to be here.
Perhaps I was once an oracle and it was calling me there for some reason?
Are there energies at these sacred sites that activate parts of us?
Or maybe we are just clearing old energies from other lives there?

Maybe.

Sometimes, I wish that I would have been an archeologist so that I could have traveled the world exploring ancients sites.

Anyways, I don't like that Bruce is gone fifteen or so days a month and it is hard on me. My abandonment issues kick in from time to time and I get really mad at him for leaving me.

But, we do make up sex well though.

Our friends begin to have kids and this puts a damper on our party life. I begin to feel like I want to have kids, but I am super afraid to. Bruce wants kids and is just waiting for me to give him the green light.

Yep.
Another one of my "vows" to myself.
Never have kids.
Broken and discarded.
I am happy I broke this one though.

At about thirty-one, it kicks in for me and I am pregnant within a few months. I am shocked as I was on "the pill" for about ten years. Bruce is super excited and I am too, but I am afraid that I will do to my kids what was done to me.

I find out that we are having a boy and I am just so jazzed.
My pregnancy is easy as is the birth.
Yay!

It's funny the way having a child changes you.
You "grow up" somewhat.

Well, at least, I wanted to keep this kid perfect just as he came out, so I had to "grow up."

I found that I didn't want to drink much anymore or party. I still loved having fun, but it wasn't about staying up all night with friends anymore. I didn't like feeling like shit the next morning and having to take care of my son all day.

Bruce didn't dig this at all.

He still wanted things to be as they were and drink as much as he wanted. This put a huge strain on our marriage as the main focus became clear to me about what was important to Bruce.

Beer. Beer.
And more beer.

I saw things so much more clearly as I rarely drank anymore. Bruce's main focus when going to someone's house was to get beer or make sure they had at least a twelve pack of beer. He couldn't drink just one or two beers. It was six, eight, twelve beers depending on how much he could consume.

I began to realize that when he got upset, he would crack open a beer.
If anything got tough, he went for a beer.
If he got anxious, more beer.

Something was tapping me on the shoulder and I began to wonder if he was addicted to alcohol. I looked into what was behind an alcoholic as to why they couldn't stop. I found something that made sense to me.

It said, "Behind every addiction is pain."

This made so much sense to me as it didn't matter what type of addiction it was, there was pain underneath it. So, someone could be an alcoholic, drug addict, sex addict, workaholic, foodaholic, etc...

They numbed out their unresolved pain with their addiction.

I began to learn more and I could see the deep unresolved pain Bruce had. He began drinking at age eight. His parents got divorced at age eight. Bruce was beaten physically and verbally by his dad. His mom showed him how she numbed out her pain with alcohol.

Bruce wasn't ready to stop drinking and it turns out that when I was working, he was drinking. My mom helped to care for our son, so that helped, but my mom was also worried about his drinking.

Things would go up and down and I pulled my energy from Bruce and put it into raising our son. I wasn't sure how to get him to stop drinking and even our friends began commenting that they didn't like to be around him when he is drinking.

So, what do you do when your marriage is in trouble?

Have another child.
Yep!?
It was a girl!
I cried.

I was excited and scared at the same time.

I was really freaked out about this as I knew it was the mother/daughter lineage in our family that fostered big emotional and verbal abuse. I didn't want to continue the pattern. I fell in love with this little girl and vowed to never harm her the way I was harmed.

Now, I realize that I am telling you this story like I am a victim in all of this.
I am not.
I was a very willing participant in all of this.
My issue of abandonment kept me needy and co-dependent.

About six months into my pregnancy with her, I caught Bruce lying about many things. Little things. Big things. He said he lied to me because he didn't like it when I was mad.

Mother fucker.
What a pussy.

Now, hold on here.

I know this word triggers most of us women because there is a negative intent behind it. It is not talking about a kitty cat, either. Just take a second though and think about words. I have often thought about words and the energy behind them. I have thought about the "bad" words and how we are the ones that decide this, but they are just words.

Take for instance, the word "Shit." It came from when they would ship manure across the ocean and they would write on the crate, "ship high in transit" aka SHIT. A bad word? I used to get a bar of soap in my mouth if I said a word that my mom thought was "bad."

Anyways, I don't like to use that word in a demeaning way as I know it refers to men being weak as they think women are, yet women are some of the strongest people I know on this planet. It is like the word, "Bitch" which is really just a female dog which I find them to be cute and loveable, but people use the word "Bitch" as a put down as well.

Words are fascinating when you look at them. It is the energy and intent behind them that triggers us. Look at the deeper meaning within ourselves as they have much to teach us.

Anyways, I use to think that women were weak and men were strong. I wanted to be a man because it seemed that they had it better in this world. I wanted to be like my dad and not like my mom.

It wasn't until my late thirties that I realized women are so fucking strong!

They are strong physically, mentally, emotionally, spiritually. Some of my closest women friends had gone through so much in their lives and came out even stronger. They dove into their fear and didn't run from it. I worked with all men for twenty plus years and I saw how vulnerable they really were underneath. They acted strong around others, but I could see through them. Of course, not all men and I don't mean to bash men either as I am just stating my observations.

This reminds me of Captain Jay who used to tell me that I was one of the only real "guys" on our fire department because I had "big balls." I thought this was funny. He used to say this because I had no fear of going up against our fire chiefs or politicians when there was an issue. Most of the other guys would never go against the "establishment." I stood for truth and there was so much dysfunction in the fire department and government.

Captain Jay would go on and say this "pussy" thing is all wrong. He would say that vaginas are so strong that they should make tires out of them because they can take a beating with sex and giving birth. Then, he would say how "balls" are so sensitive and weak.

He was quite a character and I loved him.

Back to mother fucker…

Bruce lied to me and I was pissed. I was done and I was over his lies over the years. I was done with his drinking and I was done period.

I knew it was over.
He knew it was over.
And I was six months pregnant and had a three year old boy.

I didn't know what to do or where to go.
I was broken and hurt.
Deeply sad.
I sobbed.

I called my sister-in-law who I was close with and she had married the same type of husband. She loved her brother, but also knew what I was going through. She told me to go to a therapist before I filed for divorce.

A therapist?
I was desperate.
I didn't like therapists.
I didn't know how they could help.
I agreed to go to one she recommended.

Bruce and I went together to see the therapist and we were both anxious. We both wanted to make our marriage work, but I didn't know how we would get through all our issues. We both sat on the couch as the therapist asked us questions.

Then, the therapist threw out a "Fuck."
I was shocked as she looked so professional.
She threw out another fuck.
I loved her already.
I knew this person was going to work for me!

Towards the end of our first session, she told Bruce and I that our issues are unresolved childhood issues and wanted us to work separately with her for a while. She said that I had issues with trust and abandonment. Bruce also had issues as well, but needed to deal with his drinking first. Then, she would get us back together as needed for couple's therapy.

Therapy helped me tons and we worked with EMDR which helps to process traumas quickly. I dove in and went regularly for about a year and a half. Bruce wasn't so excited about therapy and said that I was the one with all the issues.

Gotta love it.

With therapy, I became stronger emotionally and my PTSD was gone. This was big for my abandonment issues. I was also developing trusting my therapist which was helping my mistrust issues. My need for adrenaline rushes also left.

Fascinating!

When Bruce was not wanting to look at any of his deeper issues, I told him that I wasn't going to be with him any longer if he continued drinking. I told him that I couldn't as I loved myself too much to continue with a life like this.

I didn't want to give him an ultimatum and yet, I was just being honest. I wanted him to quit drinking because he wanted to quit drinking. I knew that was the only way it would stick.

I also knew that he was scared.
Scared because alcohol was a tool for him to get through life.
I didn't know what he would pick, but I was choosing me.

A few days later, Bruce ended up running into some friends of his that all used to be alcoholics and now attended meetings at AA. They talked him into going. This was big and Bruce was apprehensive. He went and decided to quit drinking a few meetings later. He also started doing therapy more regularly and looking deeper inside himself.

We were both healing so much and it felt like we were healing our ancestor's lineage as well. Neither of us wanted to treat our kids the way we were treated.

It's interesting as we both healed, we came closer together and also further apart. It's like we didn't really know each other anymore. We worked a lot and didn't see each other much. Kids also took up much of our time.

Is it possible that we accomplished what we came in to do together?
Did we finish our contracts with each other?
But, aren't we supposed to stay married till death do us part?
More on all this later…

CHAPTER 25
BAREFOOT AND PREGNANT?

Give up defining yourself — to yourself or to others. You won't die. You will come to life.
And don't be concerned with how others define you. When they define you, they are
limiting themselves, so it's their problem. Whenever you interact with people, don't be
there primarily as a function or a role, but as the field of conscious Presence. You can only
lose something that you have, but you cannot lose something that you are."
~Eckhart Tolle

So, it's 1997 in Southern California and I am now hired as a firefighter/paramedic. Done with the fire academy, I am now sworn in to protect and serve the community of Sparrow City. I am so excited to do a good job and help people.

I am one of three women on the fire department of about one hundred people. I am working on the "Avenue" for my first assignment which is the "bad" part of town. Really, it is where the poorer people live and many homeless. Some gangs and drugs run this part of town.

My captain is a cross between an old cowboy and a soldier. He is about forty and yet he looks like he will retire any day. His name is Jay and he is everything "bad boy."

I like him already.

I also heard that he likes to yell at new recruits, so I am a bit nervous about this and yet, I know it will just roll off my back. It's just a power trip to try to break you down. It is so wild that this still goes on today.

Why?

I have my last name hyphenated because I kept my maiden name. Jay doesn't like this at all and berates me for being a feminist.

This makes me laugh.
He continues with his comments and I laugh harder as they are so absurd.

It just feels so absurd to me about being a feminist and I get it, too. Stand up for women and our rights. Stand up against the abuses and wanting equality. Is this why I am here in the fire department? To show that I can do the job as good as a man?

No.

I just wanted a job that suited me. One where I got to help people, be a part of a team, be physically active, and have fun. This was being a firefighter. I kept my dad's last name because he is Cuban and he said it was a good idea. It is part of the Cuban tradition. I was into pleasing him, so I kept it.

Back to Jay...

I realize that he likes to try and find what upsets someone and then continue there where the wound is. He is good at this. I see his game and don't give anything he says much emotion except my laughter at his comments.

We get along well and he seems to know everything about everything. The other guys at the station know him well and give him shit. I just love the bantering that goes on back and forth and the off color humor. Sexual jokes are some of Jay's favorites and he is actually quite amusing. I don't take any of it personally and I can see that I am winning Jay over.

He is rude and hilarious at the same time.
I also see that Jay has a huge heart.
He is really a "softie" inside.

We are pretty busy with calls on the "Avenue." Lots of medical calls and some big fires too. I stay calm during calls and as a firefighter/paramedic, I am in charge of telling my crew what to do if it is a medical call.

Jay loves to tell the story of how we went on a call for a woman stabbed with scissors. We arrived and sure enough, there is an older woman standing in front of us with a pair of scissors buried in the middle her chest.

The other firefighter/paramedic on the call with us looks at me and says in a very panicked way, "Hydee, there is a pair of scissors in her chest!"

I say, "Well, she's standing up talking to us, so let's stabilize it and put her on the gurney."

I am thinking that she must have hit her lung and may have trouble breathing soon. I am wondering how this happened when the woman says to us that she tried to kill herself with sewing scissors. She buried the scissors all the way up to the handle!

Wow.

We all get her on the gurney and stabilize the scissors. We ride in the ambulance to the hospital with her, starting IVs and such, going Code 3. We get to the emergency room and she is doing well. They do an x-ray to see what she hit. Turns out, she missed all her vital organs and arteries!

Amazing.

We see the x-ray come back and the scissors were angled, so it stayed away from her heart and lungs! She's gonna live.

Anyways, Jay loves to tell that story because in all the years I worked with him, he never saw me lose my cool.

And really, I was able to keep my cool on the outside, yet my insides were sometimes freaking out. Somehow, I always felt like I was guided. Perhaps my guardian angel was always by my side whispering to me?

Captain Jay loved to give me shit about my cooking, too. He often told the story of when I cooked broccoli one time. I put the broccoli in the steamer with no water. He was watching me and asked me how the broccoli was going to cook.

I told him, "I washed the broccoli with water and it will cook that way."

He laughed out loud saying, "You went to USC and don't know how food is streamed?!"

Ha ha!
I didn't know!
So funny.

Needless to say, I eventually learned how to cook in the fire department as many guys were great cooks.

I loved the guys on the fire department. Many of them were like my dad and older. Some of them had been in Vietnam or in the military. Some were old hippies. Most of them were really helpful and nice to me. The young guys were great, too.

One of my favorite off color firefighters was a guy by the name of Stan. He was in his late fifties. He was working in place of my engineer that day and he was constantly telling stories. He was quite racist and very opinionated.

I listened and asked questions. I found him quite amusing.

He was telling me how he thought we should nuke certain places and turn it into "green glass." I thought that term was funny and just kept laughing. He was dead serious though.

He followed me around most of the day and into the evening. I went out to the apparatus floor and decided to do another weight workout. He followed me out there and was telling more stories watching me workout.

He then stopped and looked at me.

He says, "I just don't understand you women. Why do you want to come and work alongside us men? You should be home in the kitchen, barefoot, and pregnant! We are supposed to protect you and take care of you, not work alongside you."

I look at him with a smirk on my face realizing that this is how he was brought up and taught. I am giggling.

I say, "Stan, this is just who I am. I don't know how else to be."

We both laugh as we understand each other completely.

CHAPTER 26
GREG

The clearest way into the Universe is through a forest wilderness.
~John Muir

There are so many amazing men and women that I got to know and love while working in the fire department. One of those people was my first engineer, Greg.

Greg was twenty years older than me. He was about 6'5", kind, and soft spoken. He was friendly and funny as well. I first began working with him when I got hired as a paramedic on the ambulance. I was on his crew with four other guys.

I loved these days when the five of us would laugh and play pranks on each other. We were always laughing while running calls in between. We also spend time as a crew together off duty. Sam and I were on the ambulance. Jay, Greg, and Andy were on the fire engine. Greg drove the engine.

Jay, Greg, and Andy all seemed like old cowboys. They all were hunters and had horses. They all had big cowboy hats and watched "The Duke" (John Wayne) on television all the time while at the station. They took Sam and I horseback riding a few times which was always a good time.

Greg had the kind of humor where you didn't even know that he had just insulted you in the funniest of ways. He was also going through a divorce when I got hired in 1996 and he had two young girls.

I was twenty-five years old and Greg was like a father figure to me. He was good at listening and giving advice. He liked teaching me things. He was hoping to retire at fifty, but not with two young girls and a divorce.

I got hired a year later as a firefighter/paramedic and worked with Greg for part of my probationary year. I got to stay at the same station with him during that time and even though we were on other shifts, we would still sling insults at each other, laugh, and talk about life.

We would talk a lot about money stuff as I was learning about the stock market and our retirements. He was trying to figure out how to get the most money he could while retiring as soon as possible.

This all shifted when he found a lump in his throat.

It was 1999 and everyone was devastated to hear the news especially me. Greg was optimistic and knew he could beat it even if it was cancer. The whole fire department came together and we rallied around in support for him. Other guys started working his shifts for him so he could concentrate on healing his body.

I drove him down to UCLA hospital to get the lump removed and biopsied. We took a whole day and it was great to be there with him. Unfortunately, the news came back that it was cancerous and was the worst type. It had also progressed to stage three. All of us were devastated to hear this news, especially Greg.

He began chemotherapy and radiation while also changing his diet. He was dating a woman who loved him and was helping him make amazing, healing food. Greg knew he could beat the cancer. He was doing well and I would meet him sometimes before his chemotherapy or up at his house. We would catch up and talk about what was going on at the fire station.

One day, we met after his chemotherapy and treatment. He was super excited because the next day, he was going to go hunting with Jay in Nevada. He was optimistic that the cancer was gone and that he would return to the fire department soon.

It was great to feel how wonderful he was doing.

I worked that next day which was Halloween and it was around 6 pm when a phone call came in for my captain, Adam. He answered and seemed to get really somber. I wondered what was up. He got off the phone and told Bob and I that he has some bad news. He said that Greg had died around 2 am this morning.

I was shocked and said, "No. Can't be. He is on his way to Nevada with Jay today. I saw him yesterday. He was doing great!"

Adam said, "He had to cancel his hunting trip with Jay as last night he got really sick and went into the hospital. He died from the chemotherapy treatment."

We were all shocked and no one knew what to say.

I left and went to my room where I just cried and cried.
"It can't be!" I thought. "I just saw him. He looked amazing."
I just couldn't wrap my head around it.

Greg…
Dead?

Really?

And on Halloween?!
The Day of the Dead?!
Fuck!

I just couldn't wrap my head around him being dead especially since I just saw him yesterday doing so great. He was so excited and the best that I had seen him in a long time.

I was devastated.
Someone that I loved and cared about…gone.
I had never really lost someone this close to me.

I was pissed.
Mad at life.
Mad at God.
Why would you take such a good person!?
He is too young!

I wrestled with all this in my head while trying to shut down my emotions and act like everything was okay. I wasn't good at dealing with sadness and tears.

This was the first death for Sparrow City Fire Department since he was still technically working for the department, but on leave. Cancer was presumptive for firefighters, so this was a line of duty death. All of the firefighters were saddened by the sudden loss.

We had a fire department funeral for Greg to honor him and all that he did. It was a huge turnout and other fire departments helped. I was part of the Honor Guard which brought the casket out and folded the flag. We also stood on stage in front of everyone for the whole funeral.

I probably should have not been on the Honor Guard for this one. I could barely keep it together. I wanted to lie on the floor and sob my heart out. Instead, I choked back tears and cried silent tears throughout the entire funeral.

When it was finally over, I went into the bathroom and sobbed. As I came out, I saw Andy. He gave me one look, grabbed me, and hugged me tight. I just sobbed and sobbed in his arms. He did too. He loved Greg as much as I did.

I was deeply sad.

Sad to lose a close friend and father figure.
Sad to think about his girls not having a father anymore.
Sad because I didn't understand life or death.
Sad because I had forgotten that death is only a transition.

It would be another five years or so before I began to remember more again.

My son's middle name is Greg.
He is named after an amazing soul who I know I will see again.
Actually, I have spoken to Greg on the other side, but I will get to that later in this book.

I love you, Greg.
May you have exciting travels on your next journey.

CHAPTER 27
JUST ANOTHER CHRISTMAS DAY

Do you want to know what my secret is? You see, I just don't mind what happens.
~Krishnamurti

Before I had kids, I would offer to work Christmas for the guys that had to work that day that had kids. I didn't really care about that day and it always seemed hectic to me to try to see all of the family.

So, work was a good option and it was usually it was a pretty mellow day.

I was working in the middle of town with a couple of guys who weren't much older than me. We all had fun laughing and planning our day of what we would cook for dinner.

A call came in mid-morning for a person not breathing at the jail.

We got there pretty quick, but we had to go through many locked doors. We finally got to where the man wasn't breathing and they had him sitting up in a chair with oxygen on him.

I quickly recognized this as I was the firefighter/paramedic on the engine and we moved him to the floor. Tyler, my engineer, began to get an ambu bag out to breath for him. I checked a pulse and he didn't have one. Billy, my captain, began compressions on his chest.

This guy looked like he was maybe twenty-five and I was asking the staff what happened while putting him on our heart monitor. He was not in a shockable rhythm, so I began starting an IV on his arm to give him medications.

The staff was telling us how they just received him today and he could have snuck drugs in with him. This fit as it looked like he had overdosed on heroin and stopped breathing.

The ambulance guys arrived and we loaded up our patient onto the gurney to take to the hospital. While enroute to the hospital, I noticed a rhythm change on the heart monitor and I checked for a pulse.

He had a pulse!
A really strong pulse.

We stopped CPR and continued to assist him with his breathing. By the time we got to the hospital, he was grabbing at the tube in his throat to pull it out.

The hospital staff was ready for him and he continued to thrive. Billy, Tyler, and I cleaned up, restocked our medical bags, and did paperwork for the next call. We were all jazzed that he came back. It felt like a gift being Christmas and all.

It was a pretty slow day, call wise, and we watched television while stuffing our faces with food. I went to bed around 930 pm hoping to sleep all night.

Not so lucky, around 1130 pm, we received a call for a woman not breathing. We got dressed quickly and headed to the home. It was up in the hills and took about five minutes to get there.

When we arrived, the scene was chaos.
The street didn't have street lights, so it was really dark.

I grabbed my bags and headed towards the house as I saw a police officer who looked wide eyed. She said to hurry.

I entered the house first and I could hear the husband yelling and screaming. He was yelling, "Shit! Fuck! Shit! Fuck!" He kept saying this over and over as he grabbed his head.

A little three year old boy was up walking around in his pjs and following his dad around. He was copying everything his dad was doing. He was yelling, "Shit! Fuck! Shit! Fuck!"

The police officer led us to a room where we found his wife in bed.

She wasn't breathing.
In fact, she looked like she may have been dead for a while.
She was still warm though.

We got her to the floor and began CPR. I got the heart monitor and hooked her up. She was flatline.

Damn!

We continued and I put a tube down her throat to help her breathe. The ambulance was there fast and one of the other paramedics started the IV. He began to give her epinephrine to see if we could get her heart to start again.

You could feel the urgency in the room to get her to come back into her body. She had a husband and young son…and it was Christmas, damn it!

We all wanted her to live.
Moms can't die on Christmas.
It is just not okay.

We continued for twenty minutes giving her medications and doing CPR. We loaded her up on the gurney and headed to the hospital continuing our efforts.

The hospital staff continued trying to revive her without any luck. The staff said that she had been in the hospital earlier that day with chest pain. They couldn't find anything, so they let her go home for Christmas around noon.

Billy, Tyler, and I were all super somber and bummed. None of us spoke as we gathered our things together for the next call. We were all cleaned up with our stuff back on the engine when the little boy whose mother had just died came up to us with his grandmother.

The grandmother asked if she was okay and I replied that the hospital staff can help them. I couldn't tell her or I would burst into tears. This little boy had no idea that he had just lost his mother. I gave him a stuffed teddy bear that we had on the engine and led them inside the hospital.

I was on the verge of tears.

I came back to the engine and looked at Billy and Tyler. They were on the verge of tears as well. This was a heartbreaking call. I cried silent tears on the way back to the station. None of us said a word.

My thoughts were going crazy on the way.

Why?
I don't understand.
Why?
It just doesn't make sense.

"God, why would you take a young mother from her family on Christmas and let a druggie come back from the dead that was in jail?" I asked in my head. "It's not fair!"

I was twenty-nine years old and this was hard for me to take.
It was years later before I ever found closure around it.

CHAPTER 28
9/11

This new world should be the world in which the strong won't exploit the weak, the bad won't exploit the good, where the poor won't be humiliated by the rich. It will be the world in which the children of intellect, science, and skills will serve to the community in order to make lives easier and nicer. And not to the individuals for gaining wealth.
~Nikola Tesla

It was just another morning at the fire station.
I was still asleep around 630 am when I heard a loud knock on my door.

"Hydee! Get up! Get out here! You have to come see this! I think we are under attack!" Rod says.

Rod is my engineer and I am a firefighter.

I am so tired from a long night of calls, but I can hear the panic in his voice and I rush out of the dorms to the kitchen area where the television is on.

My captain, Dave, and Rod are glued to the television saying a plane just hit the World Trade Center. I am watching for a moment when the next plane hit the other tower.

Fuck.

I am rubbing my eyes in disbelief.
Something isn't right.

We all continue to watch for the next few hours and we know that the New York City firefighters are rushing into those buildings. People are jumping from the towers with the intense fires.

Is this for real?

Then, one of the towers comes down.

What?!
These buildings are built to withstand plane crashes.
Then, the next tower comes down.

People are rushing and panicking. We can feel their fear as we watch. We don't know what to say. We know that there were firefighters, police officers, and civilians inside those towers when they came crumbling down.

Another building comes down later…WTC 7.
Huh?
This makes no sense.

We finally decide that it is time for us to go home. The oncoming shift had shown up a few hours before and we were all glued to watching the chaos. The freeways are empty. It reminds me of when the Los Angeles riots happened. No one was going to work or school. Everyone was in the safety of their home.

I finally got home and I couldn't wrap my head around all that was happening.

Are we in a war?
Did we just get attacked?

As I walked around the neighborhood, I tried to get a grip on what was happening. My husband was at work with the fire academy and probably had no idea. I saw a neighbor who looked just as distraught as me. He was trying to figure out what was happening as well.

Finally, I went back inside my house with my two dogs. We sat and watched the television as more news came out. I stayed there for hours until Bruce came home.

I think I was traumatized and it felt as though I was there in New York. Bruce hugged me and I cried. He had not seen anything on television as he had been training new recruits all day. He heard about it, but had not seen anything. He didn't think it was a big deal.

How fascinating really that we can be feeling so different just because I watched it and he didn't. Can we get traumatized from watching something on television even though we weren't there?

I learned many years later that we can and we do. So, now we have a nation full of millions of traumatized people who watched it even though we weren't there. It's in our psyche. Our "fight or flight" has been triggered.

Bruce and I went back to New York about three weeks later with about twenty other firefighters from our surrounding fire departments to help out any way we could. We went to help our brother and sister New York City firefighters as many of their families had been devastated. They were having lots of funerals and mourning continuously for their loved ones.

We were welcomed by the New York City firefighters and you could feel their disbelief and sadness. Whole crews were killed. We went to the fire station right next to the WTC and stood on the roof looking at the twisted metal still being pulled out and put on trucks to be hauled away. You could see the destruction of other nearby buildings with holes in them. It looked like a war zone and the smell was horrible. Signs of missing people were posted everywhere.

We went to some of the funerals and listened to their stories. We drank with them at some of the oldest bars in New York. It was basic humanity reaching the depths of our souls.

Some of the stories being told by the New York City firefighters were that the towers should have never come down. They talked about how they had been in numerous high rise fires and that something isn't right. These towers were built to withstand plane crashes.

Then, they mentioned explosives.
Whuuuttt?

They talked about how the building came down perfectly as if whole floors had explosives on them. They said to look at the pictures of the towers coming down on television. You could see the explosions of explosives going off and then the towers coming down. Then, they questioned why WTC 7 came down on its own a block away.

Perhaps it had explosives inside it as well?

This was all being told quietly away from their management as the New York City firefighters were told to not question anything they saw that day or they would lose their jobs. Even the wives of firefighters that were killed were asking questions.

Something reeks of a cover-up!
WTF?!
Why?

I came back from this trip and all the firefighters were talking about it. They knew something wasn't right, but no one could understand it.

It wasn't until some years later when one of the guys at the fire station brought in the movie, Fahrenheit 911.

Talk about blowing your mind...

CHAPTER 29
CLEAR!

If you want to find the secrets of the universe, think in terms of energy, frequency, and vibration.
~ Nikola Tesla

I had been on the fire department for about three years now. I was mentoring a new firefighter/paramedic from another fire department to sign off on that his paramedic skills were above average. I had to make sure that he was ready to run calls on his own.

It was fun having four people on the fire engine as it gave more to talk about and give each other shit about as usually there were only three of us. His name was Ed and he would work with us for about two months while I assessed his paramedic skills.

He hadn't been a paramedic very long and had been a firefighter for about three years. He was doing okay on calls, but lacked experience as all new paramedics do.

One morning, we were working out at the beach and running when a medical call came in for a man with chest pain. We all hurried back to the engine and drove to the call which was not far away.

It was at a grocery store and the man who looked to be in his thirties was sitting down where they bag your groceries. He looked to be in severe distress and breathing heavily. Ed was in charge and he was telling us what to do. We put him on our heart monitor and oxygen. Suddenly, the man just looked at us.

We knew his heart had just stopped.
Ed was still trying to talk to him.
He didn't realize this man just coded (died).

Brian, the engineer, and I immediately got the man to the ground and I told Ed to grab the paddles on the heart monitor. He was in ventricular fibrillation which means the heart is there quivering and not pumping any blood. We had a chance getting him back if we could shock his heart with our defibrillator quickly. We charged the monitor and Ed put the paddles on the man's chest.

"Clear!" He yelled.

We all backed away to not get shocked.
Nothing.
No changes to his heart.
We charged the monitor again at a higher shock.

"Clear!" Ed yelled again.

Suddenly, the heart rhythm changed.

It looked to be regular and fast.
We checked for a pulse.
He had a pulse!
Sweet!

We get him on the gurney as the ambulance just arrived. He still is not breathing, so we assist his ventilations. Ed is grinning from ear to ear as are we. It isn't often that we get someone back from the dead.

We are in the back of the ambulance driving to the hospital when the man begins to move more and sits up! He is now looking at us all wondering what happened. We tell him that his heart stopped and he doesn't believe us. He said he just stopped into the grocery store.

Wild!

The heart is so fascinating to me with its electrical wiring. Why does it beat? What causes that electrical spark to constantly beat and keep us alive? What causes it to stop? Is it purely the intent of the soul and wanting to experience a different reality when it stops?

We are electrical beings.

I wonder why he chose to have that experience of death? Did he "go to the light" and they sent him back because it wasn't his time? Did he switch souls with another soul who "walked in?" Perhaps he needed to be reminded of his mission here on Earth?

Love to have all the answers!

CHAPTER 30
HAVING MINI-ME'S

Parenthood is an inner change. We ourselves grow because parenting is so deep and intense.
~Mr. Rogers

I love kids.
Always have.
I see them.
Their purity of being.

They still embody the energy of the other realms.
I love their spirit and freedom that they express.

I had two nieces that were about eight years younger than me in high school. I loved playing with them. I just love the way they laugh and giggle. I felt like I could just be a little kid again or maybe I never grew up!

Kids are doorways to the other realities. They still see what else is out there and haven't shut it down yet. They still talk to their "imaginary" friends which I feel, are really their spirit guides or helper spirits.

I love kids so much that I had decided I should not have them once I was an adult. I didn't want to do to them what had happened to me growing up. I didn't want them to feel the pain and suffering I went through as a child.

Being selfish was also my reason to not have kids. I was too selfish and wanted to experience life. I wanted to travel and feel like I wasn't tied down. If I had kids, I wanted to really nurture their spirit.

I have always felt that I was about eight years old at heart and really maybe even four or five years old. My dad would play like a kid and was always so fun. I wanted to be like him when I grew up. I wanted to be that FUN adult!

Somehow, I equated having kids with being divorced.

Did I, on some level, feel that I was responsible for the divorce of my parents?

I know lots of kids feel that way. To me, it felt like if you had kids, then you forget about your partner and your energy goes to the kids. I never realized that you could balance this.

When my son was born, I fell deeply in love with this little being. He was just so "gorgeous."

Every time I looked at him, I would just smile and call him "gorgeous."
The amount of love you have for your child is just indescribable.
He was just so perfect.
Nothing had messed him up in this world yet.

The same goes for my daughter when she was born. Her smile and sparkle in her eye made me melt. They both felt like they were not from this world and I wondered how I could support their mission in life this time around.

Wow.
How do I be a good parent?
Where do I start?
Is there a manual on how to raise kids?
I had so many questions!

Raising kids really needs to be important in our society as this shapes the next generation. We need a license to have a dog, a license to drive a car ...shouldn't we need a license to have a child? Should just anyone have a child or those who have evolved their consciousness?

Such an important decision!
And I don't want to take away anyone's freedom as it is just a thought to ponder.

One of the best things I ever did was becoming a parent.
It made me want to become a better person in this crazy world.
They soothed my soul.
Truly, they are my teachers.

CHAPTER 31
HANGING BY A THREAD

You are here to create the world around you that YOU choose, while you allow the world as others choose it to be to exist also. And while their choices in no way hinder your choices, your attention to what they are choosing does affect your vibration, and therefore your own point of attraction.
~Abraham-Hicks

It's 2 am in the early morning.

Why is it that we have so many crazy calls at this time of the morning?

I know the bars close around this time and lots of drunks hit the street. It can be a rather still time of night where the veils are thin making it a good time for those spirits not in a body to contact those in a body.

Anyways, it's one of those nights.
Not much sleep as people are quite restless.
We keep getting call after call.
I finally lay down to sleep at 1 am.
How glorious is that!

I am rudely awakened with eyes burning an hour later to dispatch coming over the loud speaker.

Fire!

It's a house on fire and it sounds like it has been "cooking" for some time. Dispatch is describing neighbors out of their houses trying to use their garden hoses to put the fire out and lots of smoke. I am always excited to go on a fire as is my crew. I am working for a new captain, Billy, and Tyler is my engineer. I have been on the department for about three years now.

We throw on our turnouts and jump on the engine as we scream out of the fire station blaring our lights and sirens. The fire is in the next sector from ours and we will either be the second or third engine to arrive which is about seven or eight minutes away.

I am hoping that we are the third engine because that means we get to go inside the house and back up the guys on the initial fire attack. The second engine will take over commanding the incoming units and will stay outside the house as a backup rescue team as per our policies.

I wanna go play!

We can see a large header of smoke coming from the beach area as we get closer. Another engine arrives on scene just before us, so I am excited because we are just a minute behind them. We will get to be back up and go inside the house on fire.

Fun!

We pull up and it is chaos everywhere. It is a one story beach house with flames and smoke coming up from the house. Neighbors yelling and people everywhere. We hear a report that the owner is still inside the house and hasn't been found.

My captain tells me to grab a hoseline and we are going in to look for the missing person.

We get to the door and go "on air" (putting our facemasks on and connecting to our SCBA bottle, so that we can breathe in the smoke). I have a hoseline in hand and Billy is right behind me. It is dark and smoky. I can barely see as the smoke is almost to the ground as I enter through the door.

I crawl a few feet and suddenly, I fall through the floor!

Thankfully, it is only a few feet down that I sink in with one of my legs. I am able to pull myself up and out. I yell for Billy to be careful and he radios everyone on scene about the hole.

We continue. I feel around and some of the floor is spongy, but intact. We make a left hand search as the initial engine company did a right hand search of the home. This will help us cover the whole house.

It's hot!
It's loud and I can hear the fire crackling.

I feel around with one hand and pull the hose with the other. Billy is pulling the hose, too. We are running into tables, couches, etc.. as we go in and out of rooms. We can't see anything. Before going into a house, I try to look at the house and guess the layout. It helps to know where the windows are and where the kitchen and bedrooms may be.

Nothing found yet and we have gone through what feels like one side of the house. I open a door. It's the garage and there is no fire. It is full of light smoke as we enter and something hits me in the head.

It keeps swinging back and forth hitting me as try to stand up.
I finally get out of the way to see what it is.

We found the owner of the house.

He has hung himself in the garage and is dead. Billy and I look at him almost in disbelief wondering if it is a real person.

It is.
We cut him down and lay him on the ground.

Billy lets the incident commander know that we found him. As he is talking on the radio, I am looking around at the multiple open gas containers on the ground. There are also books of matches everywhere. I also open the garage door to the outside.

This guy wanted this place to burn.
He wanted to die.
I wonder why?
What was so bad?

I didn't think about it being arson until later, but that is probably why I fell through the floor. It probably has gasoline trails and burned super hot. Other crews are helping to put the fire out and ventilating the structure. We finally get the fire out and now it's time for the fire investigator to do his thing. Once the investigation is over and we all know it is arson, we start to hear the story of what happened.

The couple that owned the house were going through a nasty divorce. The wife was about to get the house and the husband decided otherwise. He left notes and we saw some of them in the backyard that hadn't burn. They were pretty angry notes and this was his "fuck you" to her.

Really though?
Burn your house down?
Kill yourself?
A fuck you to who?

I know sometimes we can't see a way out.
Sometimes we get locked in one way of thinking.
We humans can get into some crazy states of mind.
Nothing surprises me anymore.

Oh, the human condition!

CHAPTER 32
HIGH VOLTAGE

Earth is a realm. It is not a planet. It is not an object. Therefore, it has no edge. Earth would be more easily defined as a system environment. Earth is also a machine. It is a Tesla coil. The sun and the moon are powered wirelessly with electromagnetic field (the Aether). This field also suspends the celestial spheres with electro-magnetic levitation. Electromagnetic levitation disproves gravity because the only force you need to counter is the electromagnetic force, not gravity. The stars are attached to the firmament.
~Nikola Tesla

Electrical calls usually made most firefighters more aware and cautious. We didn't go on these calls that often and we weren't experts on electricity. This was better left to the electrical company.

However, sometimes electrical wires would come down from storms and such and the fire department was more available than the electrical company. We would typically close off the area and wait for the electrical company to come and shut down the power.

Captain Jay would tell me when I got hired that this and freeway calls are the most dangerous for firefighters. He would go on to say, "These electrical calls are low frequency, high risk calls. They could kill us instantly."

One time, when I was a new firefighter, we got called for a line down. This was from an electrical pole and was going across a street still energized.

Captain Jay was off that day and I had a different captain, Captain Robert.

When we pulled up, Captain Robert told me to grab the electrician gloves and a pike pole. He went on and told me to move the energized electrical line off to the side of the road, so cars could go through while we waited for the electrical company. It was a residential street with little traffic.

My engineer, Greg, looked at me while I was getting this stuff and said this wasn't a good idea. Captain Jay would never do this. The other firefighter there handed me the pike pole and said, "Good luck!"

The hair on the back of my neck was standing up. I didn't have a good feeling about this, but I was being ordered to move the line out of the street. I could see the electrical line had zapped the asphalt a few times already on the street. It was most likely still energized.

Fuck!
What do I do?
Do I disobey an order?
Would I get fired since I am on probation?

I remember learning in the fire academy that once a line is down, the electrical company sends electrical impulses through the line trying to figure out which one is down, so they aren't always continuously charged.

I think to myself, "Maybe I can just move the line super fast to the other side and it won't be charged. I can do one big sweep."

I take a deep breath and move the line over fast.
So fast.
Done and I am still alive!

My captain is pleased and we wait for the electrical company. I am grateful that I am still alive as is Greg. About thirty minutes later, the electrical company pulls up. A guy gets out and my captain goes up to him. He tells him that we moved the line out of the street.

The guy is shocked and says loudly, "Who don't you guys like on your crew? Whoever moved that line could have been killed. It's a high voltage line of 10,000 volts!"

I am shocked and pissed at the same time. I knew I should have listened to my inner guidance and disobeyed the order.

Lesson learned.

Valuable lesson learned within my first month on the job. I learned that captains don't know everything and to think for yourself. I realized I needed to learn to pay attention to my inner alarm telling me when something isn't right.

The kicker is that when Captain Jay comes back from being off duty, he yelled at Greg and I. He talked about how Greg knew better and should have stood up to Captain Robert. He told me that I was too smart to let this kind of thing happen. This made my lesson learned even stronger.

A few years later, I got promoted and was an engineer. My main job was driving the fire engine and getting water to the guys on fires. I loved this job as it was so much fun. As an engineer, you were also insulated from the chiefs telling you what to do and you weren't the firefighter, so you didn't have to do the "grunt" work. Some guys loved this job so much that once they promoted to engineer, they would stay there the rest of their careers.

Anyways, I digress...

One time, I was working with this firefighter named Judah and he told me a wild story that had happened to him a month earlier with electricity where he almost died. He was hoping the fire department would do a training on it, so that it would never happen to anyone else again.

Here it goes...

Judah was working with his regular crew, Engineer Tim and Captain Dave. They got called to a broken fire hydrant that was blowing water about a hundred feet into the sky. A car had hit the fire hydrant and now they need to shut the water off until the water department got there to fix it.

Judah was told to grab the large fire hydrant key and shut down the hydrant. As a firefighter, to shut off the water, you go in and find the valve (which is about six feet down underground) in a hole in the street which is under a heavy cover. You are getting soaked while looking for this cover as hundreds of gallons of water pour down upon you.

He found the cover, removed it, and put the large key in the hole. Judah began to turn the key to turn it off which can take ten minutes or so. You stand upright to do this.

Now, the water is shooting really high and into high voltage power lines. These lines are moving and zapping around. As Judah shuts down the water, the water that is streaming high up into the air is coming down more and more.

It is still in the power lines though.

Captain Dave and Engineer Tim are watching Judah and staying dry over by the fire engine. Judah is looking into the hole, shutting it down as he twists the key around and around. Suddenly, he sees a huge bright light coming up from the hole.

In that instant, Judah sees his whole life flash before him.

The next thing he remembers, he was twenty feet away and on his back. He is completely dry whereas before, he was soaking wet. Captain Dave and Engineer Tim run over to him to see if he is okay as they saw the whole thing.

Judah is disoriented, but okay.

Captain Dave and Engineer Tim go over quickly and finish shutting off the broken hydrant. There are no other issues.

As I listened to the story, I was shocked that Judah was sitting here able to tell me this story. I kept thinking about the light coming up from the hole and his life flashing in front of him. He should have been dead.

Somehow, it wasn't Judah's time to cross the veil.

CHAPTER 33
MAMA BEAR

Bless your enemy, and you will rob him of his ammunition. His arrows will be transmuted into blessings. This law is true of nations as well as individuals. Bless nations, send love and good will to every inhabitant and its robbed of its power to harm.
~Florence Scovel Shinn

I have always heard stories about moms protecting their babies especially in the animal kingdom. Animal mamas were especially protective of their young and would attack if need be. This carried over to human mamas just as intensely which I didn't realize.

I was a fairly new mom with an eighteen month old son. He was my pride and joy. I loved being with him and I had no idea how much you could love another being.

The first words out of my mouth when I saw him was "Gorgeous." Danny was gorgeous and so precious. I know every parent thinks that their baby is the most beautiful in the world. It was the same for me. I loved making him laugh and chasing him around. We would wrestle and play hide and seek. He loved sitting on top of our two older labs, Teddy Bear and Polar Bear. They were so gentle and tolerant.

One day, I had some friends over that also had little kids. A few of the kids were Danny's age (two years old) and one was five. We set up a jumper, so the kids could jump around in it. It had plastic balls inside it, too.

The kids played in it on and off while we moms would catch up chatting. Danny came and sat in my lap for a little while and then, he went back into the jumper. I got up to go and watch him since the only other kid in there was a five year old boy.

Danny was smiling and laughing as he tried to walk across it and would fall. He would pick up some of the plastic balls and then drop them for another one. I was standing outside the jumper looking through the mesh watching him when the five year old boy threw a ball hard right at Danny's face.

I was shocked.

I could see Danny was shocked as he sat on his butt.

Why is it that most kids have empathy and can feel others? Do those lacking empathy shut off their own feelings at an early age because of deep emotional pain they feel and then their anger turns to rage? I wonder if the rage becomes too much to feel and they shut off this part of themselves.

I believe this is a theory of how psychopaths are formed. They have shut off their capacity to feel empathy for others and take delight in watching others suffer. How can we make a huge shift in how we raise our children so they feel empathy?

It starts with the parents and society caring who raises children.

Anyways, running around to get into the jumper, I tried to stop him before he did it again. He threw another ball hard at his face again. Danny began to cry. I will never forget the anger, clarity, and protective power that overtook my body as I watched my little cub, Danny, get hurt. I was ready to kill this five year old.

Now, I know that may sound harsh, but I am only being honest how I felt in the moment. I was truly a mama bear ready to destroy this being as I felt like I had the strength of a hundred men.

I yelled, "Chuck, you knock that off!" As I stormed into the jumper throwing my body on the makeshift bouncing kid's playroom. Thank goddess it took me a little bit to get around the corner and into the jumper. I had a moment where the adrenaline gave me clarity to not kill this five year old or at least, not punch him in the face.

I grabbed Danny and hugged him tight. I yelled at Chuck, "It is not okay to throw balls at people's faces! It hurts!"

He shrugged and got out of the jumper walking away.
Oh, I was fucking pissed.

I didn't know his mom that well and I wondered why kids would do such things to other kids. He seemed like an angry kid and now wondered what his home life was like.

To this day, I will never forget the sheer power that came through me when I saw Danny getting hurt. It was uncontrollable, pure, raw power in an instant. I felt like I was twenty feet tall and that I could do anything. The clarity and accuracy that came out of my eyes as I honed in on the enemy was like looking through a scope of a sniper rifle.

Don't ever mess with a mama bear…

CHAPTER 34
TARZAN

All people everywhere should have free energy sources. Electric power is everywhere present in unlimited quantities and can drive the world's machinery without the need of coal, oil, gas, or any other of the common fuels.
~Nikola Tesla

So, there is this story that I heard often during my twenty plus year career as a firefighter.

The best part about it was Tom telling the story. He was actually there on the emergency call and no embellishment needed.

It goes like this...

A call comes into dispatch.
"911. What is your emergency?" A dispatcher says.

"This naked guy just came running through the gas station and jumped on top of the hood of my car screaming while I was getting gas!" A man on the line says.

Dispatch confirms the address and sends the police. The man hides inside the gas station waiting for the police.

The naked man is running all over town and freaking people out. The police are after him. Dispatch also sends a fire engine and ambulance in case anyone is injured. The man goes into a three story building and the police follow. They think they will have him now as some cops stay at the front and rear doors.

The fire engine and ambulance arrive and stay out on the street. Inside the fire engine is Tom who is the engineer and driving (this is the Tom who loves to tell the story), Chris who is the captain, and another Tom who is the firefighter.

They watch the action from the safety of their fire engine.

There are police everywhere and almost all of them are in the building trying to get this naked man. Just then, the firefighters see the man on top of the roof of the building. He is trying to escape as many cops get on the roof as well.

Suddenly, the naked man rips off the large electrical wire that comes into the building!

There are sparks everywhere!
He uses it like a rope and acts like Tarzan!
He swings down the three stories and lands!
The firefighters wonder if he is hurt...

Nope!

He gets up and begins to run.
How did he not get electrocuted or break his bones?

All the cops are up on the roof except one cop down on the ground who was guarding the door. He chases the naked man and tackles him.

Chris, Tom, and Tom are still watching all of this from the safety of their fire engine. They are told that the scene is not safe for them to enter until the naked man is apprehended. They don't have guns and are there to give medical aid.

So, the cop and the naked monkey man are wrestling around and the naked man is getting the upper hand. He has his hand on the cop's gun and is trying to pull it out of his holster. The cop is on top of the naked guy.

The other police officers are yelling for the firefighters to help their friend and Chris, the captain, is telling the two Toms to stay put. The two Toms look at each other, see the cop struggling, and get out of the engine running to help the cop.

They have just disobeyed their captain's orders.

They can see that the man now has the gun out of the holster and the cop has his finger in between the trigger so it won't go off. The man is attempting to choke out the cop.

This naked man is about 160 pounds and 5'9."

Amazing what the drug PCP can do. It can give you super human strength and make you feel burning hot. This is why they take their clothes off. I remember another story of a sixteen year old girl who was on PCP and there was a firefighter or cop on every arm and leg to try to hold her down. She was lifting them up!

Firefighter Tom, who is 6'5" and about 230 pounds begins to choke out the naked man. Engineer Tom uses his whole body weight and knees the man right in the abdomen. He does it again. Tom is about 200 pounds.

This gives cop the ability to get a small knife from his leg and he stabs the naked man in the gut. He stabs him a second time in the gut.

It finally took the wind out of this naked guy.

The cop tells Engineer Tom to put handcuffs on the guy. They get them on him, finally! Other cops are rushing to help and the cop tells the two Toms "thank you" for coming to his rescue. He said he was so close to passing out!

The crazy part is that Captain Chris is upset and when they get back to the station, he is writing both Toms up for discipline because they disobeyed his orders. As he is doing this, the police supervisor calls and says the two Toms are up for metals of honor!

Both Toms end up getting honored for saving the police officer's life and neither of them get disciplined for disobeying a direct order.

Power is a funny thing.

CHAPTER 35
JACK OF ALL TRADES

When you believe something is hard, the universe demonstrates the difficulty. When you believe something is easy, the universe demonstrates the ease.
~Abraham-Hicks

The fire department is really just an insurance policy for the city. We are there to get rid of the liability if there is any. And really, when you don't know who to call, you call "911" where typically, they send the fire department who will figure it out.

We are the jack of all trades and masters of none.

I learned a lot in the fire department on the job and it helped that I was mechanical. I understood construction, some plumbing, and electrical from when I worked for a construction company after college and also, from remodeling our home. My husband taught me lots as well.

Many of the guys on the fire department had some kind of trade under their belt before being hired which helped. Sometimes, we fixed people's plumbing for them. Typically though, we just shut their water off and had them call a plumber, so we could stay available for emergency calls.

I remember a call where this ninety year old woman had a water hose break to the back of her washer. It flooded part of her house, so we vacuumed up the water for her. Then, Captain Jay was so nice that we drove to the plumbing store, got the parts to fix the line, and came back to install them for her.

Captain Jay had a really big heart, but acted like a tough guy.

Public speaking was also something else that came with the job of a firefighter. Being in my late twenties, I was still terrified of public speaking and afraid of looking like an ass. Yet, as with all the challenges in my life, I decided to face this fear head on and become a good public speaker.

We had different programs where we taught kids about fire safety. One was a junior fire program for all the fourth graders in the city. I can remember the first time getting up on stage in front of over one hundred kids and their teachers feeling overwhelmed and stumbling through parts of my performance. Once it was over, I was actually really proud of myself for accomplishing this and I began to realize that the fear was really of me judging myself.

It got easier the more times I spoke and I realized that if I made people laugh, I was a hit! This actually became really fun for me and I looked forward to speaking in public. We also gave safety talks around fires and earthquakes and I was sometimes asked to speak about my experience of being a female in the fire department. I spoke at elderly homes, high schools, colleges, and community clubs. Sometimes, we had school tours for kids who wanted to come see the fire station and hear about what we do.

I loved to lead these tours.
Honestly, public speaking became something that I looked forward to.
It is amazing what happens when you face your fears head on!

We had other fun parts of the job and would go on many animal calls. The calls were amusing with animals like racoons, birds, opossums, and bats in people's homes. It was always entertaining to watch us in action as the three of us tried to catch an animal or bird. Opossums were funny because they played dead when you tried to catch them. Racoons would hiss at you. Birds and bats were always a challenge because they had wings!

One time while working with my engineer, Tom, we had a hummingbird inside a house. She was up high and hard to catch. My firefighter and I tried and tried. Finally Tom, who was outside, came in and asked if we wanted help.

Of course, we did.

Tom came in and began making bird noises. He clapped his hands holding his arms out again and again. My firefighter and I thought he was nuts!

Funny though.
She came and landed on his hand.
We were shocked.
We called him the "bird whisperer" after that!

CHAPTER 36
SUICIDAL

In oneself lies the whole world and if you know how to look and learn, the door is there and the key is in your hand. Nobody on Earth can give you either the key or the door to open, except yourself.
~Krishnamurti

Honestly, I feel like for my whole life that I wanted to die. I was never scared of death and suicide sure seemed like an easy way back to the other side.

So, what keeps me here?
Good question.

I know it is normal for people to think about killing themselves at different times in their lives. Normal to question what the fuck we are doing here. Life gets tough sometimes and we can't see a way out.

So, enter suicide…

Not to say that this is right or wrong…good or bad. It just is. We put all kinds of thoughts and feelings around it. We feel sometimes that it is selfish if someone commits suicide and say leaves a family behind while doing what they wanted to do. Maybe they wanted to get out of their personal hell and couldn't see another way out?

The feeling of wanting to kill myself was strong for me during my teenage years. I was feeling so lost and in so much pain from all that I had stuffed down. Growing up with a mother who judges you for everything and then tells you that you can't have an opinion except for hers was daunting. You aren't allowed to cry or be angry.

Then, throw crazy religion on top of it all!
So, all that is left is to be happy and this only works for so long.
Or to just be in a neutral zone.
I perfected this art of having no "bad" emotions.

Over it.

It is amazing now looking back at not allowing myself to be angry.
Stuffing this emotion again and again.
How caustic this was for myself.

Then, to feel as if crying was weak and to decide that I was never gonna let my mother see me cry again because she never cared or hugged me when I did. In fact, my mother never touched me except with a belt.

I began to hate her.
Deeply hate her.

I hoped that she would die in my teens as I didn't see another way out and really, I just wanted to go live with my dad. I felt like I was living with a monster. How did I ever get to this crazy planet?

Suicide seemed like a good option, but there was one problem…
Religion.

I was taught in military church that suicide was wrong and that you don't get to go to heaven if you do this.

Double fucked.
So, you are suffering down here and you see a way out, but you can't take it.
Fuck.

My mom must have felt this from me sometimes as she would remind me of this often. I have a feeling that she really is psychic, but is afraid of her abilities. She probably sees it as the devil.

Sometimes, I am in awe of how I have lived so long to be forty-nine now. I used to feel that I would die before I turned thirty.

Premonition?

Or maybe just being chronically traumatized over and over living with a crazy, narcissistic mother. I had major PTSD, but I never thought this until I saw a therapist in my thirties. I thought PTSD was just for war veterans or rape victims. Chronic subtle or overt emotional trauma is just as gnarly, but harder to pinpoint.

I went on many suicides while working in the fire department.
Lots of them.

People killed themselves in so many ways…hangings, drug overdoses, gunshots, traffic accidents, jumping off tall buildings, jumping in front of trains, drowning themselves in the ocean, etc…

Really there are so many ways to die.
We forget how precious life is when we get here.
Why do we "lose" our memory when we incarnate?

It was always hard to go on these suicide calls when the family was present and especially when kids were there. So much emotion...from shock to horror to sadness and anger. We would try to revive their loved one who didn't want to be here anymore, usually without success.

The whole thing feels quite ironic.

To try to bring someone back who has just made a statement to the world that they no longer want to be here. They are done.

I often wondered if they were standing next to us watching from out of their body as we tried to revive them. Sometimes, I would see or feel them close by us and I would talk to them through telepathy while doing chest compressions.

"You are okay. I can feel you," I would say in my head to them.

"Your body is dead and you are there watching us in spirit. Your family will be okay. Look around you and go towards the light with your guides if you want. Or you can come back into your body. It's your choice."

I didn't always do this. It wasn't until the middle of my career that I could feel them and sometimes see them. I could feel their shock and surprise of being out of body.

I always loved hearing and reading about near-death experiences and what people remembered from the other side. Sometimes people were told that it wasn't their time to die yet and had to go back. Others chose to go back because they hadn't danced enough! I found it fascinating about those who saw behind the veil.

We also had many emergency calls where people were threatening suicide, but really just wanted help. They would take a bottle of non-lethal pills or be standing on top of a building and not jump.

One time, I was working for Captain Jay and we went on a call for someone threatening to jump off a building. It wasn't that high up, but we thought they might break their leg unless they landed on their head. The cops were there, too trying to talk him down.

Then, Jay gets this idea as he always thought outside the box.
He came up with the best ideas.

He has the ambulance go back to our fire station and take as many mattresses from our beds as they can fit in the ambulance. They come back with a bunch of mattresses and they do this a couple times. Then, we put all these mattresses on top of the fire engine to ease his fall.

We then pull the fire engine alongside the building where the guy is standing. It almost reaches the top. There is now just a six foot drop. We are standing up there on top of the fire engine talking to the man who wants to die. He finally just jumps down and is transported to the hospital for evaluation.

Did we save him or did he save himself?
Makes me wonder if he got the help he needed or if he tried to kill himself again later?

I know I used to think about killing myself by driving off Grimes Canyon in Moorpark as it just seemed easy and people would just think that it was an accident. Or maybe I would step off a curb and into a truck.

I obviously never did this though.
And I really am grateful to be here now and see a whole different side of life.
It is really quite a colorful and amazing world.
It's just getting good!

CHAPTER 37
PUSSYCAT THEATRE

Only in the shattering can the rebuilding occur.
~Barbara Marciniak

The downtown of Sparrow City was getting cleaned up and revamped. The politicians were trying to revive the city and get new revenue. Many homeless lived there and downtown had lots of bars and drugs with some prostitution, as well.

I was on my new crew after getting off probation as a rookie firefighter. We had been together a few months and we had been getting lots of big fires. One night around midnight, an emergency call came in for a fire in the old abandoned theatre. Homeless frequently live in there. Of course, I was excited to go to the fire and first on the engine while waiting for Adam and Bob to get going.

Off we go!

We can see heavy, thick black smoke hovering around the building. Not much wind was blowing and we pull up at the same time another engine pulls up. People are up on the balcony calling for help. Adam tells me to grab a ladder and rescue them.

I grab a ladder and set it up. Adam and I go up and get three people down. Two men and a woman who seem to be okay, but have some smoke inhalation. I take them over to the ambulance for help.

Lots of fire engines and fire trucks keep arriving. This is a giant theatre and the fire is cookin'! The guys called it the "pussycat theatre" because porn used to be shown here. I guess in the 1980's, the fire chief would come down on his lunch break and watch porn.

Funny world.

Adam and I grab a hoseline to go into the theatre as there are already two crews in there. They are way at the front of the theatre and we can see them even though it is smoky. Most of the fire is above us. When we look up, we can see fire raging all through the ceilings.

Not good.

This building could come down at any moment as we didn't know how long it had been burning. Guys could be killed for an old building if the roof collapsed!

Adam tells me, "We're outta here!"

We head out and he goes to talk to the battalion chief in charge of the incident. We have been on scene for over twenty minutes. In fighting fires, twenty minutes is a marker for deciding when to pull firefighters out of a building on fire depending on the progress that has been made in extinguishing the fire or not.

"Chief, we have a problem. Fire is running through the rafters and the whole ceiling. We need to get everyone out of there now as it could collapse at any moment!" Adam says.

Just then, another captain named Austin comes out and says, "Chief, we can get this fire. We almost have it out! We just need more manpower! Send me more fire crews!"

It's all perspective, right?

I am listening to this whole thing as the two captains are arguing for what they think needs to happen next in front of the chief when the truck captain on the roof radios in and says they are getting off the roof as it is unsafe.

The roof had dropped down, but had not collapsed yet.
The chief immediately radios all crews inside the theatre to get out now!

Everyone scrambles to get out.
Hoselines are being pulled back out.
A couple minutes later, a portion of the roof collapses.
Fire shoots out of the roof and the interior becomes engulfed.

Just in time!
Everyone is safe and the operation moves from an offensive fire to a defensive fire.

I get up on the top of the fire engine and (wo)man a deck gun which is a large fire stream. I aim it onto the roof area as does many other engines. We finally get the fire out in what seems to be hours later when the sun begins to come up. I think about how we could have had many firefighters die that night if it weren't for Adam standing his ground.

Thanks, Adam.
Safe and sound for another day.
It all depends on your perspective as to how you see things...
So true for all of life!

CHAPTER 38
MY BIRTH GIVERS

To love someone is to strive to accept that person exactly the way he or she is, right here and now.
~Mr. Rogers

I love my parents.
Period.

I know I say lots of things referring to my parents and how they were lacking, but they also did good things as well.

Bottomline...
They are very human as we all are.

I'm not sure what they think of me these days as I don't follow their religion or political views, but I know they love me.

My mom grew up smack in the middle of the USA.
Iowa...the heartland of America.

She was raised in a town of less than five thousand people where life was slow and you could leave your door unlocked. They were Christian and believed people were mostly good. Lots of people farmed there and my grandfather owned a tractor dealership. My grandmother raised the kids and worked as a secretary once the kids grew up and left home.

Her parents were part German, English, and Irish. Needless to say, they didn't show much emotion about anything. My grandma loved to talk and talk which drove my mother crazy. She actually told me years later that she hated her mother.

Why?

I loved my grandmother. We got each other. She made me laugh, was a great cook, and gave me the best back rubs. It was just the opposite for my mom who said my grandma was judgmental and put her down often. Is this just a continuation of the cycle of abuse from my ancestors? Can I clear this energy?

Hmmm...

This was exactly what my mother did to me!
Gotta be from my lineage.
So interesting to have two totally different experiences from the same person.

My mother told me a story one time when she was young of how her mom would criticize her cooking and decided she was only allowed to do dishes.

As an adult, my mom hated cooking and dishes.
Fascinating.

I always felt my mom was super sensitive and traumatized at an early age. She told me she was inconsolable as a baby. I wonder if she was left alone a lot to cry. She was probably feeling the intense energies of the Earth!

She also told me a story of how she was in the corn fields with her parents at the age of three. She stepped on a corn snake and it freaked her out. Her parents yelled at her and put her in the car crying by herself.

It made me feel sad for her because I know she just wanted to be held and told she would be okay. They could have taught her about snakes and validated how she was feeling. Instead, she became a devout Christian who hated snakes and says that snakes were the devil.

Wow.
Is this how our beliefs are formed?

I know my mom loves and cares about me, but she wants to control me. She tried to keep me safe growing up and instill me with her beliefs. I feel she is just incredibly traumatized and is stuck at the age of two, emotionally.

My dad is a character who came over from Cuba when Castro was stripping the country of wealth and making it a communist/socialist country.

His family was wealthy in Cuba. My dad came to the United States when he was sixteen as his parents put him and his brother on a plane to the USA with nothing but the clothes on their backs. They landed in Florida and were in a camp for a few months with many other Cuban children waiting for their parents to come to America and pick them up.

He and his brother were just about to be sent to live with a family in America when his mother and grandmother came from Cuba to get them. They were all relocated by our government into a small town in Iowa. His father was able to leave Cuba a year later by going through Spain where he finally met up with the family.

What a hugely traumatizing ordeal!

My father had never seen snow living on a tropical island. He tells stories about how when they got to Iowa, there was a house with food and clothes in it for their family. They were so grateful.

I believe it is part of Cuban culture to never take anything too seriously. They are always making jokes about everything. I grew up with my dad always joking, but sometimes it was just too much.

I don't remember my grandmother on my dad's side as she died when I was four, but my father says she was a powerful and intelligent woman who studied in New York. She was going to marry a man in Texas, but World War II broke out and she went back to Cuba where she met my grandfather.

Funny the twists and turns of life.

My grandfather was a funny man. He loved to joke and I loved him so much for that. He was incredibly smart and was a chemist and journalist in Cuba. Life changed for him greatly in Iowa as he didn't speak much English, so he became the janitor at the high school.

Talk about being humble!

My grandmother became the Spanish teacher since she spoke both languages well. My grandfather loved to play with my brother and I when we would come to visit. He was such a kid! After my grandmother died, my grandfather remarried a year later to the principal of the high school.

He was so happy.

My dad loved his parents and I know he missed his mother. They were a close family after having lost everything in Cuba. My father was driven to excel and be successful. He taught me this. He loved the United States for all the opportunities it provided.

Truly, my parents taught me many things of working hard and not taking life too seriously. I know over the years I have had been angry with them, but I forgive them completely as I realize they are doing the best they can in this world!

I will always love them both dearly.

CHAPTER 39
TRYING TO EAT MY BURRITO

The human race has one really effective weapon, and that is laughter.
~Mark Twain

It has been a busy day at the station. Lots of calls on a Saturday. We finally get a break in the action and head down to get a burrito.

It's one of my favorite Mexican food places.
We go there often.
It's busy there and just as we get our food, another call comes out.
Damn!
I'm so hungry!

It is for a man with a gun running through the streets of Sparrow City. He was running through the downtown and there was an outside art show going on. People are freaking out as you would expect!

We head that direction and will stage somewhere close until the police apprehend him. The location keeps changing as to the man's whereabouts as he is on foot running. We keep driving around.

We are in an older fire engine. I am sitting in the back of an open cab engine. I love this engine as it is fun to sit backwards and outside except in the rain. The captain and engineer are in the front where it is enclosed.

I am so hungry and I can't hear anything that is going on since I don't have a radio. I decide that I will eat my burrito on the way as it will probably be a while. I eat a few bites and I am so happy. I wonder what is going on now as we are close to downtown. We head up to City hall and then we stop. My captain tells me they shot the suspect in front of City hall.

Oh damn.

I drop my burrito and grab my paramedic gear. The man is bleeding out and not looking good. He is shot in the chest and abdomen. There are bystanders and

143

witnesses everywhere, as well as cops.

The man takes his last breath.

We begin CPR, hook him up to the heart monitor, and start IVs to give him fluid.

The whole scene seems surreal.
I wonder where his soul is at the moment.
Does he know he is dead?

We get him into the back of the ambulance as soon as they arrive and I get in the ambulance too. We speed off to the hospital. He needs blood and surgery now. The emergency personnel are ready and they work on him for another twenty minutes before pronouncing him dead.

Their magic didn't work this time.

Life and death.
It's what we do.
I wonder why he chose to run around with a gun today?
Was he looking to die?
Death by cops?
Done with this reality?!

Back to the fire engine and my yummy burrito as another emergency call comes in.

Damn!
Busy shift!

CHAPTER 40
ALLOWING THE DEVIL BACK INTO MY LIFE

Forgiveness is the only way to heal. We can choose to forgive because we feel compassion for ourselves.
~Don Miguel Ruiz

Now, I know that the title of this chapter sounds a bit harsh. And maybe, you will judge me for what I am going to say, but I don't care. Until you have lived in my shoes, you have no room to comment. Really none of us should judge each other as we are all doing the best we can!

You just never know what circumstances you picked for this life.

Anyways...
I always knew that I would live with my mother again.
How did I know that?
I have no idea.
Some part of me just knew.

I didn't think about it much as I was so excited to move away from my mom in my teens and move in with my dad. It was a welcomed relief to be free from the oppression and tyranny. I was so rebellious that I may have not lived to be twenty if I stayed with her.

My soul knew it was time for me to leave.

So, did my soul know that later in life, I would be living with my mother again? I would have never ever said "yes" to this, but something within me knew this was going to happen. I had the same knowing that I would not be working while my son was in high school. I just knew this since he was little. I just didn't know the details.

Knowing is something that is strong within me, yet I always have wanted to see and hear spirit or my spirit guides. The knowing is always right, so maybe I should be grateful for this.

I am very grateful.

We had a nanny help us out when Danny was three months old until he was almost a year old. She ended up not following our rules when she was home with Danny, so we let her go.

I didn't know what to do.
Do we hire another nanny?
Do I quit my job and stay home with him?
I sat with the options.

Then, my mom called.

I told her about what I was dealing with and she says, "Well, I am off work for the summer. I can come out and help until you guys figure out what you need."

So many things are running through my mind.
I can't stand to be around her.
Is she going to talk about her religion all day long?
She doesn't see life the way I do.

I talk it over with Bruce and we decide to have her help out for the summer. We see the positives of having family instead of having a nanny help. We also see the negatives and decide that we will tell her that we will not be discussing religion or politics with her. Am I insane for thinking this could work?

Probably!
But, here we go!

My mom flies over with a great attitude and willingness to do as we ask. She is so excited to be a part of our lives and to be with her grandson. I am excited thinking that things will be different. I am now thirty-two years old and it's been eighteen years since I have lived with her.

Everything is working out so great all summer that Bruce and I consider asking her to move in with us. She goes about her church stuff and doesn't put anything on us. It is so great and it actually feels like she respects us to live our own lives.

We decide to ask her to live with us and she immediately is thrilled. She wants to sell her house in Iowa (which we don't want her to in case things don't work out) and move to California immediately. She ends up selling her house as she said she wants to be in California no matter what. We help her move her things.

So, what are you thinking here?
Life is peachy grand?
A new start?

There is some part of me that knows we have more shit to work through and that this is a big part of the reason she is back in my life. Another part of me hopes that she will show up to be the mother I always wanted, but never had.

Recipe for disaster?
Expectations?
What could go wrong?!
Insanity at its best.

The first six months or so go along without a hitch. She has her ways of doing things, but is respectful of our space. Bruce and I are relieved because she is there to be with Danny for the overlap of our fire schedules and for the five to six days a month where we both work.

She loves her religion and hers is the only right one if you want to go to heaven. I hope you can feel the sarcasm as I write this. She is passionate about Jesus which is great until she puts it on you. She begins listening on Sundays to a pastor on the television. At first, it's no big deal as it is only an hour. Then, she begins to turn the volume way up, so you can't escape it.

I ask her to turn it down and she does. This happens week after week. The news is her favorite, too, and we never watch the news as it is so depressing and fear-based. She also begins judging all the television shows that we watch. Bruce and I begin to retreat into our bedroom to watch television, so we don't have to listen to her commentary.

Now, all of this is pretty harmless and somewhat subtle how it all began.
She's good…she slowly infiltrates and you don't even realize what is happening.

There is always something positive in all of this and for me, it was that we cut the cable. We rarely watched television any longer with Danny around and spent more time outside with him.

I found how I didn't miss television a bit.
It was actually quite freeing and I began to read more books.
I also began realizing how television was programming us.
We saved money as well.

The best part was we didn't have to listen to my mom's religion or the news anymore. She took to her computer to find the news and began to find a church to belong to.

I was going through so much having kids as it made me think about how my parents raised me and what they taught me. I questioned everything and wondered what it must have been like for them at age twenty. I can't even imagine as I was such a mess then. I was still just a kid.

The love you feel for your child is so powerful and like nothing else. I wondered if my mom had ever felt that way towards me.

My mom continued with her subtleties and I put up with them the way I did as a kid. I knew not to confront her or she would go ballistic with anger.

Really healthy, right?

Before I knew it, years had passed and we had another child. This seemed to shift gears for my mom and she went back to being more mellow, focused on her new granddaughter, Piper.

It brought everything up for me as I was scared of having a daughter and of mind-fucking her the way my mom did to me. I was determined to have a different story with her and I knew therapy would help me with that.

Life went on, my kids got older, and I loved being a mom. It was great having my mom's help, but it came at an expense. This expense was my sanity. We couldn't say certain things or she would go off on how that was wrong in the eyes of Jesus.

One time she asked me what I was reading. I told her that it was *The Da Vinci Code* and she asked what it was about. I said it is thriller novel with some truth of how Jesus was actually married to Mary Magdalene and that they had a child named Sarah. I went on to say how the church actually buried this and made Mary out to be a prostitute, being that we are in a patriarchal dominated world.

Well, this didn't get over well.
I wasn't even thinking about her reaction as I was just being honest and excited about this book.

She listened to all of it and then said that none of this is true. She shamed me for reading it and the next day, she came home with reading material from her church saying how this book is bad.

What?
Who does this?

Better yet…who lets themselves be shamed as an adult by their parent in their own house?

Apparently, I do.

I was caught between a rock and a hard space, as they say. If I go against her, she gets crazy. If I don't say anything, I lose by not speaking my truth.

I am a prisoner in my own home.

We are also considering the Catholic Church to give the kids a basis even though we don't totally agree with it, but we do like the community. I tell my mom this and she freaks out about how the Catholic Church is evil and of the devil.

Here I thought that she might be excited that I was going back to church.

She decides to take matters into her own hands a month later. She gets the kids baptized at her church and blames Danny that he wanted to get baptized there.

I am pissed.
Beyond pissed!

I talk to her about this and she acts like she did nothing wrong. I have also learned to not lose my cool with her, but I am about to fucking rage on her!

I can't believe she would do this!
She seems to get this weird grin when I lose it and yell at her.
Something inside her enjoys this.
She's sick.

I explode with all types of fucks and shits and anger and spit and and...

Then, there it is...
Her grin showing that she got to me.
I regain my cool and tell her that I am very upset with her.

FUCK!!!

I'm done.

Bruce has been done for some time now and wants to kick her out. I would feel bad kicking her out as she needs us and we need her.

What an unhealthy co-dependent relationship!

But, we do it. We tell her the next day that she has a month to find a place to live as she is not respecting our boundaries.

This is the worst part.
I know her act.
She acts like a wounded child and just says that she understands.
She will leave.

She leaves for the rest of the day and comes back that night. We have a friend over and are talking outside. My mom walks by and I know she isn't okay. She can barely walk and is walking like a ninety year old woman.

I meet her at the door and ask, "Mom, are you okay?"

"I'm okay, Hydee. I just need to take a bath," she replies.

I leave her be and she goes into the bathroom. I hear the water running and her getting in. Then, I hear her wailing.

It's loud.
Really loud and it's escalating.
She is balling her eyes out.

Our friend decides it is a good idea to leave and Bruce and I are left trying to figure out what to do. She finally stops after about twenty minutes of this and comes out. I meet her in the hallway and ask if she's okay.

She tells me that she just needs to go and lay with Danny in his bed. He's asleep. I tell her "No!" as I know this would freak him out if Grandma is crying in bed with him. He wouldn't understand what is happening.

Deep down, I know she did this with me when I was little and she was crying.
So familiar.

Anyways, she starts crying and I hug her tight.
She begins wailing and shaking as I hold her.
I bring her to sit on the couch with me.

My mom cries and cries. I am holding her thinking to myself, "This is what I always wanted from her. To be held."

Surreal.

Doing what feels natural for me and what I do for my own kids, I put her head on my chest knowing that my heartbeat will help soothe her. This works quickly and she slowly stops crying. I continue holding her.

Bruce wants nothing to do with any of this, but he finally comes in. We all talk and she agrees that she will seek therapy to deal with some of her issues. She can still live with us while she does this.

Wow.

Looking back, I learned so much compassion for another and I realize that I am more a mom to her than she has ever been for me.

Well, therapy for her was a bust as she wasn't ready to look at any of her issues. She went once and then told me that we had to go together to a therapist from her church. I agreed, but was super cautious as I didn't want to get ambushed.

It ended up being great as the counselor at her church was open minded and called her on her stuff. My mom would tell him that I was wrong in my thinking and the way I see things. She would say that her way was the only right way. The counselor would then tell her that Hydee sees things the way that is right for her and same for my mom.

I was so excited that he said this to her and I felt empowered. It stopped her in her tracks. She didn't know what to do after that. It was a great session and I thought we would dive into our issues even more the next session. Unfortunately, we only went once as she refused after that.

Well, what do I do now?
She doesn't want to be mentally or emotionally healthy.
I am used to her quirks and she is great with the kids.
The kids love her.

If we have her move out, who will watch the kids?
Will she have another breakdown?
Oh, the drama!

So, here's what we do…

We build her a place on our property, so we can all have our own space and she can come watch the kids as we need her too. Feels like a win-win with less drama, but it is really just a bandaid for bigger issues. She continues playing passive-aggressive and I have to be so present with her to not get drawn into her stuff.

What am I doing?!
Why do I feel so guilty and feel responsible for her?
What's our past life connection?
What are we really working out?

I need to stand up for myself. I need to stand in my power no matter how many times she threatens me that I am going to hell. I need to not let her bully me.

Eventually, I do get my power back and stand up for myself. I get to do this over and over again with her. It is exhausting though. There is a part of me hoping that she will change and be the mother I want her to be. Guess I need to heal that child part of me.

As my kids got older and could see the dysfunction in their grandma, they wanted less and less to have her watch them while we were at work. My son complained that he was twelve now and didn't need her around.

I knew it was time for some other arrangement, but how do you kick out your mom after all those years? Yet, I knew it was time for something to change after eleven years of living together! It just didn't work having her live on our property with us even though we lived in separate houses. Her presence was ominous.

151

One of the final straws was when Bruce and I were at work and my mom was there watching the kids. It was a Sunday and we have given the kids permission to stay home while she went to church, since they didn't like going to her church.

We told her as well, and she acted like she was okay with this.

My mom never misses church and it came time to go. She told the kids to get ready and that they were going with her.

Danny refused saying, "Grandma, Mom and Dad said that we could stay home while you went to church. I don't want to go."

Grandma became upset with this as she sees this as a refusal of loving her God. "I don't care what they said. You both are coming to church with me. You can have a donut there," she rebutted.

"I am not going and they said that I don't have to," Danny replied.

Piper watched as her brother stood up to Grandma.

Grandma lost it at this point yelling, "Danny, you are going to turn into your uncle who does drugs and drinks too much alcohol. He refused church at the same age as you and look at where he is now. Get in the car. You are going."

Danny stood his ground and was crying. "I am not going!" He yelled. Danny ran outside to his favorite tree and climbed up in it as high as he could.

He called me as he had grabbed our portable home phone. I answered and he was sobbing telling me all the horrible insults Grandma had just said. I told him to throw the phone down to her and I will talk to her. She refused to talk to me.

Just then, I got a "911" call for a person who was not breathing.

Shit!

I told Danny that I would call Dad and see if he could come home, otherwise, I would after the emergency call. Danny was partially relieved, yet I could feel that he was traumatized.

Inside the house, Grandma was ranting horrible verbal onslots about me, my brother, Danny, and everyone else that she was upset with.

Piper stood there watching and wanted to make the craziness go away. She said, "Grandma, I will go with you."

This stopped her in her tracks.

Grandma left Danny in the tree and off she and Piper went to church.

Now, who is more traumatized?
Everyone is.
Those who watched and those who participated.

Piper also gave up her power to keep the peace when she didn't want to go either.

Or did she give up her power?
Was it more powerful for her to calm the situation?

My mom never did apologize or take responsibility for this situation. She said she was the victim. We had to pick up the pieces and talk through the whole situation with the kids.

So crazy.
Wanna know what is wild?

The universe decided that it was time for Bruce and I to get divorced a year later and we ended up selling the house. Grandma had to move out as we did, too, and we have had limited contact with her since then.

It's on our terms when we decide to see her or not.

I'm done with having traumatized, victimized people around me who don't take responsibility for what they put out there.

Done!

I love them and want the best for them, but I love myself too much to continually put myself in a position of being constantly attacked, humiliated, or hurt.

Done!

I think to myself…if my mom was a friend and she acted this way towards me, would I still keep her as a friend?

FUCK NO!
Absolutely not!

So, why do I continue to have a relationship with her?
Just because she is blood?
Enough already!
I will love her from afar.

Yet, "every cloud has a silver lining" as the saying goes and I have realized that I am incredibly appreciative for all the experiences I have had with my mother. I realize that if I had not been traumatized throughout my life, I would have never been driven to want the adrenaline rushes and "live on the edge." Because of my lack of fear around death, I experienced so much with so many important life lessons. It's amazing when you look at the bigger picture.

It's all perspective.
My mom has been one of my greatest teachers.
You picked a tough role in this lifetime, Mom.
Let's change our scripts now.

CHAPTER 41
RIVER BOTTOM WARS

Life has everything in it. But you only see what your perception allows you to see.
~Dr. Bruce Lipton

On the north end of Sparrow City is Sparrow River. It is a big river bottom that comes down to the ocean. Sometimes, it has lots of water in it as it is quite wide and other times, it is just a small river. It is filled with big brush in and surrounding it.

It is also filled with homeless people.
Lots of them.

In fact, they have taken over this area from the ocean to about five miles up north. Typically, the police leave this area alone as it is like the "wild west" days. There are people there who don't want to be part of society. Some are traumatized war vets and others are criminals. A younger crowd of druggies and alcoholics frequent the area as well.

They have their own city there with their own rules. Yet, when "911" is called, we go down there for medical issues and do quite a bit of hiking. River bottom fires are quite common as well here since they cook their own food down there and have warming fires.

When I was new to the job, I loved fighting fires there. They were huge and raging. Typically, it would be in the middle of the night and seeing fire at night was incredible.

Then, one of our firefighters got hurt.

At one point, we were having these fires often and all of us were getting tired of it. We weren't sure why this was happening and arson was mentioned. It wasn't very safe and the brush was dry. We would be up all night working our asses off into the next day or more.

And no one mentioned that there were "boobie traps" in the river bottom.

It was late at night in the river bottom and fire once again was raging. It is hard to see sometimes and one of the firefighters fell partially into a hole twisting his ankle. When others came to help, they saw what looked like a trap.

It was about a six foot deep hole and was about four feet by four feet wide. It even had some sharp bamboo spikes coming up from the bottom. Some of the guys who were in Vietnam mentioned they hadn't seen these traps since being in the war there.

The incident commander immediately let everyone know to be careful and to watch your footing. We all knew there may be more out here. We even began to question if we should be out there as we didn't need to save anyone and we could let the brush burn to the ocean. We ended up continuing until daylight hours getting the fire under control.

The police were out there because of these traps and possible arson. They were talking to the homeless people and gathering information.

Well, we finally figured out why all the fires and traps.

The homeless people were getting into fights with each other. Some of them were old war vets and dug the traps to keep others out of their camp. If they got pissed at someone in a neighboring camp, they would light their camp on fire that night.

One minor detail these homeless people forgot is that fire spreads and it often ended up burning down their camp, too.

Funny people.

After our firefighter got hurt, the police began doing "river bottom sweeps," kicking out the homeless people. Turns out, they arrested many people from there, too, as many of them had warrants out for their arrest.

It's the wild, wild west!

CHAPTER 42
BECOMING A FIRE CAPTAIN

There are no limitations, unless you create them yourselves. Anything is possible. You are only limited by your own imagination.
~Delores Cannon

There is so much to learn being in the fire department. Every day is different and every emergency call is different too. Of course, some of them have a similar type of theme and you can store them in the hard drive of your brain for when you need them.

When I began to study for the captain's test, there was so much to learn. You had to know the job below you and above you. So, you had to know the engineer's job of driving the fire engine with all the math and mechanics. Then, you had to know how to run a major incident as the incident commander until the battalion chief showed up.

I was already an engineer, so I knew that job well. I loved driving the fire engine and it was fun driving lights and sirens. It was just pure excitement and I really felt like a kid in a candy store when I drove. People waved to us and loved us. It was kinda like we were in our own private parade.

I didn't think that I would want to be a fire captain until much later in my career as I wanted to have at least ten years on. It began to change when many of the "old" fire captains began to retire. They had so much experience and were leaving with thirty plus years on the department. The "new" guys began to promote and I found myself not wanting to work for many of them as many were micromanagers.

I don't work well with anyone who gives me a job to do and then tells me exactly how to do it. I want to know what the bottom line is that they want done and I will deal with the details of how to get it done.

In the fire department, there are so many different personalities with so many different backgrounds. Some guys have military backgrounds, some are incredibly intelligent, and others have experience in the "trades" like plumbing and electrical.

And I am not saying anyone with military or trades background are not intelligent. I know they are and there are just some guys that I worked with that were incredibly smart. They could figure out how to do a job with the least amount of effort and really think "outside the box."

When I got hired as a firefighter, there were a bunch of us "newer" guys who were paramedics. We were used to being in charge of a scene with a patient, so to become a fire captain didn't seem like that big of a deal. We liked to figure things out and to be in charge.

It came easy for me.

The fire department really doesn't like change and when I got hired, I asked lots of questions. I just wanted to understand why we did certain things and I found out that guys didn't know why. They just did them because that is what we always did.

Fascinating, right?

I can see why in any job that older and more seasoned employees would get annoyed with the new hires. It threatens them and their way of being. They didn't like change. This is what they have always done and now some new yahoo comes in questioning everything.

I was twenty-six and really just eager to learn.

Some captains did get upset at me questioning why they did things. Typically, I phrased things when I asked as me just wanting to learn, but I realized some of them took it as criticism. I actually realized some were just insecure in their decision making and didn't want to be questioned. Most didn't mind me asking questions and were happy to teach me by describing their thought processes.

Anyways, back to micromanaging.

We did have some captains who would tell the engineer how to drive and this didn't go over well with those seasoned engineers. Other guys seemed to like being told what to do. Maybe they weren't comfortable standing up for themselves or didn't like to think for themselves?

There was this one captain who was famous for telling the firefighters exactly how to do something once he gave them a job to do. He would stand there and watch until it was done instructing them in every move.

And I don't mean just with emergency calls.
It drove people crazy.

One time, he told someone to sweep the apparatus floor and then he instructed them on exactly how to sweep the floor. He stood there the whole time.

What is that, really?
Power trip?
Lack of feeling in control?
Lack of trust?

There was always a joke about captains and chiefs who were micromanagers or power trippers. Guys used to say that their wives bossed them around at home, so then they had to come to work and boss everyone else around.

I think there was some truth to this.

There were many different captains that I worked with over the years. On overtime shifts, I worked with many that were not with my regular captain. This was great because I got to learn lots of what I liked and didn't like on how they ran their crew and calls.

I really believe that I learned more from being with captains who didn't know what they were doing than from those that did know.

One captain that I especially learned a lot from was a captain that I worked with for about a year who would disappear as soon as we got to a fire. I was just off probation as a rookie firefighter and had no captain to tell me what to do. So, I took what I had learned and would decide for myself with my engineer's help sometimes. We had lots of fires that year and I became quite comfortable making decisions myself.

I would decide what size hose to bring into the fire and how I was going to put it out. I learned that it wasn't so hard to figure out what to do and eventually, when I would get the fire out, my captain would show back up.

Funny and not so funny.
I always wondered where he went.
Perhaps he was scared?

Regardless, I learned so much from that experience and it gave me the confidence to want to be a captain early on. I just knew that I could run a crew and emergency calls.

So, with about five years on, I began to dive into studying for the captain's test. There was so much book knowledge to know and I figured that I would see how I could do. I know I needed more experience though.

Preparing for the test, I thought of how I studied for the engineer's test as I put a lot of time and energy into that test. I would see myself grabbing the hoses, adjusting the levers, picking the right adapters, and setting the right pressures to pump the water. I visioned many different hose evolutions, driving the engine through the cone course, doing the math portion perfectly, and answering the questions on the oral interview with the best answer. I saw myself in the driver's seat with my engineer's helmet on.

Practicing this over and over again was what I did all day long until the test came. When the results came out, I was number one on the engineer's test.

I was so excited.
Visioning was key.
Doing this mentally helped me immensely when it came to the "real" test.
This is the same type of technique that many athletes use.
I would do this again for the captain's test.

I took the captain's test twice. I did well the first time passing all parts of the test which included the written, fire simulators, and oral interviews. There were lots of guys taking the test and I came in fifth for my first test. I was excited and I knew though that I wasn't ready. There weren't enough openings to get promoted, so I stayed engineer.

Something inside me had decided that even if they offered me the job as captain this time, I would turn it down because I didn't feel that I was ready.

When the next test came around, I was ready and I scored third. I was so excited and two guys that I had initially gotten hired with as firefighters also took the test. They beat me out by a couple points and took first and second.

The three of us got promoted the same day in 2004.
I was the first woman captain in Sparrow City Fire Department.
When my first shift as captain came, I was nervous, but I knew I could do it.

I was a go-getter and wanted to do a good job. I worked hard and had fun. Guys wanted to work on my shift and respected me. It had been seven and a half years of working on the fire department when I got promoted to fire captain.

I met with my crew that first day as captain and told them what I expected. I have always been easy going and they knew this. Reminding my crew that I would support them as best I could, I also said, "More eyes are better than one set of eyes and even though I am 'in charge', I want you to speak up if you don't agree with the decision I make or if you see something is unsafe. I want us all to go home safely after every shift."

I would take the heat for any decision made, of course.
That was my job.

I felt confident on just about any emergency call. Fire calls and medical calls were the easiest as I had been on so many. It was the calls that were unknown and you had to figure out what to do that were more challenging.

People called "911" for anything.
Firefighters are the "jack of all trades and masters of none" as I mentioned before.

I had an old captain once tell me, "On those calls where you don't know what to do, make sure you get rid of the liability." This made total sense to me. If you can pass the liability or get rid of the liability, then the city is covered and my butt is covered.

As the years past, I grew more and more confident. I knew what to do and I always made sure that I was open with my crew, so if there was something that I didn't see, they could chime in. It is all about going home to our families as our safety is first priority.

I loved being a fire captain.
It just felt like who I was.

CHAPTER 43
HE JUST NEEDS A FLOWER

Imagination is more important than knowledge. Knowledge is limited. Imagination encircles the world.
~Albert Einstein

Bruce and I were playing catch one summer's day in the front yard as we watched our kids play. The kids were little, around one and four years old. We were having fun throwing the ball back and forth and catching it in our mitts.

Really, this is one of my favorite things.
I love playing catch.
So simple.
Reminds me of being a kid.

Bruce threw a high ball up and across into the trees towards me. Unfortunately, there was a hummingbird sitting on a branch and the baseball hit her. I watched the hummingbird fall out of the tree and onto the grass.

"Awww! The ball hit a hummingbird." I said out loud.

Bruce walked over as did Danny. They both looked at the dead bird as I picked her up.

She is just so tiny and beautiful.
So colorful.
I felt sad to have contributed to her death.

I told Danny what happened and I was thinking that I would put her in the trash can when Danny says, "Mom! I know what she needs!"

"What?" I respond.
"She needs a flower!" He says matter-of-fact.

I was surprised by this and responded, "Of course she does, Danny!"

"Come follow me!" He says.

I have the hummingbird in my hands and he takes me to a flower. He picks the flower and gives it to her in my hands.

I say, "Why don't we lay her down with the flowers here, Danny?"
Danny says, "Okay."

So, in my mind, I am thinking that this bird is dead and that we will lay her in the flowers on the dirt. As I go to put her on the dirt, she suddenly springs to life and hovers at eye level to Danny and I!

I am so shocked that this bird is now looking at both of us and buzzing her wings. It is like she is saying, "Thank you" to us while I am also saying, "Sorry for hitting you."

A moment, so precious with just no words.

Life and death.
It can change in an instant.
One moment, you are alive and the next moment, you are dead.
I just witnessed both.

Danny is not surprised at all that she is alive. I say to Danny, "Hey buddy, you were right! She just needed a flower."

He smiles and off he goes to play...

CHAPTER 44
WE CAN HANDLE

When you don't do your best, you are denying yourself the right to be you.
~Don Miguel Ruiz

I have been a fire captain now for six months and I am really loving this job. There is lots of action and some challenging calls. I enjoy being in charge as it feels like it comes naturally. I attempt to be a good leader and not a tyrant.

My engineer, Staci, has about fifteen years under her belt on the fire department and she knows her job. My firefighter/paramedic, Craig, has less than a year on and is on probation. We have been working together for a few months now.

We all have fun together and I have talked to them both about my philosophy as a crew. I tell them that just because I am the captain and am responsible for making the decisions, we are a team. If they see something I don't see or don't feel good about a decision that I made, I want them to speak up. I remind them that my job is to make sure that they go home safely to their families, but it is also theirs as well.

We do lots of training together and we are also very busy running calls.

One night, we have all just finished dinner and we are sitting around the table telling stories. The tones go off and dispatch's voice comes over the speaker telling us of a small fire by the hillside.

We head out. It's foggy and almost dark. I know this area well and there is a flat area behind some houses where kids play. It is flat for about hundred feet and then, it goes up to a steep hillside.

It isn't hot out and I am not worried much about a brush fire. We turn down the dead end street towards the small fire, but are unable to find it. We head down another street and see a small fire not doing much behind the houses in some grass. It takes a while for us to get the engine in the right place and to get to the fire.

Suddenly, I notice the fire is getting bigger!
Shit!

This shouldn't be happening!
It is foggy and cold out.

I tell Craig to grab the hoseline quick and help him pull the hose over a wall. I say, "Come on, Craig! Let's get this quick! We got this!"

In the back of my mind, I am thinking that if this hits the base of the hill, it's gone. It will go straight up the mountain and I am going to have to call in lots of fire resources. My ego will be crushed. It will be a huge brush fire, but I know it will stop at the top as it will run out of fuel. This is what all these fires do that burn on this hillside.

But still!
We can get this!
My pride is at hand!

Just then, dispatch calls me on the radio. "Engine 1, we are getting more reports that the fire is getting larger. Are you at the fire? Do you want us to dispatch a second engine?"

Now, this was just a single fire engine call. We "should" have been able to handle this. My ego gets the best of me and I reply, "We are just getting water on the fire. We can handle."

Another minute goes by and Craig is attempting to put the fire out. I am pulling hose for him and I can see the fire is taking off and headed up the mountain.

Damn!

Dispatch radios me again, "Engine 1, we are receiving more reports that the fire is now headed up the hillside. Do you want us to start a brush response?"

My ego is getting the best of me and yet, I know that we need help. I reply, "Affirmative, send a full brush response."

Damn.
I know I am going to take shit for this from the oncoming crews.

The fire is rippin' and headed straight up the mountain. Craig and I are chasing it, but with the elevation, the fire is leaping ahead. It is also steep and we have hose packs on our back now.

Engines begin arriving and I begin to tell them what I need and where to go. My chief arrives on scene and takes over as incident commander. More and more fire engines and crews come and help us with the fire. We are on the mountain all night and the fire does put itself out at the top. At about 5 am the next morning, we come back down the hillside.

Well, actually, we slide down parts of the hillside as it is so freakin' steep!

Craig and I are dirty, tired, hungry, and thirsty as well as the other crews. I see my chief when I get down there.

He has a smirk on his face and says to me, "We can handle?!"
We both start laughing hysterically.

I reply, "Yeh, my ego got the best of me. I was embarrassed that a little fire got away from us. We should have had it."

He says, "Hydee, it has happened to us all. It's quite humbling."

"Yes, it is," as I nod my head and reply. "Yes, it is."

CHAPTER 45
ADULTS ARE JUST BIG KIDS

Power over others is weakness disguised as strength. True power is within, and it is available to you now.
~Eckhart Tolle

After I had about three years on the fire department as a firefighter, I was asked to be on the union board. I asked lots of questions about why our chiefs and politicians did the things they did and was just curious as some of the decisions did not make any sense to me. Sometimes it even seemed that decisions were made because they didn't like someone or were vengeful.

Could this really be?
People in power abusing their power?

I was the insurance coordinator for a few years on the union board and I got to see firsthand how decisions were made. I also was the vice president for many years. This was quite an eye opener as I found there were lots of egos and "children" running our fire department and city hall.

I guess I was naïve?
Or maybe I thought people "grew up" before being in positions of power?

There were really so many "playground issues" going on.
Bullies, threats, lies, backstabbing, and "he said, she said" stuff!

Geez…
I thought people were honest?!
I mean, really!?
It's the fire department and city hall!

Citizens depend on us to make decisions in their best interest. They put their trust in us. I wondered if the police department and other departments had the same issues.

Of course, they did.

It happens wherever humans are.
It's called the "human condition."

I saw how there were special interests and if someone liked someone, then their project would happen. If chiefs or politicians didn't like someone, they didn't support them and sometimes would even go after them.

Coming from a psychology background, I could see the deeper emotional issues that our chiefs hadn't dealt with. Some of the guys knew their history when they were kids. One chief in particular, Chief Kline was gnarly. He was bullied as a kid and got beat up all the time at school. He hated women and minorities. Chief Kline would openly call black people terrible names and he didn't like women in the fire department.

Nice guy, right?

Perhaps those that get to be in power should have their mental health checked in a much deeper way? There were so many "games" being played. The chiefs would have committees where they wanted us to feel like we had a "voice" and what looked like our ideas to get us on board with something that they wanted.

For example, I was on the apparatus committee where we were researching new fire engines and fire trucks. The chiefs wanted to buy what was called a "quint" which is a combination engine and truck. It has ladders and could pump water.

It sounded like a great idea, but it was too heavy and got stuck going up some of our steep hills. The committee came back not supporting it, but the chiefs kept pushing it. We found out later that one of our chiefs' brothers-in-law was working for the company that was selling the quint. He would get the sale and a large kickback.

Ummmm…yeh.
Total corruption.
No thanks.
Come on, people!

I later found out that we had two engines that nobody liked to drive and would always break down because an earlier chief got kickbacks for buying them. The interior was way too small for the guys and we couldn't fit our gear. It is so interesting to witness the selfishness mentality in our leaders.

I saw firsthand how politicians used their position of power for their selfish reasons instead of putting the citizens safety first. There was a time when I was first hired that the fire department was running their own ambulances because it was better service for the citizens. The private ambulance that used to do the service was "for profit" and would take over ten minutes to get to emergency calls most of the time.

This is important because the human brain can only live for six to eight minutes with no oxygen before there is damage.

The private ambulance didn't like that they lost money and contracts with the cities. They ended up fighting the decision. Other cities and counties were getting their own ambulances as it was better service for the citizens.

So, it went to a vote by the city council and board of supervisors.

The fire departments all over California lost their ambulances because of a court decision and in our county, the board of supervisors voted to give the contract to the private ambulance company.

I couldn't believe it.
I was dumbfounded.
Just didn't make sense!

It was better and cheaper for the citizens to have their fire department run the ambulance service. This is where I began to learn how the private ambulance company had padded the pockets of the politicians to make decisions. They gave some of them paid vacations or other kickbacks.

I wondered…if this is happening at the city and county level, what is happening at the state and federal level?

Is anybody honest?

Being on the union board, I also saw how we had special interests and used our good name as firefighters with the public to help get politicians into office that would support us. Sometimes it helped the public and sometimes it helped ourselves.

So, am I really any different?
Am I just as selfish?
Is that the nature of the human being?
What about for the common good?
We have a long way to go in our evolution!

Many politicians didn't like the fire department. They saw us as wasting the taxpayer's money because we were such a big expense and didn't bring in much revenue. Many tried to figure out how to scale back the fire department's budget.

As I said before, the fire department is really just an insurance policy.

Before I got hired, a new city manager was hired as well as a new fire chief. She was brought in by city council to cut as much as she could from all the departments. The city manager got the new fire chief to cut the fire department budget by over twenty-five percent and he reduced staffing to bare bones on all levels.

We used to have four firefighters on each fire engine and he cut it to three which was a big safety issue for fighting fires. Many guys were outraged, but there was nothing they could do.

I enjoyed being on the union board and being outspoken for truth. The chiefs began to not like me so much because I called out lies when I saw them. I didn't care as I was a fire captain and wasn't planning on ever promoting to battalion chief, so there was nothing they could hold over me.

I loved the guys and fighting for their rights came naturally.

It was tough sometimes though as there were five of us on the union board and sometimes other guys would be swayed by the chiefs telling them that they would promote them if they voted a certain way.

The corruption was just nonstop!

I knew who I was and knew my job.
I was good at my job and would get compliments from citizens sometimes.
I was outspoken and not in an "asshole" type way.
I would just speak up for the truth.

As a fire captain, my boss was a battalion chief. I got along great with the chiefs that left me alone and trusted me to do a good job. It was the micromanagers that caused me problems.

I had this one battalion chief named Dave who would call me so many times during the day that it became ridiculous. He was a "type A" personality who was such a busy body. It drove me crazy. He would even call me on the way to a call and try to tell me what to do.

So, I stopped answering the cellphone which pissed him off.

He was constantly telling me what to do and also wanted me to discipline my engineer because the chiefs didn't like him. I knew their game and stood up for my engineer which really pissed off the chiefs.

My chief's background was also interesting as he grew up with alcoholic parents and I wondered if this was why he was so anal and controlling. Dave finally retired and I was hopeful that I would get a mellow chief.

Not so lucky.
I got another micromanaging chief.
Perhaps it is my energy that is drawing this type of person to me?
What did I need to learn or clear?

This time his name was Brandon. We were good friends as he was president on the union board for a while when I was vice president. He knew how I worked and we had conversations about him leaving me alone to do my job. I promised to call him when I needed him to help.

This lasted for some time, but he began to put pressure on me. He began to come by the station all the time and wanted to talk. He was questioning me on things and trying to find things to discipline me for. He never could and I knew the other chiefs had put him up to this as things were heated between the chiefs and the union board.

So fucked up, really.

One time, Brandon had called me numerous times throughout the day and I had really had enough of him and his micromanaging. It had been a busy day with calls and training. We also had to get our station ready to be fumigated for termites.

We had just eaten dinner around 7 pm and were still bagging stuff for the fumigation. We had to pack up the whole kitchen as they were coming the next day. Brandon had called me about this a few times throughout the day.

Then, he drives up.

"You have got to be kidding!" I think to myself as my blood begins to boil.

He walks into the fire station kitchen where I am busy working. The other guys are working on other parts of the station. It's late to be still working on station stuff. This is our time usually to relax if we are not running calls.

He says, "Hey Hydee! How's it going?"
Friendly enough, right, but I am not amused.

I fire back, "Brandon, I don't know if you are my husband or my mother, but I have had enough of you telling me what to do and you checking up on me all the time! So, from now on, I am going to call you every time I do anything. When I go to change my clothes, I will call you. When I go to workout, I will call you. When I go to eat, I will call you. When I go to take a shit, I will call you so that you never have to bother wondering what I am doing ever again. I can play this game, too, Brandon."

And with that, he spins on his heels and leaves. He gets in his car and drives away.

Enough said.

From that day forward, he stopped fucking with me. I know I am not telling you (the reader) all the other times this kind of stuff happened, so it may seem harsh to you.

But really, it was well deserved.
Perhaps, I am just one of those big adult kids, as well.
Oh, the games we play…

CHAPTER 46
ARSON FIRE

True intelligence operates silently. Stillness is where creativity and solutions to problems are found.
~Eckhart Tolle

Arson fires are one of the most difficult crimes to prove as most of the evidence is burned up at the scene. Most fires are accidental or electrical in nature, so the police don't put a ton of resources to solving arson fires as they are so hard to prove.

We would get "fire bugs" from time to time that were arsonists going around lighting things on fire. They usually had their signature call as around the same time of night in a specific area. Often times, the arsonists would stay around in the crowd to watch us work putting their fire out. They are infatuated with fire. These fires caused safety issues for firefighters.

Being a new fire captain on the "Avenue," we were busy with calls and getting lots of fires. I had been on a number of arson fires during my years on the fire department. They often had an element of surprise associated with them.

One particular shift sticks out in the realm of arson fires. I had a new "rookie" (probationary firefighter) with me whose name was Craig. He had been out of the academy and on "the floor" (at the station) for about five months. Craig was a "go getter" and loved doing a good job. He was strong, wise, and intuitive.

It was a busy shift and I was happy to go to bed around 10 pm.
At about 1 am in the early morning, the tones went off.
"Structure fire. Flames seen."

I shot out of bed and threw on my turnouts. From half asleep to wide awake now with adrenaline pumping, I let dispatch know that we were responding while looking to find the address. It was in our first in and it was at the top of our sector, so it would be some time before the next in engine showed up to help.

From what dispatch said, it sounds like this will be a rippin' fire!

I am nervous and excited at the same time.

My engineer, Tyler, was seasoned and had about twenty years on the department. I knew he was good at getting us water and I trusted him. This would be Craig's first big fire and we had been talking a few shifts before of what I expected from him. He was ready.

We drove fast and had our emergency lights going. We didn't need the siren much as there weren't any cars on the road. The fire was in a wood flooring manufacturing company according to the address details. As we got close, we could see heavy, black smoke laying down. There wasn't much wind and the smoke was thick in the area.

We pulled up to the fire and I gave my onscene report to dispatch so the incoming units knew what to expect.

"Sparrow, Engine 1 is onscene. We have a one-story wood flooring manufacturing business with fire coming out of the tactical front in two separate locations. Engine 1 will be attack. Have the next in engine take command and set up RIC. Initiate a second alarm."

We are all still in the engine and I see powerlines down across the front part of the business. We stay clear of these and I get on the radio to let dispatch know as well as incoming units. I know dispatch will contact the electrical company and get them to shut down power to this area and the business.

In my head, I am thinking we need to stay very present to live wires down, especially at night. We don't need to fry anyone this evening!

My crew knows what to do as we were talking about it in the cab of the engine as we pulled up.

I know Craig is grabbing a hoseline and meeting me at the front of the building on fire where it appears the main fire is. Tyler is hooking up to the hydrant and getting us water. I am doing a quick walk around of the building to see the bigger picture of what we have.

This is all happening at lightning speed.
Adrenaline does amazing things.
We are doing everything just as we trained.

It is really like "clockwork" as they say when you "fight" a fire. We train day after day so that when the "real" fire call comes in, we don't have to think much (especially in the middle of the night!). Our bodies know what to do. Of course, I do need to take many nuances into consideration, but really, the structure of a fire call is basic.

You put the fire out!

We get taught little acronyms like REVAS to help remind us of the strategy and tactics on fire calls. In REVAS, it stands for rescue, exposures, ventilation, attack and salvage. These are broad categories for what we need to accomplish on a structure fire call. REVAS serves as a good reminder if too much adrenaline is flowing.

Back to the fire…

I come around the building noting that there are two points where fire started and they are far away from each other. One is a smaller and detached building. I radioed that another engine can attack this fire and I also see that Tyler is pulling another line towards this fire.

I know what he is thinking…once he gets us water, he can put water on this other fire until another crew comes.

Damn, he's good!

I walk up to the front of the building on fire where Craig is. He is going "on air" and I am doing the same. We are connecting our facemasks to the lines of our air bottles, so that we breathe air when inside the smoky building. We also make sure that our bodies are fully covered with our protective gear with no skin showing.

Don't want to get burned!

Craig and I head into the building with Craig in front on the nozzle. I am pulling the hose for him as we go in deeper and around corners. We can see somewhat as the smoke level is not all the way to the floor yet. We head in deeper to get to the "head" of the fire and are now crawling on our hands and knees as the smoke got hotter and thicker.

Craig is putting out fire along the way and we are making good progress. The fire is loud and I move back on the hoseline to pull more as it is stuck on a corner.

Then, something then tells me to look up.

Shit!
How did this happen?!
I see fire above and behind us.
It is running the ceiling.

I know instantly that we need to get out or the fire is going to flash with us inside and cook us! I don't need to be in a second flashover this lifetime! I don't know what told me to look up, but I know that someone or something bigger than me is always protecting me and guiding me.

It is a deep inner knowing.
It has kept me safe many times and I trust it.

I drop the hoseline as I know that if it won't move than Craig can't go any further. I move back towards the main fire to tell him that we have to leave now! I find him and I point to the fire above and behind us. I can see that he knows we need to leave quickly.

He still has the nozzle in his hands and I grab the hose as we make our way back to the front door that we came through. We are booking it and just get outside the door when the whole place explodes with fire blowing out the windows.

Fire is everywhere.

We stand in awe and look at each other.
Less than a minute ago, we were deep in the building.
Somehow, we got out just in time.

Another engine company had just pulled up and saw everything. The captain ran over to us to make sure we were okay.

"We're okay," I say as I pull off my mask.

The other captain says, "You guys are so lucky. We saw the explosion of fire. You got out of there just in time. We were worried that you guys were in there."

I know we were seconds from being burned alive inside the building.
I wonder to myself what happened as I am very aware of not letting fire get behind us. I have talked to Craig about this as well.

Hmmmm...

More engine and truck companies are beginning to pull up on scene. The downed powerlines are not energized any longer and not an issue. Craig and I go to work blasting water in through the windows as fire shoots out of them.

I give an update to the incident commander and we continue putting water on the fire as well as other crews do, too. The truck crews are headed up to the roof to cut holes in the roof to alleviate some of the heat and smoke. Lots of fire crews are on scene and we are getting a handle on the fire. This is a big facility with two big buildings in the front and one huge manufacturing plant in the back. Luckily, we were able to keep the fire from spreading to the back building.

We get the fire out and before we go into savage and overhaul operations (saving things that are okay and removing things that are burned), the fire investigator needs to take a look to see what started it. Shiela, the fire investigator, comes over to interview me. She wants to know what I saw when I pulled up. I tell her and show her where the fires were. She continues to gather information while interviewing my crew as to what they saw. Shiela is piecing it all together.

My crew and I take a much needed break. We are tired and exhausted from all the adrenaline and work. We grab some energy bars, waters, and relax.

The investigation takes over an hour as she goes through the building looking for the cause. The incident commander calls all the captains to have a meeting. He wants us to walk through the building with the investigator.

We start at the unburned part of the building and Shiela is telling us that she knows this is arson. She shows us that the fire was started simply with gasoline and match books. There were multiple sets, so that as one goes off and catches the room on fire, it will spread with gasoline and reach another room catching that on fire with another set of matches and gasoline.

Doesn't take a rocket scientist to start fires!

This explains so much to me as to why Craig and I were making progress on the fire and then having fire get behind us and above us. It was the gasoline making things spread quickly with multiple sets ready to go off.

The arsonist didn't expect that some of his props would fail and that we would get a handle on it. I wonder who it was…usually it is a disgruntled employee.

Arson is a big killer of firefighters.
So, who is watching over me anyways?
Somehow, I am very protected.
And I am very appreciative!

CHAPTER 47
TOMMY

The mountains are calling, I must go.
~John Muir

We all have those favorite people in the world. Those who love us just for us with all our faults and funnies. They seem to accept us wherever we are at in life. I always found that saying fascinating about friends. "People come in our lives for a reason, a season, or a lifetime."

It's just so true.

No need to try to hold onto what was. Some friends are there for a short time and others for longer times. Some teach us lessons or fulfill karmic roles. Others are there for our whole lives. I've learned to just be grateful however long they are in my life.

Tom, or as I called him, "Tommy," is one of those friends who seems to accept me right where I am no matter what. He is one of those lifetime friends. I met him when I first began working in the fire department back in 1996. He was really funny and always made me laugh. He was more than twenty years older than me and had this fatherly feel.

We connected instantly and I always loved when I got to work with him. He would call me, "Hydacious" or many other nicknames over the years. Tommy was a long-time engineer who knew his job well. He loved to drive the fire engine and was good at it.

Tommy was one of the best story tellers around. He had a way with telling stories and I would listen again and again when he would repeat them. Most of them were hilarious. We also had these traditions in the fire department. One of those was to "roll the pees" after dinner for dollars. It was like poker, but with dice. Tommy loved this game and we would laugh making fun of each other during it.

He had been in the Navy and worked on a ship. Tommy was so intelligent and could see the absurdity of it all. He learned how to act like he was busy in the Navy while really doing as little as possible. This routine followed him in the fire department. In fact, he wanted to write a book about how to get out of work. We kidded him saying that it would be called "The lazy man's guide to looking busy and getting out of work."

He was a professional at this.

Now, this isn't to say that he was always lazy because when he really needed to work, he did. Tommy just didn't see the reasons for always keeping us busy with work. It didn't make sense to him. He was great on emergency calls and would go beyond what was asked of him to help the public.

Because he was such a great storyteller, if he didn't want to work, he would tell his stories. Guys loved them, so often our trainings would get interrupted with story time. He also was a great joke teller.

About a year after I became a captain, I ended up on Tommy's crew. Some captains didn't like to work with Tommy because they said he was too lazy and strong willed. I decided that I was up for the challenge as I liked to figure out how people work inside. I enjoyed the psychology of it all.

I learned really quick how he worked and I made a deal with him. He liked to have down time, so he could get his naps in and read. I told him that he could have longer lunches to nap, but that we needed to get done what was expected of us first.

Firefighters work for twenty-four hours, so we may not get much sleep at night. I wanted my crew to be well rested and to take care of themselves during the day. Tommy also liked to eat well, so the other part of the deal was that he would be the shift cook and we would pay for his meals.

He loved this!
Sleep and eat!
I was happy because I got him to do his job and to eat yummy food.
He was happy because he got to rest and cook yummy food!

One of his mottos was "to eat till your sleepy and sleep till you're hungry."

So great.
He had lots more of those mottos.

I was happy and so was he. This made for a great friendship and working relationship. He became my engineer for over eleven years. We were buddies. When I first came on Tommy's crew, it was Tommy and Mark. Mark was the firefighter and loved to talk. He could talk about anything. This would drive Tommy crazy, so Mark and I would talk for a long time until I had enough and needed some peace and quiet.

Little did I know though that there was a feud going on between the two of them. It took me a few weeks before I realized they didn't stay in the same room for too long with each other. One would come in and the other would leave.

Early one morning, I was still sleeping and I heard some yelling outside in the hallway. I was in my bed and heard doors opening and slamming. I wondered what was going on and by the time I got up and looked outside my room, there was no one there.

Hmmm…I wondered and didn't give it another thought.

During the next shift, it was lunch and I had just finished some reports. I came to sit down and watch some television with Mark. As I sat down, I noticed a note on a table next to me.

It was written with a sharpie in big letters, "GO FUCK YOURSELF."

I picked it up and asked Mark what it was. Mark replied matter-of-fact, "Oh, that is Mofo and my new contract." He always called Tommy, "Mofo." Yes, it is short for mother fucker.

I laughed and said, "What?"

Mark laughed and said that they have been having some issues lately. Mark likes the central heating on and Tommy doesn't. Tommy likes it cold in his room and doesn't want the central heating on. Mark is cold and wants the heater on.

Mark goes on to tell me that the other morning, they got in an argument about turning the heater on. Mark turned it on and went back in his room. Tommy came out and turned it off. This continued a few more times until Tommy waited for Mark to come out of his room where they yelled at each other. Tommy shoved a space heater in Mark's face and told him he was "gonna shove this where the sun don't shine" if he didn't knock it off.

So, Mark knew enough to stop and now he is asking Mofo for a contract on how and when the heater is used. Mofo wasn't too amused and wrote Mark a contract.

"Go fuck yourself."

I had to laugh at the whole thing. Grown men fighting over a heater. Now, I also know Mark well enough that he likes to do things that piss people off. So, I am sure he is fucking with Tommy just because he is bored.

Realizing that I have to deal with this issue between the two of them, I talk more to Mark to hear his side of the story before I go and talk to Tommy.

Can't we just all get along?
Another example that adults are really just kids in adult bodies.
Most of us haven't left the school playground.

I make my way after lunch to talk to Tommy and hear his side of the story. Tommy agrees with all of it and says that Mark purposely does things to piss him off.

Just as I suspected.

Tommy goes on to say that he can't stand country music, so Mark blares country music when he works out or when he goes to shower. Mark takes a radio into the bathroom and cranks up country music. The bathroom is directly across from Tommy's room. Tommy has threatened Mark that if he doesn't stop, he will take a baseball bat to the radio.

Good times.

This whole thing amuses me, and yet, I know how real it is for both of them. I tell them both the next shift that we need to have a shift meeting.

It goes well and I have both of them tell their sides of the story, so they both feel heard. They both agree to knock off the fighting and get along. They ask me to figure out the heater issue. I decide that no one uses the central heating and everyone has a space heater in their rooms. Everyone can decide their own level of comfort when it comes to temperature.

They agree to this and it seems we have peace again. Sometimes these personnel issues in the fire station were harder than the emergency calls!

One thing I love about Tommy is that he wears his emotions. You know if he is happy, sad, mad, etc... There is no hiding them. I just love this about him. We had a great working relationship and friendship. We had great, deep talks.

When I first came to work with him, I had a year on as a new captain. I was also vice president on the union board and majorly stressed out. We had so much fighting with our chiefs and politicians. They were cutting our budget and firefighters. The chiefs were attempting to change many policies that hurt the firefighter's safety.

I would come to work ranting and raving about all these union issues. He would listen and listen. He never added fuel to the fire I was raging. This went on for the first six months of working together. I had come from a very busy station and now, I had more down time. My system was still in shock from constantly working as I didn't know how to slow down.

One morning, Tommy and I went for a walk during workout. I was busy talking about union issues and he was listening. Then, Tommy says, "Look. The Topa Topas."

"Huh?" I say not understanding.

"The Topa Topa mountains. They are just so majestic," he says.

I am so confused.
I stand there and just look at them.
My mind can't wrap itself around what is happening.

I will never forget this moment as it shook me out of what I had been missing. Tommy didn't feed my story I was telling. I had long forgotten my connection to nature. I had forgotten to look out at all the beauty around me. Instead, I was busy fighting internal battles within the fire department and myself. I began to question things more and wonder what really mattered in life.

Was I here to fight with management and politicians? I was angry with everyone and I had lost myself somewhere.

Tommy would talk about his grandson and the fun stuff they did together. He would talk about spiritual gurus and his awakenings on mushrooms back in the hippie days. Nature was very connected with him and I began to listen. We often walked in the mornings at work and our conversations went deep into exploring consciousness.

Getting off the union board that next year, I began to read more. I spent more time at home and began going to therapy. My thirst to better understand myself and why I was here opened again.

With downtime at the fire station, I dove into metaphysical books reading everything I could. Tommy and I would read and discuss everything from Eckart Tolle to Shamanism to Toltec to hypnotherapy to Yogananda to Jesus to Buddha to Krishna to goddess cultures to energy medicine to beliefs to extraterrestrials to quantum physics to conspiracy theories, and on and on.

Studying religious beliefs was eye opening for me as I realized that almost all religions had some type of creation event, flood story, virgin birth, messiah/teacher, and some type of heaven place. They all preached the same thing about evolving the human being back to their original condition of love, joy, and peace. They just all used different terms.

Fascinating.

Really, we talked about everything and questioned everything. Our marriages weren't in the best shape either, so we had common ground with the volatility of our spouses. I began to process so much personally and internally with therapy, as well. I was learning about myself and my fears. I understood the shortcomings of my parents and grieved my childhood.

I began to look forward to downtime at the fire station.
It was a gift to myself.
I stopped watching television and put my energy into healing myself.

This was a time of great transformation for me and my dreams were very prophetic.

I can remember two snake dreams signifying that I was beginning to transform and coming into my power. They were scary and I didn't learn the meaning of these dreams until much later.

One dream, I was at fire station one working with Staci and Robert. I was at the back of the station and a rattlesnake came up and bit me on the side of my right hand. I yelled and they went to grab a snake stick to get it off of me. We had snake sticks on the engine which were long sticks to grab a rattlesnake with when we got snake calls.

The rattlesnake looked me deep in the eyes as his fangs were buried in my hand. I stared back into his eyes.

Suddenly, I knew what to do. I took my arm and flung it up and down hard. The rattlesnake turned into glass and broke into millions of pieces on the ground. I knew I wasn't hurt, but I was stunned that I was okay. Then, I woke up.

About a month later, I had another dream with snakes and this time, I was walking in a rural area. I came upon a mama snake and her babies. They all chased me as I ran fast. The mama snake was gaining speed on me like a black mamba could and then I woke up in a sweat.

So much meaning in dreams and I loved learning about them.

Tommy, Mark, and I were a crew for about four years together before Mark promoted. They would watch movies often together and one time they told me that I had to watch this movie with them. It was called *What the Bleep Do We Know?* They had just finished watching it and wanted to watch it again with me. I was reluctant as I wanted to read as much as I could, but I gave in and sat down with them.

It was a really great movie about quantum physics and also emphasized how our thoughts impact our realities and our bodies. They showed how we are made of water and how Dr. Masaru Emoto studied the molecular structure in water finding that water transforms when it is exposed to human intentions, thoughts, and words.

Dr. Emoto would take pictures of frozen water crystals with the words written down on the bottle of water. He found beautiful molecular formations when there were loving words on them. The opposite was true when the water had fearful and negative words on the bottle. It looked like a disfigured molecular formation.

Can you imagine all the thoughts we think about our bodies every day?
Makes you want to be conscious of every thought.
And what thoughts are we sending to others in our environment?
We can change so much with just our thoughts!

All of this reflection and slowing down made me realize what an adrenaline junkie I was because of all my PTSD. I even began to see that many of us firefighters were really traumatized and used adrenaline type scenarios to continually re-traumatize ourselves again and again.

Just fascinating!
We humans!

The time came for Tommy to retire.
He was sixty-seven years old.
He loved the fire department and had over thirty-five years working there.
It was a happy and sad day for me, indeed.

Tommy tells me that I really helped him throughout his life, yet he helped me greatly as well. I will be forever grateful for his friendship and waking me up. He reminded me that there is more to this human life underneath it all. Perhaps we had a contract prior to incarnating that we would trigger each other into remembering more of who we are?

Of course we did.
Truly, we deeply helped each other in many ways.

CHAPTER 48
REPEATING PAST LIVES AGAIN AND AGAIN

The most interesting moment of a person's life is what happens to them when all their certainties go away. Then who do you become? And then what do you look for? That's the moment when the universe is offering up an invitation saying, 'come and find me'…
~Elizabeth Gilbert

You just never know who your friends, siblings, parents, or enemies were in your past lives.

Some of us know. Most of us don't, but those who "see" may know. I hadn't really given this much thought until this one firefighter that I worked with kept telling me about a book called, *Many Lives, Many Masters* by Brian Weiss. He said that we live many lives and just keep reincarnating.

Huh?
Or better yet…
Why?
Why would we ever keep coming to this crazy place?

I was always open to this idea of reincarnation, but I was looking to be done with life when I died. I didn't want to keep coming down here as I thought life on Earth was hell! There is so much pain and suffering here. I didn't want to go through bad stuff over and over again.

Plus, I was raised on Christianity which believed in heaven after you die, not reincarnation.

Little did I know that heaven is a state of inner being…as is hell.

I always felt that I had been on this Earth before.
I just didn't understand how I knew this.
It all felt vaguely familiar.

I read the book within a day or two. I just couldn't put it down.

It was about this psychiatrist who was using hypnosis to help heal his patients when ordinary therapy didn't work. A woman was referred to him that couldn't heal her depression or anxiety. He hypnotized her and she went back to where the problem all began.

She regressed to a time in Egypt when there was a flood and her baby was ripped from her arms. She drowned in that life. She continued to talk about other lives, too. The crazy thing was that after regressing with hypnosis, all her symptoms of depression and anxiety were healed.

Totally gone!

The psychiatrist was shocked by all this and didn't believe in reincarnation. His research led him to realize it was true.

This book led me to reading many other books by Brian Weiss and others about reincarnation. I even found references in *The Bible* showing reincarnation. Apparently, it was in the third century AD, from the Council of Nassiem, where "they" stripped almost all references to reincarnation from the books "they" decided to put in *The Bible*.

I was blown away, yet other religions like Buddhism know and teach reincarnation.

If you really think about it, we are all energy.
Everything is energy.
Energy cannot be created or destroyed, just transformed.

Is this really what we are doing here? Are we really just experiencing everything in a variety of bodies and settings? Are there lessons to be learned? Are we just here for the experience?

We could be a dog one lifetime.
A tree in another.
A butterfly, a hawk, a fish, a rock...anything?!

Is this why we shouldn't kill unless we ask permission from that spirit? There is a spirit in everything. The indigenous people know this and when they take or kill anything from the Earth, they ask for permission and give thanks.

Everything is alive and connected.

I have majorly forgotten and we humans (or most of us) are taught to dominate nature and all of the Earth. No wonder the Earth is so out of balance.

We forgot that we are just one part of the whole.

I often think that humans are the dumb ones. We are the ones who don't communicate with telepathy as the animals do. We are the ones that don't know how to "just be." Time for us to come back into our power.

We could learn a lot sitting with the trees or our pets.

Anyways, I have a story to tell on the subject of past lives. Some of this you heard in an earlier chapter, so I will try not to repeat much.

My husband and I were headed for divorce as he was lying about everything to me. I didn't trust him and I was six months pregnant with our second child. I was done with our marriage and had no idea what to do.

Crying, I called my sister-in-law, Helen, and told her I was leaving him. She told me to hold on and try therapy first before I throw in the towel. I was skeptical, but agreed to as she was working with a great therapist named Jane.

The first day I went into therapy with Bruce, we sat down on her couch and I heard in my head, "You will make love with this woman."

What?!

I ignored this and Jane began to ask us questions. She talked about how our childhood traumas and parents affect the way we do relationships. She threw out a couple "fucks" while speaking and I was hooked. This was the therapist for me.

Bruce and I worked with her separately on our issues. I first began working on trust and my parent's divorce as well as mother issues around always being blamed for everything and father issues of him not rescuing me from her.

I was skeptical at first, and the first month really was about me learning to trust Jane as I didn't even trust myself. Then, I dove in and moved through so much with EMDR. It was a powerful year.

Something else began to happen that I didn't expect while being in therapy. My feelings and emotions were coming back strong and it was overwhelming. I had been good at shutting off my feelings all my life. Little did I know that they were still there waiting for me right where I left them.

It was intense and I felt so much anxiety. I began working out twice a day instead of once, and this helped. After I finished working out, the anxious feelings kept coming back. This was my feeling body coming back online and I began to really feel. I didn't even really know what I was feeling except overwhelm and move overwhelm.

Our planet Earth is a playground of feelings and emotions.
The suppression of emotion is not a healthy thing.
Feelings are not good or bad, but just part of being human.
Emotions are just reporting on what is happening in your energy system.

Feeling my feelings, I felt so free and I began letting go of old beliefs I had been taught. I found that friends that I had for so long didn't really appeal to me any longer. I began reading everything I could get my hands on about religion, psychology, spirituality, new age, etc...

As therapy continued, I found that Bruce wasn't really wanting to dive in like I was. He did join AA and quit drinking which was awesome, but he wanted things to be my fault. I was scared that we were going to part ways and I did everything I could to keep our marriage together.

With him not drinking anymore, he became very angry and bitter. He ate instead of drank and put on lots of weight. He still wasn't ready to deal with his deep, emotional pain.

In therapy, I noticed within myself that I had a crush on Jane. She was so pretty and I didn't know what to do with this. One day, I worked up to telling her and she said that it is common for patients to be attracted to their therapists. She said to feel the sexual component is to feel the love for her and wanting to express it.

Okay.
I get it.
I accepted this explanation and moved on.

Telling her how I felt lessened the feeling. I also felt that I was done with therapy. I had moved past some of my major traumas and found that I was teaching her more things, such as subjects about reincarnation and beliefs.

So, I stopped therapy and later on, we just became friends. We began to hang out and so did our husbands and kids. We had lots of fun together and I also began going back to school to get my master's degree in psychology. I considered being a therapist after firefighting as I wanted to help people move through their traumas the way I was able to.

Jane and I had great talks and had similar interests in psychology stuff. She was interested in learning more spiritual things as she was Catholic. We continued to get closer as did our husbands. They really enjoyed hanging out together, too.

One day while driving, Jane tells me that she has feelings for me and is attracted to me. I don't miss a beat and tell her that we love each other. It's just part of love. She grabs my hand and tells me that she really loves me.

I sit with all this later and think how it's funny how it has gone full circle. We both felt this way towards each other. Yet, I don't feel this way with my other girlfriends.

Wonder why?

Then, I remember the day I walked into her office and heard that voice in my head that said, "You will make love with this woman."

Huh?
Where does that even come from?

We continue to hang out as families and friends. I realize that Jane and I are closer to each other than we are to our husbands. We are just on different playing fields and have different interests. Life goes on and one day when Jane and I are having dinner together, I just can't take my eyes off her. I really want to kiss her.

Now, I know what you are thinking…
I'm married.
I know I am and I don't want to hurt Bruce.

So, I told Bruce a few weeks before when he asked me if I was attracted to Jane. I said that we were. Now, guess what he replies…

"That's hot!"
"You wouldn't care if we kissed or were together?" I say.
"Nope! I would just want to watch," he says.

Most men's response, right? We just laughed and he said that it is different if women are together as he can't compete and it's sexy. Now, if it was another man, then…look out! He's not okay with that.

So, back to dinner…

I tell her that I want to kiss her and she smiles. She looks at me as she drinks her wine. I know she wants to kiss me.

We finish dinner and go to her car to drive home. Instead of driving, we talk. We talk about our feelings towards each other and how her husband would be upset even though Bruce wouldn't. I don't want to upset their relationship.

Then, she leans over and kisses me.
Really kisses me.
It's one of those really yummy kisses as she pulls me close.

This goes on for a while until I stop and say, "I can't do this. I don't want to hurt Neil."

Inside though, I am saying, "Please! Kiss me again. Let's find a hotel room."

She understands and doesn't want to hurt her husband either.

After this night, the pull for us to be together is just too strong. We find ways to kiss and fondle each other as much as possible throughout the next few weeks.

Then, Jane decides to tell her husband about us and he freaks out.
I freak out as now he won't let Jane see or talk to me.
I tell Bruce and he is pissed because I didn't tell him sooner so he could watch!

Damn.
It's rough.
I'm anxious and depressed.
I go through devastation and wanting to die.
What was I thinking?!

The crazy thing is that week that Jane told her husband about us, we had planned to see a past life regression therapist to find out if there was a past life connection with us. We both wanted to be regressed and explore our past lives.

I kept the appointment and went to see this therapist named Steve. He began with a hypnosis technique with my intention to see past lives with Jane. As I went under, I immediately saw myself in a male Indian's (native American) body with no shoes or shirt on. I was running through a forest next to a river and I ran into the river by a waterfall. As I did, I saw a female Indian who I innately knew was Jane and she was from another tribe. I was in love with her. Yet, our love was forbidden from her father, the Chief.

She ran into the water with me and we embraced.
We kissed and made love by the river.

Steve had me speed this life up and the next thing I am doing is running for my life. I am being chased by the Indian chief as he found out about us. I know this energy of the chief to be Jane's husband, Neil. He catches me and kills me with brutal anger. I see his tomahawk.

I see myself float out of my body and up to the light. I am immediately embraced by the light and I feel the oneness that I have wanted to feel since I was born in this life.

I feel peace and bliss.
I have no other thought.
Just pulsing…like a heartbeat.

Steve eventually interrupts this and asks me what happened to Jane. I don't want to leave this bliss, but I go and look for her. I see her. She is on a cliff and she knows I am dead. She jumps off and kills herself. I see her spirit coming for me in bliss.

We are together again.

Is that really what we are doing?
We reincarnate into different bodies and we find each other?
Is it because we were killed?
Did we not finish what we came to do?

We have relationships with so many people over and over again?

Why?
For the experience of it all?
Until we heal it somehow?

Oh, so many questions.
The past life regression felt so real.
I was really there and I would swear it was Jane and I.

In the book, *Only Love is Real* by Brian Weiss, he talks about how we are meant to meet again and again. Sometimes we meet to be together again and other times, we move on.

Interesting.
Why?!

I didn't talk to Jane for a couple weeks as she wasn't allowed to talk to me. She finally saw me in a parking lot and she seemed paranoid. Jane gave me a hug and told me that Neil is forbidding us from ever talking again. She is as upset as I am, but neither of us want to leave our husbands to be together.

It just doesn't feel right.

Then, she tells me that she kept the past life regression appointment with Steve and that she saw us together in a lifetime during the knights of the roundtable. She was a woman and I was a man. She and I were in love, but she was married to Neil (her current husband) who was a powerful knight. He killed me on the battlefield.

She was devastated.
So, is this what we keep doing?

Are we repeating these same scenarios over and over again until we transform the energy of this scene?

Does he kill me in this lifetime or is that why I came in as a woman this time?
This way, he won't kill me?

It explains why I have felt afraid he would kill me since he found out. It is leftover fear from past lives.

I get it.
Time to change the scene.
It has a different ending.
A forgiving one.

Time goes on and the four of us talk many different times forgiving each other each time. I can feel the depth of the transformation of energy around all of us. We all take responsibility for our part as we are not victims.

Love yourself and love each other.
I am never reincarnating to play this out again!
Lessoned learned!
Forgive.

PART TWO

CHAPTER 49
MY BRAIN

Unfortunately, as a society, we do not teach our children that they need to tend carefully the garden of their minds. Without structure, censorship, or discipline, our thoughts run rampant on automatic. Because we have not learned how to more carefully manage what goes on inside our brains, we remain vulnerable to not only what other people think about us, but also to advertising and/or political manipulation.
~Dr. Jill Bolte Taylor

An interesting book that I read in eighth grade was about a neurosurgeon and his surgeries that he did on people's brains. He described in his book how some people would have memories come up based on the parts of the brain that he touched during the surgeries. They were actually awake during surgery.

I have always loved the brain and have been so curious as to how it works. This jumbled mass that sits in our skulls is like a computer and processes so much. It is so fascinating how little we know about the brain and that we only use less than ten percent of it. Knowing this, I decided in eighth grade that I would be a doctor, a neurosurgeon.

Well, I changed my mind in college after volunteering in the hospital finding out that many doctors were not happy with their profession. Many complained about the schooling and some were chasing the money. I just really wanted to help people, but I didn't like being indoors for twelve hours at a time for my volunteer shift. Many doctors worked this type of shift and my being needed to be outdoors breathing fresh air!

So, I became a firefighter instead.

It was the perfect blend for me of being physically active, adrenaline rushes, helping people, and doing something different every day. I still had a huge curiosity about the brain though and learned a lot in college being a psychology major. I loved psychology and studying why people are the way they are.

We are so strange and fascinating.

I mean really, right?!

What other than the human brain can be so sweet taking care of the sick and feeble and also mastermind torturing and killing millions of human beings?

What is really behind it all?
Is it just energy and we can use it for positive or negative outcomes?
Energy doesn't care how it is used?

It makes me wonder if it is the traumatized brain that is really to blame for all darkness in the world?

What is a balanced brain?
Is there such a thing as a healthy human brain?

After going through my own therapy and dealing with a lot of my traumatic past, I thought about becoming a therapist to be able to help people see that there is another way to live. I saw how quickly people could move through issues that caused them to be stuck in their life. The psychotherapy called EMDR was amazing to me as things that kept me stuck in life moved out quickly while my brain processed it like it never happened or it had a different outcome.

In fact, after being in my own therapy for about a year, I began to notice that I didn't have the need for my adrenaline rushes any longer. I lived for this and it was strange for me to not live in "fight or flight" all the time.

What was happening?
Is this really how I have been living my life?
Living on the edge?

No wonder I always thought I would die before I turned thirty years old.
Maybe this is why I secretly had a death wish?
I had a traumatized brain?

I thought about how PTSD from subtle or not so subtle chronic abuse had been affecting my life. I always thought that trauma was typically from a single, gnarly event.

Never did I realize that it can be from emotional abuse. I thought it was from physical or sexual abuse and not from subtle abuse that was chronic. I wondered how many others out there had traumatized brains and I realized that there are millions or billions of us out there.

I mean really, a mother who constantly judges you is subtly abusing you emotionally by putting you down.

I had this for years. Not to mention that she would get angry and accuse me of things while yelling at me. I see how young kids who are sensitive take all this energy in and don't know exactly what to do with it. They put it in their bodies which comes out in so many other ways...physically or mentally or both.

I also learned more about the body and that it is good to shake. Often, on traumatic calls like car accidents and such, I would see people shaking. Their whole body would shake. Some would try to stop it and others allowed it to continue. It is the leftover adrenaline from "fight, flight, or freeze" that was moving through.

If we allowed this, the trauma from the event did not settle into our cells. Animals often shake as do children. If you watch a zebra after it gets away from a lion, it will stand there and just shake. Our bodies know how to stay healthy. They are conscious in themselves. We just need to ask what it needs.

When did we adults learn to shut off this physiological response of shaking? Probably when we were young?!

After having my daughter, Piper, I knew I wanted to go back to school and get my therapist license. I thought I could bring EMDR into the fire department to help the guys as so many of us had traumatized brains.

Speaking of traumatized brains, I read a fascinating book called *My Stroke of Insight* by Jill Bolte Taylor which was about her having a stroke. She was a neuroanatomist who studied the brain and actually studied her own brain from the inside out while having the stroke. Jill described her experience of going from her left brain (where the blood vessel blew) to her right brain as the bleed got worse.

Jill spoke of how when her left brain was not functioning properly, she was completely in her right brain becoming one with everything. She described her body merging with the exercise machine and the wall. Jill didn't care about anything when she was in this state of oneness. When her left brain would come back online temporarily, it would tell her to call "911." It was really interesting to see the functions of the left and right brain hemispheres and how most of us are more left brain dominate.

Reading this book left me with wanting a balanced brain!

How do we bring in more right brained functions back into this world? Why is art and music (right brain) taken out of most schools? Who decides that we need more math and science (left brain) in schools? Why don't we change this as a society?

At work, I was surrounded by traumatized guys who were all high on adrenaline. Listening to their stories over the years, I could see how their childhood affected their present day life. I wanted to bring EMDR to the fire department and I wondered how to un-traumatize the world on a global scale.

So, I started with getting my master's degree in marriage and family counseling. I loved these classes and learned even more about humans and the way we operate as well as the brain. In fact, I loved all this psychology so much, that I got straight A's all three years.

This was quite different than my bachelor's degree grades!

Carl Jung was fascinating to me with symbols and dreams. Gestalt therapy, cognitive behavioral therapy, psychodynamic therapy, sex therapy, family therapy, etc... So many different theories that many psychologists had about the human condition.

I found it funny that we label all these different psychological disorders depending on what the symptoms were. To me, all I could see was a traumatized brain acting out in different ways and we were labeling it to give them medications. It is really the same in the medical field as we give diseases different names, but really it is the lack of nutrients or toxins in our bodies causing different symptoms.

I obtained a master's degree and found it to be lacking so much in the spiritual realm. It seemed to leave that whole part out. I was busy reading so much in this metaphysical/spiritual realm while studying for my degree. Some of the books I read were by Eckhardt Tolle, Don Miguel Ruiz, Sandra Ingerman, Jack Kornfield, Barbara Marciniak, Tom Kenyon, Abraham-Hicks, etc... I was looking for missing pieces in the human psyche.

I also found that my psychology teachers were not open to EMDR. They said it fixed people and that talk therapy was better because they would keep coming back to therapy. They were worried there wouldn't be enough traumatized people to fix anymore!

OMG!
Really?
We live in a traumatizing world!
It's all about money.
I was appalled and pissed.
We have something really wrong here.

Wanting to keep people sick and unhappy because they are worried about not having clients?

I was wanting the opposite. I wanted to help people see a different way. I had visions of what the world would be like without all of us traumatized. People wouldn't yell and scream at each other. We wouldn't immediately be triggered and need to discharge our anger. We would be understanding and loving towards one another.

I began fantasizing about being in front of a large crowd and being able to do EMDR to all of them. Then, I thought, since sound is so powerful, what sound or sounds do we need to un-traumatize the masses? This would be amazing.

I know it is possible.
Can you imagine a world of healthy brains?
Healthy people?

Well, I decided that, for now, I could at least try to help one person at a time.

I began to see clients to get my marriage and family therapist license and I needed three thousand hours to achieve this. At the same time, I was still working in the fire department and raising my two kids while also being married. I don't know how I found the time, but I did.

I also got my EMDR certificate after graduating since they didn't teach it in my master's program. I began to use this skill with all of my clients as much as I could. My clients were fascinating. Some really wanted to do life different. Some wanted to just complain. Some were in the middle. I loved the ones that were looking for a deeper meaning to life. They were the most fun to work with besides the kids who always amused me.

I had fun with child therapy as I always feel like I am a big kid. We would play and I could see how much impact parents were having on their kids. The parents often just wanted me to fix the kids, but really the parents needed to be in therapy.

Michael was a client I had who was ten years old when he initially came to see me. His adoptive parents were having trouble controlling him and needed help. He had been born to a woman who was a prostitute and was also sexually abused as a baby. Michael was adopted at eleven months old.

We did play therapy, sand tray therapy, and guided imagery which helped him quite a bit. He enjoyed coming to therapy and his parents came sometimes, too. As he got older, he came less often because he was doing better accessing his emotions.

One day, when he was thirteen, he came in and had all kinds of sexual questions. Michael had a crush on a girl, but she didn't like him. He had hit puberty and we had a really good relationship where he felt safe to ask me anything.

Yet, I wasn't totally prepared for what he asked next.

Michael asked me if I would "get naked" for him. Needless to say, I was a bit shocked and it really takes a lot to shock me. I asked him why he needed me to do this and he said he wanted to see a "real woman" naked.

So many things were going through my head as I processed the deeper meaning of all of it. Here, you have a boy who had been sexually abused as a baby and a dad who had given him *Playboys* to look at when he turned nine. Now, puberty had kicked into gear.

We had a great discussion around it all and I never shamed him for asking me to "get naked." We talked about what was appropriate and not appropriate in regard to women and sexuality. Still, I wondered how being sexually abused as a baby had affected his development.

After three years or more, I got all my hours and received my license. I thought I would eventually retire from the fire department and just be a therapist, but I ended up using my therapy skills in the fire department with the guys, while still being a fire captain.

In fact, realizing that I was not to be a therapist full time and leave the fire department came on strong. It was one of those times when I kept receiving a message from inside myself. For me, my inner guidance comes on strong until I acknowledge it. I just knew I was to complete my hours, get my license, and then to stop. I kept feeling this for a day or so. I knew this was not my path and that there would be others to do this work for the world.

I was doubting this message that I received over and over again. I was still learning how my intuition worked and how my guides spoke to me, so I decided to ask the universe for a really clear message.

Asking for clarity.
It always amazes me how it shows up.
I love how the information comes as it is always amusing to me the form that it takes.

I had less than a hundred hours left and I went to see clients for the morning. The first client I saw was rather psychic and she sits down. She's distraught and I ask her what's going on. She tells me that she feels I am going to leave her. I have been seeing her for four months or so and we had lots of progress in her healing. I am surprised by her comment and ask her more.

She says, "You are almost done with your hours and then, you are going to move on."

I respond saying, "Well, I was just thinking about that the last day or so. I was getting the same message."

She shifts her body and it is like it's not her anymore. She replies, "You are done with seeing clients. It is not your path. There will be others that do this work."

I sit in amazement.
She said exactly what I have been getting.
It's like she just channeled what I needed to hear.
Message received.

She shifts her body again and I tell her that I appreciate her message to me. It verified everything I was feeling. We continue the session processing what happens when I leave and we talk about referring her to another therapist. It was a tough session as she had become attached.

So wild how that worked out.
Somehow the message always comes through to me.
The universe always makes me laugh.

It was perfect timing to leave seeing clients and bring some tools into the fire department as the guys weren't happy with CISD (critical incident stress debriefing). This was a type of talk therapy used after we witnessed horrible things on emergency calls. It turns out that CISD actually re-traumatizes the brain over and over again. The brain needs to process the emergency call and needs to transform it, otherwise the brain feels like it keeps happening over and over again.

I was able to bring in EMDR with TRM (trauma resource model) and other somatic therapies into the fire department. These incorporated the mind and the body, not just the mind. Other fire departments were open to new ways of helping the firefighters and were interested in starting programs to help the firefighters. We also trained firefighters to become peer counselors. I was excited to see this and hopeful that this would be a start to un-traumatize firefighters and perhaps move into helping the police and military.

One day at a time though...

CHAPTER 50
BELIEF SYSTEMS BLOWN UP

It's not your work to make anything happen. It's your work to dream it and let it happen. Law of Attraction will make it happen. In your joy, you create something and then you maintain your vibrational harmony with it, and the Universe must find a way to bring it about.
~Abraham-Hicks

As I got more mentally and emotionally healthy, I began to question everything I was taught. I questioned everything I believed.

For example, why did I decide that I liked Republicans instead of Democrats or the other party? It is because my parents were Republican. I didn't even know what those political parties believed in. How many other beliefs did I have like this?

Having kids made me question what life is all about and what I am doing here. I began to look at what I grew up with and question religion. I questioned who and what God is. I attended a few different churches to see what they were all about since I grew up in a military Evangelical church. Funny how things come full circle.

I went to a love-based church, Evangelical church, Lutheran church, Baptist church, Buddhist temple, and Catholic church. I looked at the Jewish synagogue and Islam religions. I took what I liked from those institutions and realized that church is really about community and being with like-minded people who believe the same thing.

There is just so much guilt and shame built into religions! I wanted nothing to do with this. Catholicism is built on guilt. Buddhism is built on shame. Islam is built on suppression. All of them seemed to have core fear built into them.

What an invention to control the masses.
Use fear in many different ways and the population is controlled.
Invisible enslavement.

I noticed how all the big religions had the same things with different names. I even studied older religions and found similarities of their stories. They had wrathful gods and jealous gods.

Where was the god of love that I felt existed?

Egyptian religion even had a mother goddess who had a daughter of the goddess to save the people. I couldn't help but wonder if the Christian religion took that and made it a father god with a son of god to save the people since modern religions had virtually destroyed the goddess religions.

Real history is fascinating once you really research it. So much of what we are taught about history in school is full of lies and written by the ones who won. What about the ones they conquered? Who were they? Is there missing time in history?

What is real?

Did you know that mathematicians are responsible for our timelines of history? They date things using the positions of the sun, moon, and the stars at the time and you can put events in order on a timeline. This is what we call history. Anatoly Fomenko is a Russian mathematician specializing in astronomy and wrote a series of books called *History: Fiction or Science*. I found his research fascinating as it blew my mind.

Anatoly found that history was fabricated by the scholars of the time who were working for the Catholic church to back up *The Bible* and many other events. He found events to be off by hundreds of years and many stories falsified. His research shows that there are eighteen to twenty-three hundred years added onto our historical timeline. Some things that Anatoly found that were fabricated are that Jesus wasn't real but was made up by the Church, the Roman Empire emerged in the late Middle Ages not in the eighth century BC, and the "holy land" was a false story.

Well, this will sure cause you to question everything you were taught!

Think of all the things that you are taught in school. Who decided what we learn in schools? Does school systematically get you to stop trusting yourself and trusting only what you are taught? You turn your inner teacher off?

When you start researching the truth for yourself, you will be amazed what you find. I found it fascinating to learn how socialism is just another name for communism. Another interesting fact that I found was that it was the Republican party who freed the slaves and wanted to give women the right to vote. I was shocked that it was the Democrats who believed in owning people instead of freedom.

And just for the record, I don't consider myself part of any political party as there is just so much corruption within politics. It also divides the people instead of uniting.

How do we change this?

By being open to seeing the truth with may rock our beliefs!

I even began to wonder more about extraterrestrials and how we really got here. Reading stories about the Dogones in Africa and how they had contact with beings from Sirius who told them so much were fascinating to me. Another civilization I learned about was the ancient Hawaiians. They had a deep connection to the Pleiades who guided them and also to the star system of Arcturus.

I went on a never-ending search for truth about everything.

I realized that television was just people's opinions. The news was people's opinions which were full of propaganda. There was an agenda going on and I didn't want any part of the subconscious programming within the television programs.

Who is in control here?

As I healed more traumas of my life, a friend of mine gave me one of the greatest gifts that changed my life. A book by Eckart Tolle called *A New Earth: Awakening to Your Life's Purpose*. This book blew me away as I devoured it slowly. It was new thinking or maybe old truth that had been overlooked.

He talked about the ego and the pain body which is really just unprocessed traumas in our bodies that get triggered over and over again until we transform the old energy. He went on to talk about being programmed by our parents, teachers, clergy, and society to conform to a specific way of being.

My foundation was not just cracked after reading this book, it was leveled.

There was so much more in this book and I read it again and again as it was so far out there to what I had ever been taught. I wanted to reprogram my subconscious to one of love and not fear. My brain began to integrate this new way of thinking.

I was exploring different healing modalities during this time as well and I tried everything that I heard of. I was getting healthier on the physical level by doing chelation to clean out my body of heavy metals. A byproduct of chelation was that it got rid of plaque in my arteries and it turns out that in other countries, chelation is the first thing they do for chest pain. Getting mercury out of my mouth and doing many cleanses to help my body became a priority. I learned more about nutrition and food, in general.

There were so many types of energy healing and I enjoyed seeing what people had to offer. Reiki and cranial sacral therapy were amazing as I could feel them working on a subtle level. I dove deep into meditation and breathing techniques.

I fell deeply in love with shamanism when I was in New York for a past lives conference. They had a smorgasbord of different types of healing and I signed up for as many of them as I could. I even signed up for a shamanic journey with a woman named Fraukie not having any clue to what this was.

She told me all about shamanism and how it helped her heal after she lost her daughter. Fraukie had tried everything to heal and nothing worked. Shamanism brought soul pieces of herself back that she had lost due to traumatic incidents. She said whenever we have a traumatic event, often a part of ourselves gets fragmented. Shamanic journeying could bring that piece of yourself back integrating it into the whole.

Fraukie drummed and had me go on a journey for my own soul parts from my parents' divorce. It was powerful and I found my little girl there. Also on my journey, I found a tiger that kept following me. I ended up going down waterfalls to a place where I saw a black panther looking directly at me.

I wanted to run from the panther, but she stared at me. Then, Fraukie brought me back. This shamanic session sparked my desire to read many shamanic authors' books as and it felt so natural to me. It was like I had been a shaman in many lifetimes.

Taking this shamanic experience, I began listening to drumming on my own and journeying. I learned so much about many worlds and that there is so much out there. I also joined a drumming group where we journeyed once a month.

All of this was so powerful for me.

Another book that had such simple truths in it also and filled my being with new information was called *The Four Agreements* by Don Miguel Ruiz. It made such sense to me. It was Toltec wisdom.

Be impeccable with your word.
Don't take anything personally.
Don't make assumptions.
Always do your best.

So simple, right?

Why are these simple truths not taught in schools? It would get rid of name calling and thinking that everything someone does is because of you. We would not take it personally and realize it is their projection of what is going on inside of them. What someone says is because of them and their programs that they are running in their subconscious.

We would honor and be true to our word.
No more lies.
Can you imagine that?
What would politics do?!

This really makes me laugh out loud!
Politics!

I began to realize that there is something bigger out there running our world. It is something that wants us to stay unhealthy, be traumatized, and live in chaos. They don't want us to know the truth of who we are or how powerful we are.

Why?

I wondered about this and all I could figure was it was those into power and money.

Such a small percentage of humanity.
Are they even human?
Perhaps they are an evil alien race from another dimension?
Or just out of control humans who feed on power?

It seems this one percent are truly evil and corrupt humans who forgot their connection to Source.

But, they are controlling the masses?!
What a crazy planet.
Would love for the truth to be shown.

I continued to read many other amazing books and fantasize about working with sound to release trauma from people. What if television and movies were traumatizing the masses? It would be easy to reverse all of this and have people wake up using sound frequencies!

Then, to read the book by Bruce Lipton called *The Biology of Belief*. He is a scientist and researcher who used to teach medical students. The book is all about how whatever we believe becomes true for us, and influences our cells.

So simple.
So, it's not genetics and DNA?!
That can all be influenced?
It's our fucking beliefs?!

Mind blowing really.

Belief systems are really so fascinating and when you start to look at your own, it makes you question what you have created around you. When we begin to see things that challenge our beliefs, we may not be open to it because we fear the collapse of our belief system and the picture we have created of our world.

So really, we fear this change as we have to reorganize our thoughts and beliefs. Our foundation has cracked, yet change is the only thing constant in this world. We are meant to change and evolve constantly. When we begin to embrace change, we begin to release fear.

Take this one step further...

If someone doesn't believe in elves, fairies, or extraterrestrials, it is really not about their fear of them. It is about the fear of change and the collapse of their belief system. Their picture of the world has to reorganize to new beliefs.

Beliefs are such fascinating constructs!
They are just thoughts we keep thinking over and over.

My beliefs and perceptions are creating my reality.
I am co-creating my reality with Source.
If I don't like how I am creating, time to choose again!
Possibilities are endless!

Oh, to dream!
I know it will happen one day.
The masses will wake up and wonder what happened.
We just need to turn off the fear vibration that is so prevalent on this planet.

Until then, I can only change myself and my beliefs which are always changing as I realize there are no absolute truths! There are so many perspectives especially, when you start looking at things from the higher dimensions.

And you wanna know a little secret?
You are God!
You are the creator.
Oh, the places we can go!

CHAPTER 51
FUN AND SIMPLE

Play is often talked about as if it were a relief from serious learning. But for children, play is serious learning. Play is really the work of childhood.
~Mr. Rogers

Having kids really rocks your world if you let it. I am constantly amazed at these small beings in my life and how they are really my teachers. I am just here to help guide them in this Earth life. They are reminding me to have fun and to be in the moment.

I realized that they are always laughing.
Well, maybe not always, but tons more than adults.
Everything is funny to them.
I love listening to Danny and Piper giggle and run around.
Just so much fun.

Where did adults go wrong? When did we start making such a big deal of things and getting stressed out? Why don't we laugh at the little things like we do as kids?

I love being with my kids. I love playing with them and doing things with them. I feel like a big kid, too…maybe eight years old or so!?

One thing I know…
Life is meant to be fun and simple.
I am convinced of this.
Somehow, we made life complicated and stressful.

As I reflect on things that happened in my life, I wonder why my parents did the things they did. They did the best they could with the tools they had. I love them for who they are.

Kids and dogs.
Simple and in the present moment.
I love dogs and I can feel their soul.

You can just look in their eyes and see the depth of who they are.

You can feel their love.
Their connection to Source.
What have we forgotten?
A lot apparently!

Piper tells me around age four or five that she visits her "Sparkle" planet at night. I ask her about it and what they do there. She says, "We just shoot light and love at each other."

I am blown away that she goes here at night and that she remembers where she came from. I ask her more about it and if she wants to draw it.

She says, "Maybe."

About a month later, Piper comes up to me and shows me a picture she drew.

"What's this?" I ask.

"This is my 'Sparkle' planet and this is what we do at night. We fly around shooting light from our hearts to each other," she replies.

The picture she drew looks to me like a giant crystal cathedral only in two-dimensional form and there are beings with wings shooting yellow light from their hearts to each other.

I wanna go there.
I wanna remember.
If she is from there, am I from there?

I ask her if I ever go there at night with her.
She replies with this surprised look like "duh!" and says, "Yes, Mommy."

Is this what we do while we sleep? Do we travel to other worlds and dimensions? Is this what the other ninety percent (that we supposedly don't use) of our brains are tapped into?

I want her to teach me more.
What have I forgotten?

A couple years later, it is Piper's seventh birthday. She wants to get her ears pierced with her best friend. I would rather her wait till she is older to keep it from getting infected, but I am open to what she wants, too.

I take her and Cindy (her best friend) to get their ears pierced around her birthday. They are both excited and nervous. They get them done and we go get ice cream.

The lady that did the piercing says to keep it clean for the next few months and no wrestling. She didn't want the earrings to come out.

Later that night, Danny and Piper were running around like kids do and of course, they started wrestling. I reminded both of them that Piper can't do this for a while because of her earrings.

About an hour later, Piper comes up to me crying and saying her earring fell out. She and Danny were wrestling. We go to look for it in the carpet. I can't find it anywhere and Piper is so upset. She doesn't want the hole to close.

We keep looking.
I find the earring and try to put it in her ear.
No luck.
Damn!

I am frustrated and tell her we have to go back to the store to get them to put it back in. They close in an hour and we need to hurry. I get both kids in the car and we boogie down to the store.

Along the way, Piper says to me in tears, "See Mommy, this is why I don't like this planet!"

"What do you mean?" I ask.

She replies, "Bad things happen to you here! On my planet, nothing bad ever happens to anyone!"

I am enthralled and shocked by what she said.
Imagine a planet where nothing bad ever happens.
That would be amazing!

I am ready to remember more as I have completely forgotten.
Did I remember where I came from when I was little?
When did I shut it down?
So many questions!
I just love these kiddos.

CHAPTER 52
STRUNG UP

The primary cause of unhappiness is never the situation, but your thoughts about it. Be aware of the thoughts you are thinking.
~Eckhart Tolle

I went on many emergency calls over the years where people hung themselves. It always seemed so violent and I always felt sad for those who found their loved one this way. It was always so traumatic.

Really, any suicide is very traumatic.

I remember going on a call where a woman hung herself in the garage after having a fight with her husband. Her husband and kids were home when she did this. He went out to the garage to find his wife hanging from the ceiling rafters with an electrical extension cord wrapped around her neck.

He grabbed her and pushed her back up releasing tension on the cord around her neck. He yelled for his kids to call "911."

We arrived and were led straight to the garage. We helped the husband and released tension on the cord to cut it. We then lowered her to the ground. She was not breathing and has no pulse. We began CPR while checking the rhythm of her heart to see if we could shock it back into a viable rhythm. We see ventricular fibrillation on the monitor which is a shockable rhythm.

We charged up the defibrillator and shock her heart.
Immediately, her rhythm changes into a viable rhythm and we check for a heartbeat.

She has one!
Yes!

She still was not breathing and we use an ambu bag to breath for her. The family was hysterical and off to the side as the police arrive to help the family.

We start an IV and load her up for the hospital. We overhear her husband say that they were drinking and got into an argument. She went out to the garage and he found her not long after hanging from the rafter. She still had a pulse when we got to the hospital and had a burn around her neck from the cord. I wonder if that will always be there?

We heard later that she began to breathe on her own, but they didn't know how her mental status was going to be with the lack of oxygen. It may be a long road to recovery or not.

Another hanging that I went on was a man in his thirties who decided to hang himself because he couldn't provide for his family. His wife had just given birth to their new baby.

She was devastated.

So many other hangings that I have gone on where we cut them down after they had been there for a night or so. They were long gone to the other side and I often wondered if they were still there with their body, watching us to process their death. Their necks were always stretched.

They merely left their bodies, but their consciousness is still there. Is this just moving from one dimension to another?

Hmmm…

Anyways, there was also the artist who tried to hang herself and then changed her mind at the last second. The rope had tightened around her neck, but she had been able to get her footing back on a table to prop herself back up. Her roommate walked in and found her trying to get the rope off. She had the rope burn scar across her neck.

She decided to live another day.

On a personal note, I had someone close to me who tried to hang himself. He was going through tough times with his second wife and decided to end it all. My friend said he was going to hang himself on the doorknob in his room because he was super angry with his mother. He had decided he would do it on her birthday to show her.

Yikes.

My friend told me that just before he passed out, he saw his young daughter flash before his eyes and knew that she would be devastated. He was on his knees and pulled back enough so he could breathe.

So many ways for us to kill ourselves.
Life is so precious and we forget that.

Death happens in an instant.

I think of all the hangings over the centuries. It has been a way for criminals and people who go against the establishment to be killed. Lynchings were common in the United States and were public.

Even in the recent movie, *A Star is Born*, he hangs himself in the end. I ponder this as the movie is basically subconsciously telling us that there is room for only one star.

REALLY?

Can't we all shine and all be stars?
Absolutely.
So, how do you want to shine?

CHAPTER 53
MOTHER AYAHUASCA

The endocrine system can secrete psychedelic-like chemical substances that catapult you into new forms of intelligence. You have a conflict in your society about how you view drugs. Anything having to do with mind expansion has been promoted as very bad and fearful. Yet, at the same time, a good portion of the world is addicted to prescription drugs that keep people sedated. In your society, prescribed drugs that suppress the natural chemical process are fine, while drugs that activate the mind and open other realities are bad. Major control is in effect concerning your ideas about what you can and cannot take into your body. Take a look at this.
~Barbara Marciniak

So, one day I am talking to my therapist, Steve, who is also a shaman. I have known him for about a year now and he has helped me through my relationship with Jane as well as repairing my relationship with my husband. He has also helped me find my power animal guide and we like exploring consciousness together.

He says to me, "Are you interested in doing a journey with me?"
I look at him inquisitively, "Isn't that what we have been doing all year?"

"This is different," he says.

Steve explains how the shamans of the Amazon have been helping people remember. To remember who they really are and why they are here on Earth. They help people remember why their soul chose to come here and to see beyond death.

He continues, "It is from a tree and she is knowledgeable. Her name is Mother Ayahuasca. You take the tree medicine and have a journey for about six to eight hours more or less."

Hmmm…

I am interested and scared at the same time, yet I stopped doing drugs sometime after college. Pot was always fun and I did love those hallucinogens like LSD and mushrooms. I gravitated towards the ones that help you to see into the other worlds around us that we forgot existed.

Those that opened your mind more into other realms.
I have forgotten.
Hmmm…
Maybe?

A year goes by and I tell Steve that I am interested in this journey of Ayahuasca. I would like to do a journey with him and I ask more of the details. He says that it is at his house in the valley with his wife, and sometimes one or two other people.

"It is totally safe and I will be there to help you if you start to have a bad experience," he continues.

I know that people have bad "trips" while doing LSD and sometimes it is nice to have someone who is experienced in this to help you out of it. My body is excited to experience this Ayahuasca, and yet, I have no idea what to expect.

It is just the three of us at his house, Steve, his wife, and myself. I feel totally safe with both of them and they tell me that they can help me if needed. They don't tell me much about their prior Ayahuasca trips so that I can have my own experience.

Being a shaman, Steve first opens up a sacred space and then he brings out "the drink." I am to drink it all. He says that it happens fairly quickly and that I can lie down if I want to on their couch.

As I am talking to Steve, he suddenly begins to form into geometric shapes. I know the medicine is taking effect on me. Then, I see these shapes all connecting to each other. It's everywhere. Electric blue. I can see…

The web.
I can see our connectedness to everything.
It is beautiful.
This is what people talk about, how we are all connected.
The web of consciousness.
I know all of this in an instant.

Steve tells his wife that I see the web. They both get really excited and I say that I gotta lay down. I get cozy on the couch and pull blankets on top of me. I even pull them over my head. I am in my own cocoon. Steve says he will check on me later.

I feel these light beings around me.
They feel sweet and loving.
Then, I can see them.
We began to talk telepathically and some verbally.

I talk to them and ask tons of questions. They patiently answer them and I can feel their love for me. I ask why I experienced this relationship or that relationship. I ask what is this "life" thing. I ask why I have the mother that I do.

This answer stops me in my tracks.

They said to me, "You picked your mother."
I argue, "I did not!"
They giggle, "Yes, you did."
"No fucking way!" I retort.

They don't stop, and then say, "You picked everything in your life, Hydee."

This is too much to take and I reply, "Bullshit! I would have never picked a mother who emotionally and physically abused me. She was cold to me my whole life and judged me for everything I did."

They continue to surround me and lovingly say, "Well, you did."

I feel like a three year old having a tantrum, as I simply don't believe this. I want to be a victim and they just pulled the rug out from under me.

I chose this?
I chose my mother?

These thoughts run through my mind and I can't seem to take it in. My head was spinning. I always wanted a warm, loving mother who would hold me. Hug me. Touch me lovingly. Tell me that she loves me and that I am amazing.

I sat there pouting as I knew what they were saying was truth. I could feel it in my whole being.

Truth.

"Okay…fine then," I say with my arms crossed. "But why would I ever choose this? Why would I ever pick all these 'bad' things to happen to me?"

They look at me…
These loving light beings.

They look at each other and say, "She's forgotten! She really has forgotten!"

Now, they are all giggling and I begin to giggle.

I say, "Yes! I have forgotten! Why am I here? What in the hell am I doing here?!"
They look at me and surround me again.

"Hydee, you just wanted to EXPERIENCE all of this!"

Whuuuttt?!
No way.
No fucking way.
Bull shit!

I would have never decided to experience all this crap.
I further cross my arms in defiance and disbelief.
I say outloud, "NO!"

The love that I feel from these light beings is incredible and palpable. I feel so supported and cared for. I know that I am one of them, but somehow, I ended up in this body because they said I wanted to "experience life!"

Well, that was sure dumb of me if this is true!

I end up with so many other amazing experiences this night with Mother Ayahuasca. The light beings took me all over the universe. I knew everything and understood everything in the universe. Everything finally made sense.

I only wish it lasted forever, yet it changed me forever.
Perhaps this is the "Tree of knowledge of good and evil?"
You know everything!?

I sat with this amazing experience of Mother Ayahuasca for the next year. I was in awe and gratitude for this experience. I still did not want to accept what the light beings said as I still wanted to play victim for some reason.

I pondered this for the next year while arguing with myself.
Then, one day, it all made sense and I completely integrated it into my being.

Was me wanting to play victim keeping me from stepping into my power as a creator?!

I could just feel the truth.
I chose to experience all of this.
I did.

Thank you, Mother Ayahuasca.
Thank you for showing me the web and so much more.
Thank you, light beings for being my guides and lovingly showing me truth.
I am in complete gratitude.

CHAPTER 54
KIDS KNOW

The most interesting information comes from children, for they tell all they know and then stop.
~Mark Twain

To all you parents out there...

Kids know everything whether you tell them or not. They feel energy and know what is happening with you. They may not be able to voice the exact words, but they know. Talk to them because they feel everything already.

I found this out one day after I brought home Danny and Piper from school. Piper was five and Danny was eight. They were hungry and I made them some snacks. I was standing in the kitchen with them and we were laughing and talking about their day.

As they ate their apples, Piper looks at me and says, "Mom, I feel like you and Dad are going to get divorced."

I had to steady myself as this statement hit me like a ton of bricks.
How did she know?

We had been having problems for a long time, but I had hoped the worst of it was over. Bruce and I were actually doing better or so I thought.

I took a deep breath as both kids looked at me while eating. I replied, "Well, I don't know. Someday we may or we may not. Right now, Dad and I are getting along pretty well. We have been having some issues and I hope the worst has passed."

I felt like I was having a grown-up conversation. Really, these kids are just in little bodies, but their souls know. I have always known how intelligent kids are. We adults just act like they aren't sometimes.

I continued, "Whatever happens between Dad and I, I want you guys to know that you will ALWAYS be taken care of. You are always loved no matter if we live together or not."

They looked at me and continued eating. Then, Danny looked at Piper and hit her on the arm. "You're it!" He yelled.

They both jumped off their chairs and chased each other laughing around the house. I giggled, and yet I was still in shock.

Kids…

Bruce and I were separated three months later.
Kids know.

CHAPTER 55
THE WITCH AND THE LEPRECHAUNS

When the light is green you go. When the light is red you stop. But what do you do when the light turns blue with orange and lavender spots?
~Shel Silverstein

I had to get my three thousand intern hours to become a marriage and family therapist by seeing clients and working under a licensed therapist. During all of this, I saw many interesting clients.

One that sticks out in my mind is a client named Tiffany who was married and had a new baby. She mostly wanted someone to talk to and have support with her new baby and husband. As time went on, she began to tell me stories that didn't make sense to her.

I love these kinds of stories as it feels to me like they are from the paranormal or psychic phenomena.

One day, she tells me about a time in her life where she was driving on the freeway with a friend in California headed to San Diego. She was driving fast in the fast lane to get to her dad in the hospital. Suddenly, a car pulls in front of her. She knows she will hit him. Tiffany takes her right arm and pushes the car energetically back in the other lane with a sweep of her arm.

Her friend sitting next to her in the passenger seat looks over at her in astonishment.

She says, "My mom always said you were a witch. Now, with what I have just seen and felt, I know you are a witch! You moved that car out of your lane and I felt that energy go through my body as you swiped your arm across."

Oh, how I love these stories.
I know this stuff exists.
I wonder why more people don't talk about this stuff.

We talk about this and how she felt about the whole story. I ask her if she knew what she was doing. She says she didn't really, but felt the need to get to her dad, so she would do whatever was needed to get to him.

I know stories about these things in our reality "shouldn't" happen here, but they do!

Another story that I particularly love is when a group of five friends in a car were getting on a freeway and the driver didn't see the car next to them. She merged into the next lane and instead of crashing, they ended up going through the other car to the next lane!

Every one of the occupants saw and felt the shift seeing the car disassemble its molecules to become transparent and fluid.

Amazing.

Not one person was hurt and when the cars were back in their lanes, the cars became solid again. Some people in the car thought this was amazing and others were really freaked out.

They couldn't figure out how this happened.
Ever have an experience like this?

I have heard many unexplainable experiences. When we look at life from a higher perspective, anything is truly possible!

Back to Tiffany...

Tiffany tells me a few sessions later about how badly she wants to go back to Ireland. She spent a year there about five years ago. I joke with her about seeing the leprechauns there.

She looks at me funny and says, "I have a story for you about them. I haven't told many people, but you will understand."

"Go on," I say intrigued and excited to listen.

Tiffany tells of her time in Ireland and of how the Irish people believe in these leprechauns. She says that there are stories about them everywhere.

She continues, "One night, I was walking home along a road at about dusk and I feel something following me. I walk faster and I look off to my left. When I do, out of the corner of my eye, I see something jumping up and down behind this small wall. I walk even faster and I see a pub up ahead."

I am listening with every cell of my being as she tells the story.

"I finally decide to stop and turn to see who is following me. When I do, I see this leprechaun standing on this wall!" Tiffany says.

She continues, "So, I scream and run. I run fast and go into this pub. When I tell someone in there that there are leprechauns here, they laugh." They say, "Well, of course there are leprechauns here, you are in Ireland!"

I just love her stories.
I am grateful that someone else has magical stories and shares them.
There is just so much out there if we are open to seeing and experiencing it!

CHAPTER 56
FISH FEEL

Truly wonderful, the mind of a child is.
~*Yoda*

I grew up fishing in the summers in Iowa. We would spend a few weeks there and it was my favorite to be on a boat. My uncle taught me to fish and drive a boat. We waterskied too, and I just loved it.

When I had kids, I thought it would be fun to take them fishing. I looked forward to when they were old enough. Danny turned five and I decided that I would take him fishing. I found a place that did "catch and release" which I thought was perfect.

I told Danny that he and I were going to have a "Danny/Mommy day." We were going to skip school and go fishing. He wasn't really excited and he said that he didn't want to go. I was confused, thinking that maybe he will like it once we go there. We had been with friends who had fished before and he was never really interested. I guess this day was really about me and reliving the happy times of my childhood?!

I finally asked Danny if he wanted to go fishing.

He looked at me, "Not really."
"How come?" I asked.
"I just don't want to," he stated matter-of-fact.

I was perplexed. He never wanted to eat fish and he loved the ocean. So, I said, "You don't have to eat the fish. We can just catch them and release them. It will be fun."

He looked at me with his sweet eyes feeling it all and replied, "Mom, the fish feel everything. They feel the hook in their mouth. I don't want to hurt the fish."

I was taken back.
Really, I was shocked.
This thought had never even entered my mind.

How does he know this?

Kids are really our greatest teachers.
They know so much.

It turns out that science has even proven this to be true!
Fish feel!

I tell this story to show how kids are so connected and still feel so much. They haven't turned off their intuition and knowing. All of us have psychic abilities, but do we shut them down or do we nurture them? Did our parents shame or encourage us for these abilities?

From the science perspective, I am also fascinated that science has proven that fish feel. There are so many things out there science hasn't been able to "prove" because most of science is not open to psychic phenomenon or that everything is "alive."

Or, perhaps those in power don't want science to look in that direction!

I am fascinated about the concept of plasma energy as this feels like the direction where we are headed for new concepts and technologies. Plasma is currents of energy that collect into particles and arrange themselves into patterns which become a three-dimensional physical form.

Just hearing the word "plasma" vibrates my being with truth.
Perhaps this is where our paradigm is going?
Let's just take a minute to talk about plasma as most schools don't talk about this.

According to Penny Kelly's Patreon video called *Plasma, Consciousness, and the Nature of Reality-Part One*, there are two scientists who started the plasma revolution in the late eighteen hundreds and early nineteen hundreds, Kristian Birkeland and Hannes Alfven. Birkeland said that Earth's aurora is electric and that space is filled with plasma. Alfven created plasma physics and said there was no "Big Bang."

Penny Kelly continued in her video saying there are other scientists named William Levengood, Gerald Pollack, Mehran Keshe, and Wallace Thornhill who have explored deeply into plasma physics where they talk about free energy, anti-gravity, changing the nature of matter, the electric universe, and our electric sun.

I don't want to go deep into plasma physics much more as this is not what this book is about. And I am no scientist! My intention is to show how there is so much more out there that we have no idea about or that has been suppressed by those in power.

Plasma physics also excites me as this is one step closer to concepts I love exploring like time travel, teleporting, instant manifesting, and space travel.

Did you ever learn about Nikola Tesla or just about Albert Einstein in school?

Nikola Tesla was a brilliant scientist, inventor, and knew about plasma physics. Tesla said, "Earth is a Tesla coil" and that "electromagnetic levitation disproves gravity." Plasma physics validates some of his work. Scientists are finally realizing that gravity is just magnetic attraction caused by a left-hand spin. If you have a right-hand spin, it repulses. It is plasma fields that form the initial basis of attraction and repulsion.

So, are you thinking what I am thinking?

Levitation technologies!
Spaceship technologies!
Instant manifestation!
New medical technologies!

Could we regrow limbs by utilizing plasma physics? Could we fly in spaceships instead of planes using plasma physics? Could we reverse the aging process utilizing plasma physics?

Yes, we can!
So many possibilities!

It is all plasma within this electric and magnetic universe! Our thoughts are consciousness and plasma begins to form around them as we think them over and over again until we have it manifested in the physical! Plasma currents are all around us.

Welcome to the electric universe!
We are electrical beings!
We ARE an electric universe!

CHAPTER 57
SAVING BEAR

The gift of mental power comes from God, Divine Being, and if we concentrate our minds on that truth, we become in tune with this great power.
~Nikola Tesla

Ever have one of those times when you just react and there is no thought? You look back and wonder how you even got to where you were?

Is there a bigger part of you that knows everything?
What about divine timing?
Is this the difference between third and fifth dimension?
Duality and love?

I would love to know all the answers and this is one of the things I look forward to when I die. To know and remember everything…

It would be really great to know everything and remember everything now while I am still alive.

Yes, please.
It is possible, ya know.

I have heard stories of people almost falling off a cliff and then, some force pushes them back up. Other stories of angels saving people from drowning. Earlier in the book, I shared some additional examples. It all fascinates me. It's like we have a team of guides always with us.

I have had many knee jerk reactions where I just don't even have a thought, but just react. It's wild. My body just seems to know or I have a premonition. It was always quite helpful in the fire department, of course. It's my sixth sense.

Here is a story of one of those times…

It was pouring rain outside and had been for a day or so. Our property would get clogged drains sometimes, so I went out to check. I took my dog, Bear, with me who was one year old and still such a puppy.

We walked around in the pouring rain clearing drains and I noticed that the drainage ditches out front were super full. This seemed strange as they get about half full and drain well. I walked up to the top of our property and realized that someone had plugged a couple of street drains. I went out and attempted to fix this issue, getting them about half unplugged.

I went back down and told Bruce what was going on. He came outside and both of us noticed that the front drainage ditches were now overflowing. Water was pouring into our driveway and garage.

We needed to do something quick.

Our neighbors, Billy and Aileen, were outside as well, checking on things and came over to help us. We got sandbags and wood. It was still pouring rain and we were attempting to divert water. I went back inside to check on the kids who were seven and three. They were watching cartoons.

Bear came back outside with me and we came out on the far other side of our property. I began to walk towards Billy, Aileen, and Bruce along the street and drainage ditch.

Suddenly, out of the corner of my eye, I see Bear swimming in the drainage ditch. Now, he is a black lab and loves water, but something wasn't right.

He was dog paddling, but going backwards.

The next thing I know, I am on my belly holding Bear tight in my arms as the water is pulling him into the drain under the street. I yell for help and tell Bear that I won't let him go.

The thoughts in my head go by so fast.

I can pull him up myself, but I am afraid that I will lose him as the current is powerful. I have him around his body and under his front legs with his head up. The back half of his body is in the large drain. Billy, Aileen, and Bruce came quickly to help and they tell me to hold Bear tight as they will pick me up.

Oh, I am holding him tight!
I am not gonna lose my boy.

It is still dumping rain.
They all grab me and pull me up with Bear.
Yes! We did it!
Bear is safe and sound.

I wonder what happened as he hadn't done that before.

Perhaps he slipped in?
Regardless, Bear is safe and I am relieved.

I do wonder to this day how I ended up from walking to laying on my belly holding Bear tight.

It happened in an instant.
No thought.
Just action.
Something else deep inside me was guiding me.

CHAPTER 58
PAST THE VEIL, PLEASE

One of the oldest and most generous tricks that the universe plays on human beings is to bury strange jewels within us all, and then stand back to see if we can ever find them.
~Elizabeth Gilbert

I am not sure what is happening, but I feel beings around me quite strong. This has been going on for some time now.

Who are they?
What do they want?
Are they good?
Are they ghosts?

Sometimes they were quite present and I wondered if all the people I had run emergency calls on and died were following me around?

I wondered if they were my grandparents or ancestors.
Angels?

For some reason, I had a resistance to angels. I liked them and all, but I kept them at arm's length. I associated them with religion and all the beliefs that I grew up with. I know *The Bible* talked about angels, but I wanted nothing to do with them.

NO THANKS!

Yet, I kept seeing angel books in the bookstore. When I did, I would turn and walk the other direction.

Nope!
They kept showing up.

I was at a past life conference in New York for a week learning about taking people into their past lives. I was so fascinated and wanted to learn the techniques from Dr. Brian Weiss who taught many people. At break one day, I wondered into the bookstore there and found myself face to face with angel books again.

Okay, something is trying to get my attention.
I surrendered and picked up a book.

It was a book about every Archangel there was and how they help us if we call on them. It talked about our guardian angel and how they protect us. I just kept reading and realized that I associated them with Christianity so deeply, but the book talked about how angels are in every culture and belief. It went on to say how people heard them and saw them.

I thought maybe it was time to let the angels back into my life. Was this who has been following me around and I have been feeling?

Hmmmm....

A couple of months went by and I kept feeling someone or something around me. It feels like multiple beings. I finally asked out loud, "Okay, my guides, please lead me to someone who can see who is around me and what they want."

I asked this again a few more times whenever they were present.

One day, I went to have lunch with a friend named Jean and see her new office. She was telling me all about it and that she asked a woman who does massage in the same building how the energy was in the building.

This woman replies, "Well, there were two ghosts here. I got one to go to the light and the other one doesn't want to leave yet. She's nice and doesn't cause any trouble, but you may feel her."

Whuuutttt?!

She can see them?!
I am enthralled and excited.
She's a masseuse, but she sees the other side!

Jean continues speaking as we are enjoying lunch and I forget about the whole thing.

Another month goes by and I meet up with Jean again. She used to work in Hospice and is telling me stories of dead family members who are trying to tell their loved ones that they are okay.

She talks about a husband who heard his dead wife coming up the stairs at 2 am. He saw her sit at the end of his bed and tell him that she is okay. He can move on with his life now. Jean told story after story about strange things happening after people died. The families were freaked out, yet knew somehow it was their loved one coming back to tell them that they were okay. For many people, they had a hard time accepting it because it went against their religious beliefs.

Then, Jean and I are walking back to her office to say goodbye. She tells me one last story because she says that I will understand. She is also a newly licensed marriage and family therapist.

She begins to tell me how she was getting ready to see a couple for therapy. She was meditating in her office and asking her guides and angels to help her say the right thing. Once she was done, she opened her door and began to head downstairs to get her clients.

Just then, the masseuse, Karen, comes out of her door and looks at my friend. She puts her hands in the air and over her eyes while saying to Jean, "Were you just meditating and asking for your angels? They are all around you! You can ask them to turn down their light as it is bright!"

Ummm…yeh.
That's right.

Jean is in total shock that she can see her angels around her.
As for me, I want to get this woman's card and see if she can see who is around me!
I am so excited that Source answered my request!

CHAPTER 59
LIONS, TIGERS, AND BEARS, OH MY!

The day science begins to study non-physical phenomena, it will make more progress in one decade than in all the previous centuries of its existence.
~Nikola Tesla

Continuing from the last chapter…

Once leaving my friend, Jean, I went downstairs and found this masseuse's card. It didn't say anything about medium work on it, but she did have a website. I looked on her website and she had every type of massage possible. I kept looking and towards the end, it said somatic healing massage.

Hmmm…

I read what it was and she described it as a massage with guidance from her guides and angels.

I'm in.
I have no idea what I signed up for, but maybe she can see who is around me.
All I give her is my name and I see her in two weeks.

I arrive for my appointment and am so excited. Walking up the stairs, I see her looking at me, smiling. Sitting down in her office, I tell her that I am very open and want to hear everything that she sees around me and more. Her name is Karen.

She listens and tells me what she does. Karen tells me how she is guided by spirit. She says how this isn't a normal massage, but more with energy. She will put her hands certain places on my body to remove energy blockages or cords.

We are sitting in chairs and she begins by telling me that as I came up the stairs, she saw a javelin in my lower back on the right side that goes all the way through me. An energetic javelin from a past life I had in the 1400's in Europe.

Karen goes on to tell me she is being told that I have tried to heal it many times, but it keeps coming back. This is because the healings that were done on me before removed the javelin, but then they failed to fill the energetic wound with light.

Well, nature abhors a vacuum, so it continued to put the old injury back in place!

Fascinating.

I have tried to heal that injury so many times and yet, it especially came on when I had issues with my mother or husband. It was almost as if they knew it was there and twisted it within me. Karen tells me that they are going to heal it today and that it will never come back.

Sweet.

She then asks me if my father and uncle died.

"No," I reply.

She says there are two men here that have been with me sometimes and how they seem like they are brothers. I can't think of anybody and wonder if she is the real deal. I ask her what they look like. She begins to describe one as tall with a bushy mustache and funny. The other is shorter with a bushy mustache and quiet.

Suddenly, it hits me like a ton of bricks.

Greg and Nick!

These are two guys that I worked with when I first got hired in the fire department. Greg was the tall one and he was like my father when I first got hired. We were close and I loved him dearly. He died three years later from throat cancer. I was devastated.

Nick was the shorter one and kinda moody. I worked with him, too, and later he died from pancreatic cancer. Nick and Greg were close friends and I can see why she thinks they are brothers. They were like my dad and uncle.

So, they are the ones I have been feeling around me?
Yep.

I ask Karen, "Can you ask if Greg and Nick are always around me?"

She bursts out in laughter.

She says, "Greg is really funny with his dry sense of humor. He said, 'Hydee, don't you think that I have better things to do than to hang out with you all day?!'"

I started laughing hysterically.
Yep.

This is Greg.
I loved his humor.

She continues on and keeps looking above my head. Karen says, "There is a large angel behind you. She watches over you and has been with you since birth. Sometimes your head tingles and that is because she is downloading information into you."

I know the top of my head tingles sometimes, but I never thought this was the reason.

I get on her table and she is touching certain places on my back and I feel heat. She starts telling me about my life and describing people in my life. She tells me about energetic cords and how they connect to people, but drain my energy or their energy. Karen is being guided to cut these cords now. She goes on telling me of past lives I have had and who I was.

My whole body is buzzing and coming alive. She tells me my dead family members are around me at times and describes them perfectly. I am just so totally blown away and excited by the end of the session. It had gone on for two and a half hours.

Another life changing adventure!
Past lives, dead people, and angels...oh my!

CHAPTER 60
THE AIR WE BREATHE

My stroke of insight would be: peace is only a thought away, and all we have to do to access it is silence the voice of our dominating left mind.
~Dr. Jill Bolte Taylor

I love the Earth, fire, and water, but there was something about the element of air that I have stayed away from.

Kinda funny, really, because I breathe in air every single day!

Perhaps it is because I can't really grab it and feel it in my hands. It is all around me, yet it is just empty space.

Or is it?

Living in Southern California for most of my life, we would have these winds called the "Santa Anas." When I was young, I didn't remember them much. Were they around then? I do remember them in the 1990's as we had brush fires that were pushed by these winds.

As the years went on, we seemed to have the "Santa Ana" winds in October for a few days. Then, they moved to December for a few days. Then, it seemed like they happened often and I hated them.

I began hating the wind.
And I don't like to hate anything.
The winds were hot, dry, and at extremely high speeds.
It dried everything out and it made you not want to be outside.

If there was a downed power line or arsonist around, fires would be started, and these brush fires would destroy everything in its path. It wasn't until later in my career that I heard the government had machines to manipulate the weather.

I was surprised by this and began searching to see if this was true. What I found is that Nikola Tesla had created weather machines that could make it rain or stop raining back in the 1930's. He also created free energy machines that made it so we didn't need to pay for electricity because it was created right out of thin air!

Unfortunately, those in power did not allow his inventions to be known to the general public. In fact, when Tesla died, the government came in and stole all his work.

Hmmm…
What is this really all about?
What technology did he invent?

I found other articles that mentioned the military used weather making machines in the Vietnam war to make it continuously rain and beat the Vietnamese.

Weather as a weapon?

I had never thought of such a thing as you think that it is Mother Nature who is in charge of our climates and weather. We think that there are more hurricanes and tornados because the Earth is shifting. We feel there are more droughts and floods because of humans and our destruction to the planet. Earthquakes are on the rise, as well.

What is the truth here?

It does appear that our weather is being manipulated all over the world. What is real and what is manmade? From what I read, HAARP and chemtrails are used to cause hurricanes as well as to cause droughts. "They" even have the ability to cause earthquakes and there are some people on *YouTube* reporting about this.

Who are "they?"
That is another book altogether.

If I just go back to the air element and the wind, I find that I like it when there are breezes that are cooler. It feels good.

Walking around the fire station one day, I am aggravated by the hot and dry wind. I decide that I will go for a walk anyways, but I am not happy about the weather conditions.

The wind is blowing at high speeds and I am hoping that we don't have a brush fire anytime soon. I am irritated and finally decide that I will speak with the wind.

This might sound crazy, but everything is alive. Sometimes, I can hear what "they" say back to me. I have been doing this since I was a kid and I can remember talking to the plants and trees around the schools I went to.

I tell the wind that I don't like the hot wind and that it doesn't feel good. Then, I ask the wind why it has to be this way because most people don't even want to be outside.

Hearing nothing, I ask again.
Again nothing.
Well, perhaps I need to introduce myself.

I say, "Hi wind, I am Hydee. I know I am angry at you right now, but I would like to speak with you."

Nothing.

Walking back to the fire station, I decide that before bed I will meditate to find out more about the wind. When I meditate, it comes very clear to me that I do not have a relationship with the wind, so I will not hear from the wind. I have to cultivate it just as I would with any relationship. Then, I realize that I probably didn't start off so well with the wind telling it that I was angry with it.

It is hot, dry, and windy the next day. I am still at the fire station as a brush fire broke out in another city and all of us have to stay on duty in case they need more firefighters. I go for a walk and decide to make peace with the wind. I begin by apologizing and blowing the wind kisses.

Maybe I just need to change my perspective.
I feel the air all around me swirling and twirling.
Something is different.
The air seems to be having fun and playing.

Ponder this...

When we humans are out of balance and forget who we really are or where we came from, does all of nature become out of balance? Do we begin to attack nature and see it as a threat? Do we see animals and the elements like wind as a threat? Have we forgotten how to live in harmony with ourselves and ultimately, our internal being?

So, externally, if our environment does not live in harmony with us, it is merely a reflection of what is going on inside us.

Yikes.

If we are at peace, all of nature is at peace.
I am remembering and nature is ready to help me.
Speak to me, Wind.

CHAPTER 61
GROUNDING ENERGY

Everything changes when you start to emit your own frequency rather than absorbing the frequencies around you, when you start imprinting your intent on the universe rather than receiving an imprint from existence.
~Barbara Marciniak

The Earth loves our energy and loves to transform our negative energy if we let her. There are so many ways to do this as I found out from my daughter.

We got a giant pumpkin from a school fundraiser and it sat outside our house for a few months. It was three feet tall by two feet wide.

My daughter, Piper, was six years old and not much taller than the pumpkin.

I know that my daughter feels and absorbs other people's energy as she transforms it. She doesn't always release it and sometimes carries it in her body. I remind her that it isn't hers and she can release the energy into the Earth through her feet and hands. I go on saying she can just lay on the Earth and ask the Earth to take this old energy, too.

Then, she can fill up with the sun's energy or cosmic energy to fill her back up.

One day, I was saying to the kids that we should make lots of pumpkin pie with this giant pumpkin.

Piper responded, "No, we shouldn't make pie from it."

"Why not?" I asked.

"I have been laying on the pumpkin and unloading all my bad energy into the pumpkin," she stated.

I laughed out loud and I recalled times when I had seen her outside laying her full body on the pumpkin.

Great idea…

Mother Earth transforms this energy for us if we allow her to. We can stand on the Earth and release it through the bottoms of our feet. We can put it into stones and trees asking them to transform it. So many ways for us to reboot ourselves from the stresses of life. Another one that I love is just to immerse myself in water.

The ocean, lakes, waterfalls, and any body of water.
We just need to ask and it is done.

CHAPTER 62
POLAR BEAR

Animals can always read your vibration, and if you are intent on empowering your life, they will often gift you by making special melodies of sound to balance your chakras and tune up your body.
~Barbara Marciniak

He was the cutest little ball of fur. This boy was all white and yellow with these big brown eyes. We named him Polar Bear and he was our new yellow lab.

He grew up with us and our other black lab, Teddy Bear. They were our babies before our babies.

Labs are the best.
So patient and kind.
Playful and wild.
I just love dogs.

As time went by, our pups got older and wiser. They were gentle giants when our kids came along. The kids just loved them. Danny and Piper would roll all over them and the dogs would just lick them. I loved to watch how Teddy and Polar Bear would watch over our kiddos.

One morning, I came home from work to find Polar Bear laying in the grass. He didn't come to greet me as usual and I wondered if he was okay. He was ten years old. The sprinklers went on and he didn't move. I watched him getting soaked and I went to pick him up. I carried him partly and then he walked on his own.

Something wasn't right.

I put a blanket down inside the house and had him come lay on it. He laid down and looked at me with those big eyes. I rubbed him and kissed him. I asked him if he was going to be okay and told him to rest.

The kids were running around as they were about four and seven years old. They wanted to watch cartoons, so I told Polar Bear that I would come back to check on him later. The kids were happy, so I went outside and did a few things.

About an hour had passed before I went to check on my Polar Bear.

I went to look and Polar Bear was asleep.
He appeared to be resting comfortably.
Yay!
He will feel better soon.

I went into the kitchen and did a couple more things. Something was telling me to check on Polar Bear. So, I went and laid down next to him rubbing his fur. He didn't move and I watched to see if he was breathing.

He wasn't.
Huh?!

It wasn't making sense to me.

What?!
Polar Bear died?
How could this be?
He's only ten.
I sat in shock.

Shit! My boy just died. I began to sob.

Oh, Polar Bear!
No, don't go!
I'm not ready for you to go.

I sat with him for some time. He looked so peaceful and I was grateful that he waited for me to come home from work. I knew he was a happy boy running around wherever he went.

My kids were still watching cartoons and had no idea what had happened. I knew they were going to be devastated. Bruce was at work and he would be bummed. He loved Polar Bear so much. I got up and went into the family room. I got both kids close to me and told them that Polar Bear just died. They looked at me surprised and still engrossed in their cartoons.

I said it again and told them to come with me. We all went into the den where Polar Bear was. They both laid on top of Polar Bear and cried. They sobbed and asked him to come back. Their emotions were intense and I cried with them. This went on for about fifteen minutes.

I said, "We all loved Polar Bear. We will miss you, buddy. You were a great dog."

We all hugged each other and cried.

"We will need to bury his body in the backyard, so I will dig a hole and you guys can help me if you want," I stated.

Both of them got excited to use their little shovels and said "yes." Then Danny asks, "Can we go back and watch cartoons again, Mom?"

I was so surprised.
They were both just grieving and sobbing.

Is this what happens when you allow pure emotion to move through you and to not stop it?

I said, "Sure, you guys can and I will come get you later to help me." Off they run back to the cartoons.

Kids. Dogs. Life. Death.
Really?
Is it all so simple?
What am I missing?

I shut down my emotions all through my childhood as you weren't supposed to cry or be angry. I am still learning to allow them to flow. What if I had been allowed to cry and be angry as I allow my kids to be? Did all those emotions get stuck and plague me throughout my life?

Yep.

I just let them cry and cry until they were done.
Then, it just shifted.
I am just blown away at what I just witnessed.

All these messages to not cry or be sad. We are told to be strong. What we do instead is to stuff our emotions and that energy gets stuck in our bodies. It comes out in disease either mentally or physically.

Time to train ourselves to become aware of our feelings and emotions all day long. Acknowledging the distortion or negative emotion that we are feeling allows us to be in it and to let it move through.

It is that simple.
Remember, feelings aren't good or bad.
They are just part of being human.

Kids are amazing and they remind me every day that we made up these rules in society of what we can and can't express.

Kids already know what is true for them.
We adults put our beliefs and society's beliefs onto them.

Fucking nuts!

I kiss my Polar Bear and tell him how much I love him. Gathering shovels, I go off to figure out where to bury him. My other dog, Teddy Bear, never came too close to Polar Bear. He just stayed in the other room. I wonder what he was feeling.

We buried Polar Bear and it was actually fun and sad. The kids and I talked about death and how death is just leaving a body. We talked about how our souls never die. We talked about how Polar Bear's soul is here and all around us.

It was fun wondering what new body Polar Bear would pick. Would he pick another dog body? Human body? Whale body? Bird body? So many choices!

About a week later, Danny came running in our room and said, "Mom! Polar Bear is here!"

I replied, "What? What are you talking about?"

"I was in bed and I looked down beside my bed. Polar Bear was there looking at me and wagging his tail!" He states matter-of-fact.

I grabbed Danny and hugged him. "Oh, he came to see you, Danny! Yay!"

Polar Bear was Danny's favorite.
He never left him.
His soul just entered another dimension.
Polar Bear came to visit Danny often.

Love you, Polar Bear!

CHAPTER 63
SAFETY AND CHANGE

Train yourself to let go of everything you fear to lose.
~Yoda

The decision to separate was not easy, yet we both knew in our hearts that it was the right thing to do. Somehow, it felt like there was still a chance that we could figure it out and not get divorced.

Maybe we just needed time to breathe and figure out what we both wanted.

The kids still felt so little. They were ages five and eight. Somehow, I felt like I failed them. I was headed down the road to divorce just like my parents. I wanted so badly to stuff down my feelings and fall in love with Bruce again.

What happened?
What changed?

I changed. I grew up. I healed many different parts of myself and I outgrew him. He didn't want to grow more emotionally, spiritually, or mentally. I had tried to talk to him about all that I was learning.

Sometimes he was open, but mostly he wasn't.
He thought I was nuts.
I am nuts.
And I love that about myself.
The crazier, the better.

Anyways, is this what happens to many couples? We come together to heal and help each other, and then it's time to move on? Did we just come together to heal our childhoods and have kids?

Perhaps.

It would sure be easier if religion and society didn't make it like you need to stay together forever. Perhaps it's time to change that. Instead of "till death do you part," make it "until your contract is done, then you can part."

One of the things that I love about Bruce is that he is so loving. He cares about others. He may not care about himself, but I know he loved me and the kids.

So, we decided to stay in the same house and to separate since we were rarely home together. We had opposite schedules for work and I would move into the extra bedroom. This way, the kids could have us both there and not much would change for them. On the other hand, we both set each other free to explore other people or whatever we needed.

It was time for a break.

We thought it was important to tell the kids what was going on and why we were sleeping in different rooms.

So, one night after dinner together, we told the kids that we need to talk to them. The kids got in our laps and listened as we told them that we were separating and going to sleep in different rooms. We said that we weren't getting along well, so instead of divorcing, we were going to separate for a while.

Danny being older, looked at us, and asked how this was going to affect him. I told him that it really wouldn't, except that we wouldn't be in our bed together if he comes in at night to sleep with us.

He asked if he was staying in the same room and same house. I reassured him and said "yes." It was just Dad and I changing rooms. I told him that he would still go to the same school and everything else will stay the same. Once all this made sense to him, he says, "Okay."

Within a few seconds, he got down and takes off to play with his sister. They run around playing tag and chasing the dogs.

I am kinda in shock.
Both Bruce and I stare at each other.
Fascinating...

I realize that even with changes happening all around, kids just need to know they are safe.

CHAPTER 64
THE PLEIADIANS

Extraterrestrials are living now on Earth. They are everywhere, among your friends, neighbors, even your relatives. Their blood flows through our veins. We are as much brothers and sisters to beings from the stars as we are to animals of the Earth.
~Delores Cannon

I have always loved laying on the ground to stare at the stars. It has always felt calming and knowing that there was more out there than this reality.

One of my favorite star clusters to look at was the Pleiades within the Taurus constellation.

Just something about it.
It felt so familiar.
I just couldn't put my finger on it.

In high school, my best friend Linda and I would stare up at the stars in her driveway. We both would wonder about the cluster of stars called the Pleiades.

It drew us both.

I have always believed in extraterrestrials and just thought how selfish it is of humans to think we are the only ones out there. I loved the movie *Star Wars* and its connection to outer space. I was only seven when the first *Star Wars* came out. Something so familiar about all this, too.

In my twenties, I got more into this three-dimensional reality of college, work, and marriage. Partying and traveling were top on my list, as well. I was deep into forgetting who I was.

Having my children were actually key into bringing me back out of my unconsciousness. I was thirty-two when my son, Danny, was born and I never knew how powerful it would be to be a parent. He was so little and precious. He was just so perfect that I never wanted to make a mistake in raising him.

I always questioned this life I was living, but now, I questioned life even more.

Drinking and partying didn't sound much fun anymore. I began wondering about my childhood and how my parents felt having me. Did they want me? Why did they do certain things? I wanted to do things differently.

Danny helped renew my will to live and he was just so amazing. I had so much fun making him laugh and teaching him things. I watched him at two years old look at ants crawling on the ground. He got close and just watched them. Everything was new for him.

He went through stages of loving certain things. At one point, he loved trash trucks. Danny would point and yell when they came by. Our dogs would also bark at the trash trucks, so Danny got a kick out of this as well. He also loved trash cans.

One day, Grandma was watching Danny and they got out of the car. Danny saw a trash can across the street and ran towards it. Grandma didn't see him do this as she was getting other things out of the car. Our neighbor, Billy, was in his truck leaving his house and he saw Danny in the street.

Another truck was barreling down the street and didn't see Danny. Billy pulled his truck horizontal across the street hoping the other truck would slow down and stop.

Thanks goddess!
The truck did stop.
Grandma came and grabbed Danny out of the street.
That was a close one!

Danny loved legos and building things. He would amaze me at how his mind worked. As he got older, he also loved *Star Wars* and I wondered what other connections we had before this life together. I just have such a deep love for this little guy.

His little sister, Piper, was born three and a half years later. Like I mentioned earlier, I was nervous having a girl as I didn't want to treat her the way I was treated by my mother. I realized that just this realization alone would help me raise her consciously as well as doing lots of therapy!

I feel deeply in love with this little girl, too.

Danny loved having a little sister and he would always want to play and wrestle with her. They would run around together and make me laugh. I loved playing with them.

One day, I was laying outside on the ground and I saw Piper come outside. She was three-years old and looked at me. Then, she went back inside and I wondered what she was up to. She came back outside with my small bag of crystals. Piper began putting them in between my toes, fingers, joints, and my major chakra points.

I wondered how she knew this.
She told me to leave them on until they fell off of me.
This girl is going to teach me a lot.
I just love this kid.

As I mentioned before, I had gone to a medium before named Karen and had an amazing experience. I talked about the experience to my friends and Danny and Piper overheard me talking about it one day. Danny was eight and Piper was five. They asked if they could go to her.

Hmmm…
Really?
I wondered if kids ever saw mediums.

I asked Karen and she said to bring both kids in for a session together. She had never read kids before, but she was open.

Danny went first.

Karen described his soul's journey this time around. She said he was a warrior for many lives and had died most recently in the Vietnam war. He was also a pilot who died in Pearl Harbor. She said that he and I have lived many lifetimes together.

I was fascinated by this as she described how he died in Vietnam. She said he was Vietnamese and she sees him coming from a small military boat to land. As he goes through the jungle, he hits a trip wire and blows up.

The crazy thing is that about eight months before, we were out of a boat with friends. Danny and I went up on the bow of the boat and we were looking towards the beach. He then says to me, "Mom, I feel like I am on a boat where a gun would be and we are getting ready to land in a jungle area."

This all makes sense now.
He was remembering parts of his past life.

There was also the time when Danny, Piper, and I were flying to Oahu, Hawaii. We were close to landing and Danny got this huge pain above his right eye to the point where he was crying and screaming in pain. I was holding him and trying to console him, but it was intense and non-stop.

I asked within myself what he needed. It came to me to ask him what he was "seeing." He told he saw himself as a pilot and he got shot in the head. His plane was going down.

Just then, our pilot announced that we were flying over Pearl Harbor.

Really?

Coincidence?
No way.

I stopped believing in coincidences and started believing in synchronicity a long time ago. Was this a way for him to release energy from that past life by flying over his old burial ground? Did he have to do this to move on from the past? I had so many questions.

I am not sure, but once we passed Pearl Harbor, all of his pain let up and was gone. Just like that.

Back to Karen's session with Danny…

She did some clearing around his past lives and it made me think of how he would wake up in the middle of the night screaming when he was two. He was inconsolable and I couldn't wake him up. She said he was reliving his last death when this was happening. She talked about how he "sees" like she does and he also "hears" the 'other' side.

I was loving all of this and listening intently to every word.

Piper got on the table next and she was just so excited. Karen asked her if she sees her guardian angel.

Piper says, "Yes. He is right here above me on the ceiling."
Karen continues and begins to describe him to Piper.

They go back and forth describing this giant angel together. I am just in awe listening and enjoying it all.

Then, Karen looks at me, "Hydee. Ummm… There are these beings here in my room. They are about ten to twelve feet tall and they are all healing Piper. I am not doing anything as they are doing it all. They are sending light to her and reminding her of her mission. They are so loving. They call themselves the Pleiadians and I have only seen them twice in here now."

My head is spinning.
Did she just say…the Pleiadians?
THE PLEIADIANS???

I ask, "Are they from the Pleiades?"

"Yes, but I don't know much about ETs as I never believed in them until they started showing up here." Karen replies. "They say that they are helping many humans."

I am just so excited and I ask her what they look like.

She replies saying that they are tall and humanoid looking. Karen says that they are beautiful and have longer faces. She says that they are reminding Piper that her job here is to have fun and to bring joy into this planet. Karen goes on to say that there are many like Piper incarnating here now to raise the vibration of this planet.

Wow.
The Pleiadians.
They are here in this room, right now!
I am having flashbacks of looking at the stars and staring at the Pleiades.

I knew they existed.
Now, I really know they exist.
I can feel them.
Somehow, I feel that my body can finally relax now.

CHAPTER 65
ALTERING CONSCIOUSNESS

*Realize that your brain is not your mind. If you die you no longer have a working brain,
but you still have a working mind with all its knowledge, awareness, and personality. In
fact, you don't have a mind, you are mind. Mind is the awareness property of space.
Space is the location aspect of the mind. Energy is the movement aspect of consciousness.
Consciousness is the feeling aspect of energy.*
~Penny Kelly

The nature of consciousness is to create. We are creator beings who are creating our
own realities and our collective realities. We even continue creating in our sleep as
consciousness never sleeps.

Have you ever really thought about this?
We are not victims.

We have created everything around us, whether we created it consciously or
unconsciously.

Have we forgotten?
Yep.
Most of us have.

As kids, we still remember much of our past lives and other worlds. We remember
and then our parents, society, and this reality reinforce our forgetting.

I remembered bits and pieces and enough to know that this reality sucks.

Often, I thought, what am I doing here?
How did I get here?
Perhaps I am an explorer of consciousness, as are you!

Throughout my career as a firefighter, we went on calls with many people who were
using drugs to alter their consciousness. I imagined that many were using drugs to
get rid of their pain and others used it to feel good. How many were using drugs or

alcohol because they didn't like their reality that they created?

Most of them probably.

Typically, we didn't get calls for those on hallucinogens like LSD, mushrooms, ayahuasca, etc… Instead, one of the common drug calls that I responded on was for heroin. Typically, they would inject the drug into their veins and then stop breathing. It was made on the streets, so you never knew exactly how much the right amount was to get you "high" and still keep breathing.

We would have a week or so of many "OD" (overdose) calls with someone not breathing because typically the "batch" (the heroin just made) had not been tested in a lab, so the "right" dose was not known. We would give the person a medication called "Narcan" which would reverse "their high" and make them breathe again when we arrived.

Now, do you think they were happy about this?
Oh, hell no!
They were usually pissed.

Pissed because we just took away their high, brought them back to this reality, and they wasted their money.

Sometimes, they would get angry and aggressive towards us, so we began pushing Narcan slower just to get them to breathe again. Then, we would take them to the hospital, leaving "their high" intact. The hospital personnel would take it from there.

Many of us want to incarnate and have this experience here on Earth, but we forget what we came to do.

We forget the bigger picture.

Some indigenous cultures in Africa sing a song to you when you are born. Both parents know it and sing it to you while you are in utero. It comes from the ethers and it is "your song" interpreted by the shaman. It is your imprint. Your family is taught your song and it connects you to your soul's essence.

As you go through life with all its ups and downs and forget as we do, they will sing this song back to you to help you remember.

This is awesome.
Each of us need something like this to remind us when we get caught up in this reality.

To remember who we are.

This reminds me too, of hearing the stories of how in indigenous cultures, when a person does something wrong, they don't send them to jail. They come together as a community and say loving things to them. They tell positive stories about them and remind them who they are.

Imagine that!?
No jail and being forgiven.
Putting their energy towards what they want to see.
I love this.

Back to forgetting...
Our teenagers have forgotten just as the adults in our world have forgotten.

I went on an emergency call one time as a captain for a person dead and another barely breathing. When we arrived, we found five teenagers there. One was dead and had been for a while. One was unconscious and barely breathing. Another teenager was breathing fine, but unconscious. Two other teens were conscious, but not all there mentally.

The grandmother of one of the kids had called as she had just gotten home. She found all of them like this. One of the teenagers told her that they all got their parents medications, put them in a bowl, and randomly took the pills.

Holy shit.

I radioed dispatch for more ambulances and we pronounced one dead. We began assisting ventilations for the one barely breathing and stabilized the other unconscious one. The other two were okay medically, just in another world.

I felt the spirit of the dead teenager there in the room watching us. I said to him telepathically, "I feel you here. You have died from the drugs you took and left your body. You are okay. Look around you for your light beings as they will guide you to come back into your body or not."

He seemed to want to stay around and watch us. I began to telepath with the unconscious girl who was barely breathing saying to her, "You can come back in your body if you want to. I understand. It's tough here." She felt as if she was standing next to me deciding if she would stay or go.

Sometimes I felt people go to the "light," and other times they seemed to stay with their body or family members.

These types of calls were always difficult with kids involved. When I had a moment on an emergency call, I would try to tap in and see where their spirit was, if they were dying or dead. Sometimes though, it was just too chaotic, but I did my best.

I am still learning about how this all works, so I just say what comes when speaking with the dead. Deep down, I always wanted them to come back to life for the sake of their family members.

As a captain, I was often left on scene with family members in full arrest situations. A full arrest is when someone is not breathing and has no pulse after having a heart attack, stroke, or something similar. We would do CPR, give lifesaving drugs, and shock them as per protocol. We would spend about twenty minutes on scene and then transport to the hospital or pronounce them dead on scene.

My firefighter and engineer would typically go in the ambulance with the paramedic, from the ambulance to the hospital doing CPR on the patient, so I was left cleaning up the scene and attending to the family members. This was tough as I could feel their grief and shock of having just lost a loved one, and I often cried with them.

Sometimes while talking to the family, I would feel the dead patient standing next to them. I always wanted to tell the family that their loved one was right here.

I remember a fifty year old cyclist in great shape who had just come in from riding. While he was talking to his family, he had a sudden heart attack dying in front of them. They called "911" and we did everything we could to save him. While I was doing chest compressions, I could see his energy body up in the corner of his living room ceiling, watching us.

I told him telepathically that he had died and was out of his body. He could decide if he was going to go to the light with his guides or he could come back in his body. I continued saying that it was up to him and that his family would be okay.

He stayed with his body the whole time following it to the hospital. I imagined that it was probably a shock to be out of your body with sudden death. He ended up dying, but I am always curious how long dead people stick around. Do they wait till the funeral before leaving? Do they come and go? Some never leave and this is why we see them as ghosts?

Perhaps all of the above.

One of my firefighters named Jim had a five year old niece that died suddenly and it was very traumatic for the family. They all grieved her deeply and eventually went to see a medium who helped them all get back in touch with her from the other side. The family received many messages about her reason for dying early and it gave them some peace around her death.

Jim's niece would play games with him from the other side and would hide his things sometimes. She even came to work with him and sometimes, we would hear the sounds of a girl giggling. One time, we were sitting and watching television talking about his niece when suddenly, the television screen froze. On the screen was a black and white picture that looked like his niece with her parents!

Jim freaked out.

Well, we all kinda did!
We couldn't even change the channel!
She loved to do these kinds of things to let him know that she was still with him.

I often wonder, why do we try to save people? Is it because we aren't okay with death? Most of the people that die, don't come back. So, is it the medical system that has created this? Perhaps, we have just forgotten about death. We never "really" die as our consciousness just leaves the physical body.

It is never too late to begin exploring consciousness.
To see what is out there and we don't even need drugs to do so.
Although, perhaps sometimes we do?

We went on an emergency call one time for a grandmother who was feeling strange. Her daughter had called and the granddaughter was there as well. We began asking the grandma questions and she said she felt like she was floating...like she wasn't in her body. She said her body felt tingly.

Continuing to ask her questions, we found out that her brother had come over and brought her some "special" brownies that was helping him with his cancer. She ate them and then began feeling like this.

She's high!

We began to laugh realizing that Grandma is high. She had never been high before and her daughter and granddaughter laughed. We joked saying they should turn on Pink Floyd videos and order pizza!

I love this story!

Ask for an acceleration of consciousness.
Start right where you are.
Watch what shows up!
You are never too old to explore consciousness.

CHAPTER 66
THE DREAM

Sex in 3D can provide the energy through which you can emerge to higher consciousness. It can lead to an essential part of your multidimensional development. Sometimes, it is difficult to hear about sex because you hold onto judgement of traumatic events that you are ashamed of or that you feel bad about surrounding your sexuality. Everyone has something stored away concerning the sexual part of themselves. To a large degree, there has been a plan to influence you to feel shame about sexuality and your body; this has kept you from discovering your power, purpose, bliss, and freedom.
~Barbara Marciniak

It's winter solstice.
12/21/12.

I am at the fire station and it is a clear night outside. I am around a bonfire with two firemen that I work with. We are laughing and telling jokes. We are enjoying the fire and the stars in the sky.

There is something in the air this night.
It feels powerful.

It's quiet and we just stare at the fire. Then, Kevin and Steve start telling me how much they love me and care about me. They go on telling me how beautiful I am and how much they respect me.

I laugh as this is not them. I wonder to myself that they must be up to something. Kevin says that they are just being honest.

I decide to take off my shirt and bra in front of them. They both sit there smiling and say that they want to make love with me.

There is an energy pulling us together…

I move over to Kevin and begin kissing him passionately. He pulls me in close and I am so turned on. Steve comes up behind me and kisses my neck as he touches my bare skin. He moves his hands around my back and up to my breasts. He caresses my breasts and begins to kiss them.

I now realize that the three of us are in the shower together naked.

Oh yes.

We are kissing, loving, and fondling each other.
It feels so right and natural.
There is something so familiar about all of this.

Kevin picks me up and I straddle his body with my legs wrapped around him.
Pure delight.
He is holding me up against the shower wall.
We continue making love and I feel an orgasm coming.

So yummy.

I feel like a goddess.
I feel loved and nurtured.
These gods deeply care about me and love me.

Kevin and I continue making love and we end up on a huge bed in the forest. I am on top of him and screaming with pleasure.

No words can describe how amazing this feels.
I feel like I am floating.
Our passions together are sensual and electric.
I feel like the goddess Kali or maybe, it's Aphrodite, or both!

Then, while wanting more, Steve takes me in his arms and kisses me passionately. He pulls me close to his body and I feel his love for me. He is so gorgeous and strong. We begin making love.

Heaven.
Pure bliss to be loved and feel such pleasure.
We move together as one as if we have been doing this for eons.
I have orgasm after orgasm.
Total ecstasy.

Suddenly, I awaken to my alarm going off…

What!?
Just a dream!?
It felt so real.

I smile and reminisce about what just happened.

The gods making love with the goddess.
What an honor.

I tell this story because of how powerful sex is and how sex has been so distorted in this world. Religion has made sex "bad" and that we should only have sex if we are married. It is implied to be used only for procreation and with one person. Religion uses shame and guilt against us if we have adulterous thoughts or act on these impulses.

Talk about a way to control the population!

If you look back in our ancient history into the goddess cultures, there was no shame or guilt in having sex. It was a natural part of being human.

So, what have we forgotten?
We have forgotten so much.

Just read *The Mists of Avalon*, *The Magdalen Manuscript*, or *The Evolving Human* to begin opening your mind to what we have forgotten. The priestesses would use this energy to remind us where we came from and who we truly are.

Sex is actually a connection to the god/goddess within ourselves.
This is a pathway to the evolution of consciousness.

An Awakening.

Is this really why religion has put so many restrictions and guilt trips around sex?

Sex is important for our bodies as when we orgasm, it reorganizes our cells and frequencies. This is pertinent for the human body. Also, it doesn't matter who you are having sex with whether it is a man and a woman, a woman and a woman, or a man and a man. Any type of sex reorganizes our cells and frequencies. Our whole brain literally lights up with an orgasm.

Funny how we put so many restrictions around sex and what is okay or not.

When we orgasm, we connect to the god/goddess within ourselves which puts us in our power and can awaken kundalini giving us access to so many more frequencies within the universe. Anyone picking up on the power we have been missing out on and how religion has kept us away from our power?

Anyone want their power back?

And I am not talking about power over others, but the power within ourselves. Power to open our connection to the universe. Power that opens our superpowers like teleporting, instant healing, time travel, and telepathy.

Sex is really an opening into consciousness.

Think of all the made up rules around sex. It is so subtle that you may miss them. Our society has made it okay for men to want sex, but if a woman does, they are considered a prostitute or porn star. Animals don't seem to have issues with sex. They aren't ashamed of it as it is natural. When I swim with the dolphins, often they are making love all over the place.

It's enjoyable so why not!

A friend of mine told me a story of when she was swimming with the dolphins and she was watching three male dolphins having sex with a female dolphin. She was shocked and asked telepathically to the female dolphin if she was okay with this.

This female dolphin came right over to her and looked her in the eye, then swam over to a male dolphin and had sex with him. She then went to another male dolphin and had sex with him.

Enough said.

My friend then realized how she was projecting her thoughts and beliefs onto these dolphins that these male dolphins were taking advantage of the female dolphin.

Fascinating, right?

I have some past life memories of living in the cowboy days, being a woman, and running a "cat house." I can remember how fun it was and how we loved the cowboys that came to visit us.

It's all perspective.

Going back to my dream that I had on 12/21/12.

This is the winter solstice and a very powerful time of energies coming onto the planet. It is usually a three day window. There are two equinoxes and two solstices throughout the year and have been celebrated by the ancient cultures including the pagan and goddess cultures because of the openings that happen. They are still celebrated today and sometimes, they are known as portal days.

Dreams are just other dimensions where we play out consciousness and create. Perhaps this dream was an infusing of love energy back into the Earth. The gods and goddesses coming together all over the world.

Literally and figuratively.

CHAPTER 67
HIS REALIZATION

Find something that makes you happy and fixate on it. That is the answer to all things.
It's the answer to getting everything that you want.
~Abraham-Hicks

I have always loved to do things with my kids.
It's the best.
They are always cracking me up and being so silly.

Going camping with other families was always so fun. We would go a few times a year. We were planning a trip to go camp at the beach with two other families for about five days.

We got everything packed up and were planning on leaving the following day. Sometimes the "dads" came and sometimes they didn't. We moms got used to doing things with the kids on our own while the dads either stayed at home or worked.

Bruce wanted his down time to rest and relax, so we had been doing a lot of things on our own. He didn't want to deal with kids or chaos. Plus, he didn't like the beach or camping. We were getting ready to leave in the motorhome and meet up with the other families when Danny, who was ten, found out that his dad wasn't coming again.

In frustration, he says, "Why don't dads come and have fun, too?! What is wrong with them?"

Surprised at his outburst, I hadn't really thought about the dads not coming and how it feels for boys. I can only imagine what boys think and wonder about men not being there. They are looking for role models as they grow up and how to be a man. I could feel that Danny didn't want to be the one home and not having fun.

I told Danny that sometimes the dads had to work or sometimes they were tired. I reminded him though, "You can be whatever kind of dad that you want to be when you have kids."

And with that, he went off to play with his sister.
Interesting the roles we play.
We can change them at any time!

CHAPTER 68
DOLPHINS

Joy does not come from what you do, it flows into what you do and thus into this world from deep within you.
~Eckhart Tolle

I was drawn to swim with dolphins for some time now. If I would have followed my heart and not tried to please my dad, I would have stayed in college at USD and never transferred to USC.

I loved going to school in San Diego and what I really loved was Sea World. It was the animals there and I wanted to be a marine biologist or something that would allow me to be with dolphins, whales, and such. I wanted to work at Sea World and be in the water with the orcas, dolphins, and seals. This dream was discarded to become a doctor as I thought it would please my dad and also fulfill my need to help others.

My dad didn't think you could make much money working with sea life, so I followed his opinions and transferred to USC. Funny how we don't always follow our heart's desires and instead follow somebody else's opinion of what is good for us.

Especially with our parents.

I didn't think much about dolphins and such after leaving USD and somehow turned that part of me off until I had kids. I dove headfirst into the matrix of this world and became quite entangled in it.

Going to Sea World with my kids when they were really little began to spark my love again for these ocean beings. I have always loved the ocean and loved swimming in it. Body surfing was always so much fun.

I remember walking by a sign at Sea World that said you can swim with dolphins.

What?

I saw people in the water with dolphins and they were touching them. My soul wanted to do this now! My kids were only two and six years old and couldn't swim with dolphins until they were ten. I would have to wait eight years before I could do this with both of them, I told myself.

Hmmm…
Funny how I put limits on myself.
Why didn't I just go in myself!?

I didn't think much about it after that. Two years later, my close friend, Linda, moved from San Diego to Hawaii. We went to visit her and her family on Oahu over the summer. She asked if we wanted to swim with dolphins in the wild.

Whuuut?
Ummm…
YES!

We go out on a dolphin boat tour and I am so excited to see them that I can hardly contain myself. My husband and kids are with me, as well as my friend Linda and her three girls. Everyone is excited to see the dolphins.

Suddenly, I see them!
There are in a bay.
Yes!

The boat captain has us get in and we see the dolphins way below us. We see a larger pod and they are swimming fast. I am just so grateful to be with them in their environment. We get in with them a couple more times, but they are on the move.

Something just felt right about being with them. I had no idea how deep my relationship with them really was at that time.

A couple months go by after this experience and I was looking around in a spiritual store. I found the used book section. I was looking at different books to see what resonated and this dolphin book falls out. It is a book by Joan Ocean called *Dolphins into the Future*.

Well, I like dolphins, so I buy it.

I had no idea how reading this book would begin to remind me of things I always knew existed. It reminded me of magical experiences I had as a child and I began expanding my consciousness more. Joan talked about how the dolphins showed her sacred geometry and other worlds under the water. She continued with stories about extraterrestrials, teleporting, and spaceships. Joan even realized that the dolphins are ETs since they don't live on land!

Joan spoke about how the dolphins are masters of shifting dimensions with frequency. There are many stories of people swimming with wild dolphins when suddenly, the dolphins just disappear. Sometimes, you can hear them and they sound close, but they stay invisible. Are they just in another dimension or are they in an underwater spaceship?!

I was not very far into the book when I just knew I needed to look this woman up on the internet and see if Joan did seminars.

Turns out she does!

So, I book the next seminar she has which is all about teleporting and time jumping. She teaches, leads meditations, and we also swim with wild dolphins. I can hardly wait as it is four months away.

I arrive on the Big Island of Hawaii where she leads her seminars and I feel like I am home. When I landed, I heard in my head, "Welcome home!"

I am confused because I am a California girl.
Always have been and I love California.
What is happening?!

We are on the boat at the seminar for the first day to find wild dolphins and I am so excited! We see humpback whales breaching and swimming as we go out to sea.

So majestic.

We find dolphins and there is a large pod of them swimming by. We all get in and they are close. I see one with a leaf on its pec fin.

Fun!

I had heard about the leaf game from Joan's book. She described how the dolphins love to take a leaf they find and carry it around on their fin or tail. Then, they drop it for you or another dolphin and you grab it. Then, you do the same. And on it goes!

As the dolphin with the leaf on its fin swims by me, I think to myself, "You have a leaf! Do you want to play the leaf game!?"

The dolphin keeps swimming and suddenly turns towards me, dropping the leaf close to me!

Oh my goddess!
They are telepathic!

I dive down to get the leaf and the dolphin comes back to get it just as I go to grab it. I start giggling. This game goes on for some time and I feel how intelligent they are. Do you think they play this game with us as they adjust our frequencies to what we are wanting to heal or know in our life?

Perhaps!
They are just so much fun.

Dolphins are really amazing and they never truly sleep. They can shut off half of their brain to rest while the other half is still awake and their body swims. Dolphins seem to be living in constant joy and play while they make their amazing sonar sounds reminding us who we are. There are many stories of people swimming with dolphins who wanted something healed and the dolphins helped heal them.

Love them dolphins!
They are truly amazing.
I am beginning to remember more.
Dolphins have so much to teach us.
I am so glad they love swimming with humans!

CHAPTER 69
NO NEED TO BREATHE

You are water, you understand - electrified water. The elements and balance of ocean water match the blood in your human body. Humans were made from the ocean. This is one of the greatest secrets of creation.
~Barbara Marciniak

I am on the boat and we are swimming with dolphins. It is still my first dolphin seminar and we are in a place that some locals call "ET Bay." We have been swimming with dolphins for what seems like hours.

I am just so happy.

There are hundreds of them. They are playing and I am diving down spinning with them. I love their eye contact as I feel like it takes me to other worlds and dimensions.

I know them.

At some point, I get tired and begin to just stay more at the surface and watch them. I notice lights spinning and flickering all around as I have no thoughts in my head. Becoming mesmerized by these lights, I just start to spin around with them. I wonder if this is light from the sun coming down or if this is light coming up from the bottom of the ocean.

I continue this for some time.
It is just so peaceful.

Then, three dolphins surface close to me and one makes eye contact with me.

I hear her say, "Dive down with us."
I reply, "I'm tired."
She repeats again while they begin to dive down, "Dive down with us."
I reply, "I'm really tired."

Once more, she says, "Dive down with us."

Not thinking anymore, I invert myself and dive down after them. I mermaid kick my way down while equalizing my ears. They just keep diving and diving. At a certain point, I realize that I need to breathe and need to return to the surface.

I see the same dolphin who told me to dive down, turn to look up at me. She says, "Dive deeper with us."

My body just responds.
There is no thought.
I dive deeper and deeper with the dolphins.

I am not exactly sure what happened next, but suddenly I am feeling euphoric. I feel total bliss and one with everything. No words could describe what I was feeling as it was incredible.

Dolphins were everywhere. There were hundreds of them spinning in circles at the bottom.

I am in Heaven.

Now, I have no idea how long I was down there, but eventually I had the thought, "I should have to breathe!?"

In that instant, I found myself back on the surface of the water.

Yeh.
No words.
I had a headache for two days after this.
What happened?!

What did they show me?
Humans don't need to breathe at a certain level in the ocean?
I was in a spaceship?!
Mind blown!

CHAPTER 70
SEX IS FOR WOMEN, TOO?

It is important to speak your truth, not to convince anyone else of it. Everyone must make up their own minds.
~Barbara Marciniak

I had a powerful best friend in seventh grade. We had been friends since sixth grade and we just connected as long lost buddies.

Ya know those friends you just connect with instantly like you have known them your whole life or maybe past life?

Yep.
I love it when those people come into our lives.

Her name was Renee Brown and she was an only child being raised by her divorced mother. Her dad wasn't in the picture. We were on the volleyball team together and our team was pretty good. We hung out at school, after school, and sometimes on the weekends. My mom liked her too, which was great.

Renee seemed older for her age. She just knew things and stood up for herself. I never saw her back down. Perhaps, it is because her mom taught her early on or maybe that is just who Renee was. She had so much self confidence.

One time, we were getting ready for a volleyball game and we had a break before it started. Renee and I went out to the parking lot to get something out of the bus. On our way, we ran into one of our guy friends, Jamie, who came to watch the game. He was in seventh grade, too.

Now, realize that we are only twelve years old and think we know everything.

He was talking about kissing and dating girls with us. I was just listening as it was really a conversation between Renee and him. Renee was countering everything he was saying and I was getting a good sex education from them. My parents hadn't talked to me about sex whatsoever.

Then came a point that I will never forget.

"Women have to have sex with men even though women don't like it at all. Sex is really for men." Jamie says.

Renee retorts, "Are you kidding me? Who told you that? That is stupid. Sex is just as much for women as it is for men. They both want to have sex because it feels good."

How does she know this?
I wonder...

"Well, most women don't like it because it doesn't feel good for them." Jamie responds.

"Jamie, you have no idea what you are talking about, so just shut up. I feel sorry for the woman who ever decides to have sex with you." Renee says abruptly ending this conversation.

Renee and I walk away laughing and I am taking in all the information.

I will never forget this conversation in the parking lot before my volleyball game as what sat with me most is that sex is also for women.

It makes me wonder what I thought back then with all the messages of sex around what was right or not. I found Playboy pictures of naked women all over the streets while riding my bike around when I was eight. Could I have thought sex was just for men?

By the time I was fourteen and in ninth grade, I felt I already knew everything about sex. My mom finally asked me one night before going to a dance if I wanted to talk about sex.

"Oh hell no!" I thought in my head. I didn't want an ounce of her opinions about sex in my head.

"No, mom, I'm good. I already know everything," I stated.

She looked relieved.

"Okay, well, you can always ask me questions if you need to," she replied.

Dodged that bullet!

It wasn't until my junior year in high school when my dad told me about sex. He was driving a friend of mine, Ellie, and I back from a soccer game. He started off by telling us that he knows we both have boyfriends and are having sex.

He was right.

We both start giggling and he asks if they are good in bed. He doesn't wait for us to answer and goes on saying that we should never be with a man that doesn't make us have an orgasm.

I know we are probably both beat red, but he doesn't skip a beat.

"Okay, well, so tell your boyfriends that women take longer to orgasm then men. Women need foreplay to get them aroused. Men are just ready to go. Women need to be kissed and touched before they just have sex," he states.

Ellie and I are listening intently and totally embarrassed at the same time.

He continues, "So, tell your boyfriends that they need to think about other things besides sex so they don't cum so fast. They can think of baseball and which players are on which bases. This allows you to have an orgasm before they do."

I will never forget this car ride home. We asked him questions eventually and I learned so much. I remember asking him what oral sex is and he was just not embarrassed at all.

I love that about my dad.
It showed me that sex is just a natural and normal part of life.
It's playtime for adults.

And he wanted to make sure that women get to have fun, too.

CHAPTER 71
HOMELESS ANGELS

We have the power to choose, moment by moment, who and how we want to be in the world.
~Dr. Jill Bolte Taylor

You gotta love the underdogs.
Well, at least I do.

I worked on the "Avenue" for years and I loved it. It was full of color and excitement. People walked and knew each other. Many races were there from blacks to Hispanics to Asians to whites.

And lots of homeless people.

I loved the homeless people. They were funny and amusing even when they weren't. We got to know them by name and we would run calls on many of them usually for them being drunk, overdosed, or fighting.

So much judgment in calling them "homeless" people.
They were still people.

The homeless were all over where I worked. From the river bottom, to the Avenue, to the beach, and into downtown. They slept in the bushes, the river bottom, under freeways overpasses, or just wherever they passed out.

One guy was named Mike and he was only twenty-eight, but looked like he was fifty. He would always talk to us and was amusing. Then, he would ask us for money for beer. He was very upfront about it.

Then, there was Paula who was an amazing piano player. You would see her on the streets and we would yell, "Hey Paula!" She would flip us off and tell us to "Fuck off!" We would laugh as whenever we tried to talk to her, it was always a slur of obscenities.

Scott was another homeless guy that I got to meet many times and he told me that he knew the real story of the assassination of JFK. He would go on and on telling me his theory. I was always so fascinated and wondered if there was some truth to it all.

Others would talk to themselves out loud all day having conversations with invisible beings.

I loved to get to know the homeless people. There is just something about them. I was so curious about their stories on how they got to where they were now. This one guy, Ben, always seemed so sad. He was quiet and kept to himself. We would never run calls on him. One day, I was running on the beach for workout and I stopped to talk to him.

He was a nice guy and I eventually asked him how he came to be homeless.

He said, "My wife and kids died in a car accident and I could never bring myself to be part of society again. So, here I am."

Damn.

I vowed to never judge another from that moment on.
You just never know what someone has had to deal with in their lives.
We are so quick to judge and blame another.

And how can I forget Georgia. She was a native American who was always drunk and would come by the fire station. She had no front teeth and was always so funny.

My captain, Jay, would invite her in sometimes and give her clothes and money. He had such a big heart and loved the homeless. I think most of us did if we worked at this Avenue station. Lots of other firefighters couldn't stand the homeless and didn't want to work there.

There was Sparrow River close by and many of the homeless lived there. They made their own camps and rules. Sometimes fugitives lived there, as well as Vietnam war vets. When arguments broke out, the homeless would kill each other and bury the bodies there. They had their own laws. Other times, they would light each other's camps on fire and we would have to go put these fires out.

And sometimes, we had to carry out injured or sick homeless people out long distances to get them to the hospital.

Often, I would see homeless begging for money. I would always say "hello" and sometimes give them money. Knowing they probably used it for alcohol or drugs, I still hoped maybe they would use it for food. Sometimes, I did just give them food.

But, who I am to judge how they use their money?

Everyone is learning their own lessons in this life.

When my kids were little, they would ask about a homeless man or woman that they saw. They would ask what happened or who they were. We would talk about it and then I would give them money to give to the homeless person.

One time, we were going into a large department store and a homeless man was outside sitting on a bench. He looked tired and beat up. I had seen him there a few times. This time, my kids were ages five and eight. They were asking what his name was and why he was there.

I said, "I don't know his name. I don't know why he is homeless. Sometimes, it's because life had been tough for them, they have been traumatized in wars, or they have a hard time with society. Let's ask him."

So off we went and I gave them money to give him as well. We approached him and I said, "Hi! My kids and I were talking about you."

He looked up, "All bad I am sure."

"No. We were wondering what your name was and why you are down on your luck," I answered.

He looked shocked.

"My name is Frank," he responded and smiled at the kids.

He had a sweet smile. We smiled back and gave him some money.

"Alright, Frank. Great to meet you. We will see you again later," I said.

And with that, we walked away smiling. I didn't want to probe into his life too much so I left it at that.

Ya know what's crazy?
I never saw him ever again.
And I had been seeing him for a couple months in front of that store.

I wondered what happened to him.

A couple of months later, I told the story to my friend who was a medium. She told me that many angels disguise themselves as homeless people.

Fascinating.
Really?

Did Frank leave his body and go back to his angel body?

Are they there for us to do nice things for them?
What was that experience really all about?
So many questions!

CHAPTER 72
OUT OF BODY AND IN THE COSMOS

First there was a distinct rumbling sound, then a roaring explosion, followed by a brilliant flash of light. I felt as though my body was turning inside out, ejecting me in the process. The explosion of light pulsed like a freight train up the center front of me, hit my brain, and kept right on going, carrying me into what looked like the depths of outer space."
~*Penny Kelly*

So, I read this book called *The Magdalen Manuscript: The Alchemies of Horus and The Sex Magic of Isis* by Tom Kenyon and Judy Sion where he describes communicating with Mary Magdalen from the Jesus days. His channeling of her is written down and she describes a time where she learned the ancient ways through sex in remembering the bigger picture of everything.

She describes a few different techniques in this book. My thoughts are going crazy as I read it and I am so curious. What, if anything, will happen? I felt drawn to practice these techniques.

You can do these practices by yourself or with a partner.
And yes, I am talking about sex.
Becoming aroused.
Masturbation.
Making love.

Mary Magdalen, in her book, describes a time when there was sacred sex. There were temples that taught about how sex was used to regenerate and increase one's light body. This was a time when goddess cultures dominated the world. Then, they were destroyed by the dysfunctional patriarchal cultures we have today.

I practiced the techniques by myself for some time and then asked my husband if he wanted to try something with me.

The conversation goes something like this...

"Do you want to make love tonight?" I ask Bruce.

"Sure!" he replies.

"Sweet. Do you want to try something new?" I question him.

"Oh fuck yes!" he excitedly answers.

"Okay. Well, I have been reading this book and it talks about how sex is a gateway to the universe. The book says how sex helps us to regenerate and remember everything."

I then go on to explain how to focus your energy and to bring it up to the center of our brains in the pineal gland area. I talk to him about how the energy is snakelike in it moving up our bodies. This is a much abbreviated version of it all that I hope he will understand.

He looks dumbfounded and confused.

Ummm...

"Well, how about while we make love, you just focus your energy on you and paying attention to the energy in the pineal area of your head?" I say generalizing the technique.

"Done," he agrees.

I begin by moving the energy up from my root chakra up to my pineal gland. I focus on my breathing and how everything feels as he begins to touch me. We are kissing, loving, and touching each other gently. We are now lying in bed together and removing clothing as we continue to caress and fondle each other. I continue to bring the energy up through my body.

Kissing my body all over, he begins to go down on me and is giving me oral sex when I begin to orgasm.

I keep orgasming and orgasming while focusing on my pineal gland when suddenly, I see us rocketing through the universe and we are inside the Great Pyramid of Giza. I know we are there and that the sounds coming out of me are opening more and more. I can see lights going up and down from the stars and the Earth.

As we made love, I saw us on a slab or altar inside the pyramid. We continued to make love and I could feel the Godhead. We were one with everything. More sounds kept coming out of me and I consciously let go saying "Yes" to whatever was coming.

I then heard, "Isis and Osiris" and saw a group of people chanting in a circle around us as we made love. Then I heard, "Horus."

I could feel myself completely out of my body flying through the cosmos in another world.

Then, I see us in a large grove of big green trees which reminds me of Ireland and the Celtic times. We once again are surrounded by a group of people who are chanting while we are making love in the middle of the circle.

It feels so sacred and powerful.

Sounds kept coming out of me. Sounds I never knew that I could make. The sound was deafening. I could see all this light going into our Earth and up to the stars and back and forth.

I could see everything.
I knew everything.
It was pure bliss.

Somehow, I came back into my body as we continued orgasming together. We laid there connected to everything for what seemed like eternity. I felt like I couldn't see out of my eyes. I had this feeling of ecstasy and bliss. I was so grateful for all.

Eventually, Bruce rolled over and we laid there still in bliss. I finally was able to speak and said, "I think we were in the Great Pyramid in Egypt, Ireland, and all over the universe. We became one with everything. There is really no words."

"I believe it. It was incredible!" He says as he falls deeply asleep.

I laugh.
I am still in awe of what I just experienced.
My body is buzzing, pulsing, and awake.
I am totally electrified.

I thank the universe for the experience as I replay it over and over in my mind. I don't want to forget this. I begin to fall asleep after some time when I hear, "Get up and write this down!"

"I don't want to get up," I reply to the voice.

"Write this down!" I hear again.
"Okay!" I telepathically say still not wanting to move.

This goes on for probably another fifteen minutes before I finally get up, find a pen and paper to write this all down. Back to bed and I sleep deeply. Suddenly, maybe one or two hours later, I am awakened by this light being on the side of my bed.

I stare and can feel the love coming from this being. Telepathically, the being says to me, "We, thank you for recharging the Earth's energy grid," I stare and then the being is gone.

Somehow, I know that this being is from the inner Earth. I know we were working with the Earth's energy as we made love.

Is this what happens when we consciously make love, bringing our energies up to meet the Divine? Is this the power within each human being that we aren't taught about? I know the human being is meant to unfold and evolve.

I have so many questions.

The church teaches how sex is bad or how sex is only for reproducing. Do they know that we may stumble upon this power? Is this what the goddess cultures taught? Were men threatened by this power and somehow turned it against women calling them prostitutes for this sacred sexuality? Can sex be used as a weapon and turned against us?

Yes, it can.

Was Mary Magdalen deeply in touch with the Divine and helped Jesus increase his light body through sex? Is this what helped him resurrect after the crucifixion? Were the other disciples jealous of her powers and made her out to be a prostitute?

What is the real truth here?
I don't know, but I know I stumbled onto something incredibly powerful that night.

It was 9/11/2014.
Somehow it felt as if this date was important.
Did this happen to shift the energies from 9/11/2001?
From the dark energy that happened thirteen years ago to light energy?

I know in numerology that 9 is completion, 11 is illumination, and 13 is typically associated with the goddess.

Hmmm....

CHAPTER 73
THE FIRE BEING

In every walk with nature one receives far more than he seeks.
~John Muir

Fire!
So radiant.
So powerful.
So destructive.

And so damn hot!

It would be many years after my first fire before I began talking to fire and realizing that she is alive.

A being.
The fire being.
She has a consciousness.
She isn't bad as I had been led to believe.

Who are you?
Why do you destroy everything?
You are so magical.
So majestic.
I see you.

These are the thoughts and questions that I began to ask in my mid-thirties.

What I didn't realize when I first became a firefighter is that fire has a bigger purpose connected to the whole. It keeps the Mother Earth in balance and transforms energies. I was taught that fire was the enemy and was very destructive. We did everything we could even risking our own lives to put fires out.

I found that I loved fighting fire. I loved the adrenaline rush and it was almost the part of us versus them. It was like we were at war and fire was the enemy. We were the "good" guys putting fire out and saving people.

There are so many fires of all types that I had been on before ever seeing a bigger picture as to what fire was doing. Big fires, little fires, and everything in between. I put fires out in homes, businesses, hospitals, dumpsters, cars, trucks, semi-trucks, trees, brush, etc…

Just about anything you can imagine, I have put water on it.

It wasn't until I was a fire captain with about ten years on the fire service that I began to see a bigger picture. My crew and I were on a brush fire and we were protecting fields of avocado trees from the fire because the crop was worth thousands of dollars. The fire was "cooking" pretty good and we had about four crews with us trying to keep a big break in between the fire and the avocado trees.

The fire was advancing quickly and then, we ran out of hose.

I told some of the firefighters to run back to get more hose which would take at least ten minutes. I stayed and monitored the fire's progress. It was moving up and away from the avocado trees now and I gave the incident commander a progress report as to what the fire was doing.

Standing far back in the avocado trees, I watched the fire engulf some large brush, grass, and trees. Fire is really so beautiful. She is so magical, majestic, and mesmerizing that I just stared. I watched the way she danced, spiraled, and twisted consuming everything in her path.

I backed up more because I was getting hot!

I began to wonder about fire and what she is really doing.
I decided to talk to her and to see what she would say.
Something was telling me to ask her.

Now, I haven't always thought about myself as psychic, but really we all are. I have been nurturing these gifts within myself once again and they are getting stronger. There are many psychic sensitivities that correspond to the senses of seeing, hearing, feeling, smelling, tasting, touching, and knowing. Another way to say this is: clairvoyant, clairaudient, clairsentient, clairscent, clairtangency, clairgustance, and claircognizance.

It is tapping into other information that our "normal" senses don't pick up and sometimes called our "sixth sense."

For me, my psychic gifts that have always been strong is feeling and knowing. I feel and know when someone or something is speaking truth or if it is true for me. It is like an energy that will run through my whole being giving me "goose bumps." Also, I just seem to "know" things.

I would like to be more clairvoyant and clairaudient. So, I have been working on opening those up more, but sometimes I feel like I am just imagining the whole thing. It's like I am making it all up and I begin to think that I am crazy!

As I have been playing with these gifts for some time now, I have come to realize that "imagining" is an ability that is a major clairvoyant tool. I have come to honor it and realize that it is real. Imagination is powerful and this is what we do when are creating in our own reality. Children do this all the time until they are told that it isn't real by the adults in their life.

Having learned to "clear my mind," I can ask within myself and get the answers to what it is I seek most of the time.

Talk about empowering!
To not give my power away?!
Then, to trust what I receive.
Still working on it all!

Anyways, I wonder if the fire will speak with me and what she will say...

Never thinking of fire as having a consciousness, I always seemed to see fire as destructive and an enemy. Fire was something to stop or extinguish because it was destroying homes or the environment. Just then, the fire began to engulf a large tree and the flames coming off it were massive. Still no signs of my firefighters with more hose, so I went back to attempting to communicate with the fire.

Telepathically, I said to the fire, "Fire, you are so beautiful. Really you are. So powerful. Yet, you are so destructive. Why do you destroy so much? Why do you burn up everything in your path?"

I was so drawn into the fire, feeling as if she was consuming me.
I felt as if I became one with the fire.
I could feel how powerful fire is.
She is pure, raw power.

I heard in my head, "Look deeper than what you see."

So, I took a deep breath asking within myself to be shown and to understand what the fire is trying to tell me.

The fire spoke again, "You believe that we are bad. Truly, we just follow energy. We consume old energy that is ready for transformation. We alchemize stuck energies. We keep the Earth in balance."

I stood there shocked as to what I heard.
I saw how all of life is death and rebirth.
The Phoenix!

A flurry of fires that I had been on in the past, now rolled through my head.
I could now see what fire was actually doing.
I could see fire was actually doing good.
The fire being was removing old, stuck energy that we humans held onto.

Some fires were destroying old buildings that had old, yuck energies in them from drug addicts and homeless. Other fires were old, dead brush that needed fire to actually help new brush grow.

One fire call that sticks out was a house where the garage was on fire. It destroyed the whole garage and we were able to "save" the house. The woman that owned it told me after the fire was out, "You know, my husband died a year ago. All his things that I just couldn't bear to go through were in the garage. Now, the fire destroyed it all. Maybe it is my husband telling me to move on now."

Wow.

Was this spirit trying to get her to let go and move on?
Was this her husband's spirit asking her to let him go?
I had other calls like this and they rang out loudly in my head.

I saw homes that were full of belongings and people who just couldn't throw stuff away because of attachments. The fire consumed everything. Some fires destroyed a whole house.

More alchemy.
Fire is good.
We see it as bad.
Fire is transforming old energy.
We have lost touch with its powerful essence.

It is like Pele, the volcano goddess, in Hawaii who is celebrated by the Hawaiians. If the lava begins flowing in the direction of a house, the Hawaiians open their house and invite her in. They know she is transforming old, dense energies.

We have forgotten our connection to nature. Humans have forgotten that we are to work together with nature as part of the whole, not to dominate it. We don't understand her because we have forgotten that Earth herself is a living being with a consciousness. Mother Nature will destroy us unless we come into a conscious relationship with her.

The Earth is a sacred space.
The elements are great conscious beings.
Mother Gaia is a very alive being.
Connect with all of them!

As I write this, it also reminds me of when I spoke with the Sun, our huge fireball in the sky. I said telepathically one day to the Sun, "I love and appreciate you, Sun."

I heard the Sun reply back as a multitude of beings, "You're beautiful, Hydee."

I asked what to call him and I heard, "El Sol."

I thought about this for a moment. El Sol is Spanish for "the sun." Yet, something about just the name with Sol or Soul. It was almost like my soul was speaking to me or is this Source? Same thing?

"What do you want us to know?" I asked El Sol.

"Do not be so afraid of me. I give you rays from the cosmos," El Sol replied.

El Sol was going down over the horizon and into the ocean, so I blew him a kiss and said, "Goodnight, El Sol. Thank you for all you do and I will see you tomorrow."

With that, I saw a green flash as he ducked below the ocean.
I love El Sol.

When I layout on the beach, I consciously bring in the sun's energy into my body when I breathe in and when I breathe out. I consciously send the energy to all my cells and into my light body to energize it. Sometimes, when I feel that I have had enough, I bring the sun's energy into my being and send it back out my heart to El Sol with love.

I even ask the sun to only give me the perfect amount of the sun's rays for my body, so I don't get burned. In turn, I ask my body to only take in the perfect amount of the sun's energy.

All we have to do is ask.

Fascinating to think how many people are afraid of the sun and his rays. Sunblock is constantly pushed onto us and saying the sun causes cancer.

Really?
I don't think so.
Perhaps it is the sunblock's toxic chemicals?

El Sol is giving us life.
Think of all the cultures that have worshipped the sun.
Our pineal glands are reset when we watch sunsets and sunrises.
This is our antennae to Source.
Is there another agenda here?

Anyways, when I was a kid in the seventies, we never wore sunblock. We slathered on oil and got really brown. Perhaps, we need the sun as it gives us vitamin D and fills our cells with energy. If we get too much sun, we can cover up with clothes or a hat.

Imagine that!
It is us humans that are out of balance.
We stopped communicating with nature and consciousness itself.
She is always listening to us, but we stopped listening to her.

Anyways, back to the fire...

I stood in front of the magnificent fire being as she engulfed a row of trees.

Feeling honored to hear fire speak to me, I apologize to the fire for misunderstanding her purpose and the bigger picture. I send the fire love and respect from the depth of my soul. Time to shift my beliefs around what I was taught about fire.

I realize how deeply I love fire.
Fire and I are deeply connected.
It is part of my soul.

Perhaps I am deeply connected to all the elements?
What does Earth, air, water, and fire want to say?

I need to speak with them more.

We humans have forgotten. The elements want to work together with us. They need to know what we need and we need to know what they need. The elements and elementals are waiting for us to reconnect. We are all on this planet together.

Now, I wonder how I can be a firefighter and how I can connect to the bigger picture of what fire is doing. I decide I will talk to the fire on any call I go on, so that we can work together.

Thank you, beautiful fire being.
Continue to allow me to hear you and to remember more.
To allow you to consume and know when to extinguish.
Ignite your passion inside my being.

Just then, the guys come back with more hose and the game continues...

CHAPTER 74
THE CALL OF THE WHALES

The sea, once it casts its spell, holds one in its net of wonder forever.
~Jacques Cousteau

I have always loved whales, but hadn't really thought much about them. My parents took me on a whale watching trip when I was four years old. This was probably the last time that I remember really being with them until I signed up for the dolphin seminar in Hawaii.

About a month before I left for the dolphin seminar, I had my first session with a sound healer. I didn't know much about sound healing except that it called to me. The sound healer's name was Mary. She had great energy and was very sweet.

I got on the table and closed my eyes. She was going to play some music and then move to sound bowls and tuning forks. I was open to all of it. The music began and it was mellow. Then, whale sounds came on intermixed with the music.

It was humpback whales.
My whole body vibrated and I had no thoughts.
Tears came flooding in.
Somehow, my body had deep memories and I began to sob.
I know these beings.
They are calling me from somewhere deep inside myself.

Whales?
Was it the dolphins calling me back into the ocean or the whales?
Was it Mother ocean calling me?
Perhaps all of them.

I was all about the ocean and loved her deeply. It was very much home and always inviting to me. Body surfing and swimming in the ocean was always my favorite. I hadn't been in her as much as I wanted lately. I tried surfing and paddle boarding a few times and loved them, but I would rather just be immersed in her.

I loved being by the ocean.

The dolphin seminar came and I loved being with the dolphins and in the water. The first day on the water though, the captain took us to the whales. I was so excited!

The whales were breeching out of the water. They were jumping and playing. Coming close to the boat. I wanted to be in the water with them and hear their sounds, but in Hawaiian waters, you aren't allowed to swim with them.

Whales!

The week with the dolphins was incredible, but something had awakened deep in my soul around the whales.

Their sounds.
It's unlocking things inside me.

The intelligence of the dolphins and whales is incredible and they are supersensory beings. They have much to teach us and to remind us of who we truly are. It is time for humans to join the galactic community by stepping into our power. Human DNA is actually more similar to cetaceans than to the apes.

We came from the ocean.

I found that I loved going to see Mary and experience sound healings with her. She used sound bowls, tuning forks, her voice, and her intuition. I found myself going about every three weeks to have a session with her.

We would play and experiment together how sound affected me. Every session was so different and they were always so expansive. One time, I felt myself expand and expand as I merged with the cosmos. The session ended and when I began to come back, I stayed expanded. I felt like I was Mother Earth encompassing everything. It was like I was the Earth with my head sticking out on top of the globe. This lasted for hours.

What is it about sound?
It is said that the universe was first spoken into being.
Every sound creates as it is powerful.

Just listen to the bird songs. They sing every morning and throughout the day. The plants, trees, insects, and animals respond to their sounds. Flowers open and close to certain sounds. If there were no birds, we wouldn't have our beautiful nature to admire or even food to eat. Everything works together in communication.

What about sound stopping time?

In the book, *Dolphins into the Future* by Joan Ocean, she tells a story about when she was in a bookstore looking at a book by John Lily. There was music playing in the store and she didn't like it. She moved her consciousness away from it and continued looking at the book when suddenly a tone went off in the music. She looked up and noticed everyone was frozen in position, not moving. The music continued to play and she looked around at everyone. Then, another tone played and everyone became animated again.

What is that?
Stopping time with sound?
Is that like pushing pause on a movie?
We are in a movie.
Why did that happen?

There is something about time travel and teleporting that excites my soul. I love this stuff.

Andy Basiago is a man who claims that he has time traveled and teleported. He was a child back in the late sixties and early seventies where he worked on *Project Pegasus* with his dad who was a higher up in the military. *Project Pegasus* was a time-space exploration program and they used kids with special powers in this program. Andy could levitate his toys and was telepathic.

Andy didn't remember any of this until he was an adult and his dad was on his death bed. His dad reminded him saying to Andy to tell the world about the capabilities of teleporting and time travel that the military has. Being in shock, Andy began remembering all he was involved in like his "jumps" to Mars and traveling back in time to hear the Gettysburg Address in 1863. He even has pictures to show he was there.

Just so amazing.
I just know it is real.

Time is just a grouping of specific frequencies in one location. Imagine if you could go back and forth to that frequency and gather whatever you needed in that time. Would you ever need to reincarnate? You could learn so much in the body you are in just going back and forth in time.

Imagine having teleportation stations in New York where you go into one stargate and come out in another in Los Angeles or Dublin or Honolulu within minutes!? This technology has been available since the 1960's!

It's all frequency.
We can go to locations by frequency.
Wow.

Let's go back to sound, although this is all related…

Our ancient ancestors knew about sound and many sacred sites have been shown to be engineered for sound like the Great Pyramid of Giza. I wonder if they used sound for healing and teleporting to other realms? Perhaps we are still way too primitive to understand the power of sound since we still go around killing each other.

What are the whales reminding me about?
Their sounds vibrate the cells of my whole being.
They say that whales are the "record keepers" of our Earth's history.
I just love them.

Anyways, on the last day of the dolphin seminar, I have three people ask me if I will be going on the whale seminar in the Dominican Republic the following year. I initially said "No" the first time. The second time, I said, "Maybe." Then, the third time, a woman looked me deep in the eyes and asked if I would come to the whale seminar. She said it would be life changing. I responded to her with a probable "Yes."

Something about being asked three times.
It is always a sign for me.

I went home knowing I had a week to decide as this whale seminar fills up fast. I asked my husband if he wanted to go and he said "No." Then my son, Danny says, "I want to go with you, Mom."

I am surprised by this.
He's eleven and mature for his age.
Something inside me knows he needs to go.
Let's do it!
We're going next year!

CHAPTER 75
ROLL OUT THE RED CARPET

Acknowledging the good that you already have in your life is the foundation for all abundance.
~Eckhart Tolle

It's a little after midnight when a call comes in. I am fast asleep as are the other firefighters when I hear the dispatcher's voice come over the speaker.

"Engine 4. Respond to a birth in progress. Cord around the baby's neck." I hear this and jump out of bed while the other details come over the speaker in my room.

It is summer solstice, June 21, 2015.
As we know, solstices and equinoxes happen four times a year.
They are powerful windows of time.

I never really paid much attention to these times of the year, but our ancestors sure did. The way mother Earth shifts and how the powerful energies move for three days. Much sacredness to recognize during these portal days.

My crew and I hop on the engine and I see where the call is so that I can help guide my engineer there. We head towards the house and we can all feel the sense of urgency as our adrenaline is pumping.

I am a captain and also a paramedic. Both members of my crew are paramedics as well, but the firefighter/paramedic, Ryan, says to me, "Hydee, you being a woman and all and a mom, why don't you take the lead as paramedic?"

I laugh as I know the guys gets nervous about woman issues and childbirth calls.

"No problem, Ryan. Just help assist me." I say.
"You got it." Ryan replies.

I have assisted in helping moms deliver their babies maybe ten times over the years. Usually, it isn't the mom's first baby and the baby comes too quick to get to the hospital. Other times, it has been homeless moms in a river bottom to teenage moms who didn't know they were even pregnant to moms in premature labor. Sometimes all goes well and others not so well.

I take a deep breath and ask for guidance as we pull up to the house. Grandma meets us as we get out of the engine. You can see the look of fear in her eyes.

"Hurry, the baby's head is out and the cord is around her neck!" She says.

Never a good sign.

I head into the house while the guys grab the gear to see if I can get my fingers between the cord and the baby's neck for her to breathe while assisting in helping the baby be born. Grandma is leading the way to a back bedroom.

I walk into the bedroom and I see Mom on all fours on the bed.
There is blood and fluid everywhere.
Dad looks shocked and is crying.
He just caught his new baby girl!

I announce myself to mom and dad who I am as I walk towards them and look to see about the cord. It is around her neck, but it is not tight.

Thank Goddess!

Dad hands her to me and I slip off the cord. She isn't breathing yet. Grandma hands me a blanket and I begin to warm and dry her. She starts crying and pinking up!

"Yes! Well, that is a relief," I think to myself.

My crew is here helping as well and we clamp the cord.
We ask Dad if he wants to cut the cord.
He does.
Everyone is calming down.
This is their second baby.

Mom is still on all fours and there is blood everywhere. I go to help her and get her to turn over. I begin to clean her up and hand her this beautiful baby girl. Mom is tired and excited at the same time. She smiles and holds her baby up to her breast to nurse.

"Congratulations and good work, Mom," I say.

She smiles.
I ask them if they have a name picked out for her.

"Adelaide," Mom replies.

"Beautiful," I say in agreement.

She asks me my name. I say, "It's Hydee."

She looks at me curiously, "You know that Adelaide is Heidi (Hydee) in German, right?"

I look at her dumbfounded.

Huh?!
Coincidence?!
Synchronicity?!

I have stopped believing in coincidences and started realizing that when you are in the flow with Source, synchronicities abound. It happens everywhere and things flow smoothly. People become helpful and life is easy.

It took me quite some time to learn this as I was taught to go after what I want and keep pushing till I got what I wanted. I know having kids and questioning everything that I was taught helped me to see that there is something much bigger than myself guiding me.

Something that wants to co-create with me.
I am never alone.

Back to Adelaide…

The energy in the house is so joyous and festive. Everyone is so excited to be with this new life that has come into our world. Grandmas is so jazzed that her daughter and granddaughter are okay. Mom and Dad are ecstatic that their baby is okay and Dad wants to take pictures with us. I'm sure if he had cigars, he would be passing them out to all of us.

They have another daughter who slept through the whole thing. She is two. We load Mom up onto the gurney with baby to go to the hospital making sure they are nice and warm. The ambulance takes off for the hospital and we head back to the fire station.

My crew and I are awake and excited. We stay up for a while chatting as we all still are coming down from our adrenaline rush of so much excitement. Later, they head for bed and I am still wide awake. I decide to write the whole experience down.

I want to remember this.

After I finish writing, I am just being with the energy of this experience. I think about how it is summer solstice and how the call came in just after midnight. I think of the new soul that has just graced us with her presence. It feels like an honor to be there for her birth and I am so grateful.

The energy of appreciation and joy is all I feel.
I am on a high!

I head off to bed and am walking across past the engine when another call comes in.
Birth in process!

What?
No way.
Yes way!

And it is just down the street from our fire station.
This time, it is a baby being born in a car.
What is going on tonight?

I smile and think to myself, "What an entrance!"

I get on the engine as my crew is stumbling out of the dorms half asleep. Ryan gets on the engine and says, "What is going on? Two births in one night? Within three hours of each other? You got this one again, Cap."

He then immediately jumps off the engine before I respond and says, "Shit! I forgot to put another OB kit back on the engine!" He hurriedly gets off and grabs another one.

We head down the street as the birth is less than a block away. We see a car on the side of the road at the intersection with its hazards on and Dad is waving us down. We pull up and I know Mom is in the passenger seat either giving birth or about to give birth. Dad is at the passenger side door with Mom. The ambulance pulls up just behind us.

I walk over to Dad.
He is crying and looks shocked.
"My wife just gave birth!" He yells.

I see that he has his new baby girl in his hands. The baby seems okay and isn't breathing yet. I tell the guys to grab a blanket as we need to dry and warm her. I do this and the baby begins to cry.

Yes! We are all excited to hear this.
I say congratulations to both of them.

Dad replies, "We were on our way to the hospital with our second child when my wife told me to pull over and that she is coming now! Then, I called 911!" He continues saying, "She just came so fast!"

"You did a great job, Dad!" I reply, "And Mom, good job delivering her!"

It is pretty dark on the street and cold, so we decide to get moving into the back of the ambulance fairly quickly. We get Dad to cut the cord and he is so excited.

I ask Mom what her baby's name is.
She replies, "Julietta."
"Beautiful. Another goddess born tonight," I say.

We move Mom and baby onto the gurney and into a warm ambulance. Dad begins to calm down knowing that his wife and baby are okay. In fact, you can feel how the energy of the whole situation went from panic to ecstatic. It feels amazing. There is just nothing like the energy of a new baby being born into this world.

It's just so magical!

Dad wants to take pictures with all of us and his new baby. I again think that if he had cigars, he would be passing them around to all of us in celebration. The ambulance takes off with Mom and baby to the hospital while we say goodbye to Dad.

We head back to the station wondering how this all happened. None of us have ever been on two deliveries in one shift, much less within hours apart from each other.

I don't know how I will ever sleep tonight.
Well, it's almost morning anyways.

Something feels so magical about all of this. I decide to go to my room to just sit with this energy and meditate asking inside myself what this is all about.

I breathe deeply and just feel. I begin to see what looks to me like a red carpet being rolled out. I feel divine feminine energy in the forms of fairies, mermaids, and goddesses. They are everywhere swirling around me with excitement. It is powerful, joyous, and gentle. I can feel their appreciation.

I can feel how excited they all are and I realize that I was in the presence of two powerful goddesses coming onto this planet tonight. I can see that we were holding a light for them to come through and I feel deeply honored. I begin crying tears of joy.

I sit and revel in the energy of it all.
Thank you, Adelaide and Julietta.
I am so grateful that I could hold space for you to come through.
This planet greatly needs you.
I hope someday that I will get to meet you when you are older.

And the Goddess is alive and well...

CHAPTER 76
MY LIFE AS A WHALE

The moment you change your perception, is the moment you rewrite the chemistry of your body.
~Dr. Bruce Lipton

My grandpa on my dad's side died at a hundred and one years old. I deeply loved him and he was an inspiration to me. He was from Cuba and came over to America with his family when Castro had taken over the country. He was one of those guys who has seen and been through so much, yet he was a kid at heart.

This is really why I loved him so much.
Even though he was in an adult body, he was still just that eight year old kid at heart. As kids, my brother and I loved hanging out with him and he was always making us laugh.

So, my dad and grandpa were super close. When he died, it was really hard on my dad. They used to talk every day and I think when you go from losing everything and almost losing your family, you realize how important life is.

About three weeks after my grandpa died, I almost lost my father, too.

He got really sick with some kind of unknown lung disease and ended up in the hospital with machines breathing for him. He was too young to die. He was only sixty-eight and still so full of life.

But, his dad's death was too much for him. He was so grief stricken and sad. I know in Chinese medicine, they say that lung problems mean grief issues, emotionally speaking. My dad was sure having a hard time with all his grief.

Anyways, my dad almost died and his organs were shutting down. Everyone was shocked at what was happening. Many were praying for him and miraculously, he recovered. His recovery took a long time and he was in and out of the hospital often. I spent lots of time with him.

One day at the fire station, my firefighter started telling me about this guy, John of God, in Brazil. He went on and on about how all these people were healing when they visited this guy. People who couldn't walk, walked. People who had cancer, healed.

Miracle after miracle.

I decided to read about this guy, John of God. His story was really incredible and how when he was nineteen, Mother Mary appeared to him telling him of his mission to heal people. He has been doing this ever since.

I am curious if he ever comes to the United States and I wonder if he will see my dad as he still needs to heal his lungs. John of God does come to the United States, but only to New York.

Damn.

Continuing to look online, I find out that John of God does long distance healings. You can find someone down there who can take your request in. I wonder to myself if my dad would be open to this since he is very Christian.

One day, I am visiting my dad in the hospital and I have a book with me about John of God that I am reading. I am massaging my dad's back as he says his lungs hurt inside.

He can't talk much, so mostly I am quiet and just giving him love.
Then he asks, "What book are you reading?"

I am kinda surprised because that took a lot of effort to get out since he is having such a hard time breathing. I tell him all about John of God and the healings that he does. I even tell him that he does long distance healings.

My dad says, "I will take anything, Hydee. I just want to get better."

I am shocked and excited at the same time.

Going online, I find out how to do this. Turns out, there is a woman in Ojai, California named Debbie who takes people to visit John of God at his casa in Brazil. She also can help me get the request for my dad to him.

Sweet.

Funny how things happen, but I somehow feel that I need to meet this John of God character. I wonder if I will take my dad there for a healing, yet he is too weak. My dad does begin to get better after our healing request.

Another friend of mine tells me about John of God and it seems like many people around me are suddenly talking about him. I wonder what is going on.

One day, I wake up and I just know that I need to go to Brazil. I don't know exactly why as I don't have anything that needs to be healed, or so I think. I talk to Debbie about going with her and one of her groups to see him. She has a group going in three months.

Hmmm….

I don't totally understand why this is drawing me, but I tend to follow what feels right for me. I just trust it. Maybe I can get more healing for my dad? So, I sign up and decide to go.

And I know as I write this, there are some issues now surrounding this man named, John of God, but as I said before, I follow my heart and it feels right to go.

So, it's February 2015 and I am headed to Brazil. I have never been to South America in this lifetime yet and I am excited. It is a two-week journey with John of God. I have no idea what to expect. I have two weeks at home when I get back and then I head to swim with the whales in the Dominican Republic with my son, Danny, who is eleven. I am really excited about that trip, too!

Anyways, I arrive after a long day of travel and meet my guide, Debbie. She is sweet and has been bringing people to Brazil for many years. We have to drive two hours to Abadiania which is where the casa is. The casa is the place where John of God comes three days a week to heal people.

I am staying at a hotel close by in this small town. The group with Debbie is about eight people. They are from the United States with a couple from Canada. Everyone there has something they want healed. One woman wants her heart healed after her husband's death. Another man wants to be healed from his drug addiction. Another is partially crippled. And on and on…

I am wondering why I am here.
What do I need healed?
Maybe it's not physical, but emotional for me?

Brazil is amazing with yummy food and nice people. I see toucans and macaws flying overhead. I am amazed. It is so good to see them in their native habitat and not captive in cages or as pets. They are just so beautiful.

Abadiania is a small town and people from all over the world come to see John of God here. We have two days before the casa is open for healings. I am listening to story after story of healings and I am just amazed that I have never heard of this guy until recently. I am excited to watch him work and see what my soul wants to heal.

The day comes for us to go to the casa.

It is packed.
Hundreds of people are there with huge lines coming out the door.
I had no idea.

Lots of pictures on the walls of saints and Mother Mary's picture is up there, as well.
Something so sweet about her picture and it seems to draw me in.

Anyways, there is a system to the whole thing and lines for if you have seen John of
God before or not. He also performs some type of surgery with a dull knife in your
eye if you want that or if you want something shoved up your nose.

No thanks.
Really, I'm good.
Why would anyone ever want those options?!

So, a few hours go by and I am still waiting to see him. Many people have gone back
through this door for their visit with him and he has also done some eye and nose
surgeries in front of the crowd. Apparently, when he does these surgeries, there is no
blood and different entities work through his body. Some say that Jesus has come
through him sometimes. The energy in the place feels incredible and powerful.

I finally get to go through the door to see him and I have what I want healed written
down in Portuguese. There is still a long line waiting for him and there are many
people sitting in chairs meditating near him.

I had a translator write down that I want to have any blockages removed keeping me
from my soul's purpose and life's work. I also ask to have all my super powers back
like teleporting, flying, becoming invisible, and shapeshifting!

No big whoop.

Finally, I get to see him and he looks at me. I can see he's not there and somebody
else is in there. As he looks at me, it's like he is looking through me. He reads my
paper and doesn't at the same time. He tells the translator that I need to have a crystal
bed and then to come back.

Really?
That's it?

I am somehow disappointed, yet I didn't know what to expect. Most of the others in
my group all got psychic surgery and went back to their rooms for twenty-four hours.
This is supposed to be powerful without the physical surgeries in the regular
hospitals.

Debbie finds me and gets me set up to do a crystal bed. Turns out, I can go get one
and be back to see him in the afternoon. Yet, I realize, what is it that I really want
from this guy?

What do I expect him to do?

Dunno.

A crystal bed is where you lie on a bed and they have crystals over each one of your chakras. It is to open and clear them. I go and lay there for an hour. It feels really good and I have many visions. I am apparently now ready to see John of God again?

This time, the line is shorter and I go up to him. He now tells me to go in another line to have psychic surgery. I am excited and nervous at the same time about this. There is a larger group of us and we go and sit in pews. Once the room is full, John of God comes in and says a whole bunch of stuff in Portuguese. This lasts for maybe five minutes and we are all done. I walk outside and Debbie is waiting for me.

He could be putting spells on us for all I know, but I feel the frequency of the words and it feels good.

She says that psychic surgery is powerful. Debbie says to lay down and sleep in my room for at least twenty-four hours. I am not allowed to lift anything heavy for a few weeks. She says this is real and just like if we had regular surgery. Debbie drives me back to my room and I am tired. She says she will check on me tonight and bring me dinner. I lay down and fall fast asleep. I don't wake up until I hear a knock on the door.

It's Debbie bringing me food and checking on me.

I am hungry and want to sleep more.

I eat and then fall fast asleep again.

I don't wake up until the early hours of the morning.

When I woke up, I felt this tremendous hatred for all of humanity and a huge sadness. I found myself in total tears and I just allow myself to cry and cry.

I know this feeling as I have had it sometimes before. I have never understood it though as I love people, but I love animals more. I always thought it was because humanity does mean things to each other just because. They kill just to kill. Animals kill because they need to eat. And animals don't talk back like humans do saying nasty, hurtful things. Humans can be so cruel.

I ask deep inside myself what is going on and why I hate humanity so much.

Suddenly, I am being given a vision in my mind's eye and I see myself as a whale. I am with my pod of whales and we are being killed by humans. The ocean is turning red with our blood. There is massive killing of all of our pod. It feels like we are off the coast of Spain.

I feel my hatred for humanity and what is happening to us. I see time fast forward and I see myself incarnate into a human to understand what it means to be a human. I see myself forgetting what it was to be a whale.

The feeling of hating humanity is gone.
Totally gone.
I feel it.

I am blown away at what I am being shown and not at the same time. I know this is
where it all stems from.

I am free.
Really free.
I am free to love humanity.
To really love all of them with all their flaws.

It takes a powerful soul to want to be human.
To forget everything and then to remember.

I love the whales.
Always have.
I was once a whale!?

CHAPTER 77
TOTAL MERMAID

Most of the circuits in our brains run on automatic. The more you think a thought, the more energy goes into that circuit. Eventually it gets enough energy to run the thought automatically without us needing to put more energy into it.
~Dr. Jill Bolte Taylor

After my time swimming with dolphins for a week, I told my kids and husband all about it. I wanted to take them there someday, but Bruce wasn't open to it at all. On the other hand, Danny and Piper were ready to pack their bags and go. Kids are just so ready to have fun and enjoy new experiences. I love their spontaneity.

They were both pretty young being seven and ten. I thought maybe we could all go on a whale trip together…the four of us, but my husband shot that down again.

Water and sun just aren't his thing.
Still, it's a spiritual experience.
So powerful.

So, Danny and I went to swim with the whales which was an incredible experience. When we came back from swimming with the whales, Piper kept asking me to take her to swim with the dolphins.

"Please, Mom. I need to be there," she begged.

"Danny was eleven when I took him to the whales. When you are eleven, I will take you, Piper," I said.

She begged and pleaded that it was sooner. I held to eleven.

She forgot about the dolphins for a while. Two months later, I woke up one morning and I knew I had to take Piper to swim with the dolphins.

It had to be NOW!

I sat with this energy and thought I would see if I got more signs that this was true when in walks Piper.

"Mom, you need to take me dolphins, now. They are calling me," she says.

I sit there in shock looking at her.
This is the biggest sign ever.
She is so intuitive as to her soul needs.

I look online to find out when the next seminar is and it is only four months away. I call them and they say it is okay to bring an eight year old.

Here we go!

Piper is so jazzed as we head for Hawaii for ten days. We will be spending six of those days in the seminar and four of those days will be swimming with dolphins. There are about twenty-five people in the seminar and Piper is the youngest, but there are also some teenagers there as well. The oldest is in her seventies. A very diverse group of people from all over the world and Piper fits right in.

There are swim guides on the boat and two of them, Lisa and Cyndi, have a great connection with Piper. I have known Lisa from the past two seminars and she is amazing. She connected with Danny on our whale trip.

Super fun!

Piper is a good swimmer and Lisa says that she will stay with her. Cyndi will also keep an eye on her if the dolphins take her away or me away as they love to do. She is great in the water and I have so much fun watching her interact with the dolphins. They love kids and I can't help but feel as if I am watching a reunion.

Off she goes with a pod of dolphins.
She is a total mermaid.

Somehow, deep inside me, I know she is completely safe with the dolphins.

CHAPTER 78
WAY COOL STUFF

I'm choosing happiness over suffering, I know I am. I'm making space for the unknown future to fill up my life with yet-to-come surprises.
~Elizabeth Gilbert

There are so many wonderful healers out there in this world that have many different abilities. I have gone to many, mostly because I was curious how they work. I wanted to know other ways to heal rather than the established medical system of surgery and drugs.

Some of the healers that I have worked with are shamans, reiki healers, mediums, acupuncturists, energy healers, chiropractors, etc..

I have come to realize that they are all really doing the same thing.

They are running Source energy and working with the person's own energy at the same time. We accept this energy or not and heal what we want or are ready to. One energy healer, in particular, that I have found to shift energies, release old programs, release entities, and just get back to pure love and light quickly is a healer named Michael.

Honestly, he has shown me that we are powerful and can truly do anything when we are connected with Source. It is our resistance and old energies that keep us stuck.

I found him by asking my medium friend, Karen, who clears her energy after her sessions or just for life in general. She told me about him and it was about another six months or so before I felt guided to work with him.

When my session arrived with Michael, I had no idea what to expect. Since he was in Idaho and I was in California, we did everything over the phone. He began by helping me to get me in my heart space. I put my hand over my heart and saying, "Ahhh" three times. Michael began to make different sounds and open my chakras.

I sat at my desk in my house feeling tons of energy. I was surprised since he was so far away, but I know energy knows no boundaries. Michael began cutting energetic cords and clearing energies around my parents and I. I got so hot from his energies that I took off my sweatshirt and opened the sliding glass door!

This is amazing!
How does this work?

I continue to enjoy the session when in walks my husband. Not expecting him home, I turn around and look at him not saying anything.

In that moment, Michael says, "Whoa! The energy just shifted. Who walked in your room?"

How does Michael know this?
I am blown away.
He is thousands of miles away!

I am so intrigued. Michael has helped me with so many things in my life over the years. Sometimes, when I clear something with him, I see instant results in my external reality.

My husband decided to work with Michael, as well. He thought that he needed to go to the doctor and maybe have surgery for sciatic pain in his back/butt area that was going down his leg. Bruce was quite skeptical, but thought he would give it a try as he didn't want surgery.

When Michael began working on Bruce in his session, he says, "So Bruce, who is a pain in your butt?"

Bruce replies instantly, "My dad!"

Bruce had been dealing with his sick father for a while now. Apparently, it was becoming a pain in the ass for him! Michael cleared the energy of Bruce's dad and goes on explaining to Bruce how we put emotional issues that we don't deal with in our bodies. We think it is some other issue.

So wild!

A couple days go by and Bruce and I are going to lift some hay bails out of our truck. Before we move them, I ask Bruce how his butt and leg are doing. He looks at me strangely like he has no idea what I am talking about.

"Remember, you had that sciatic pain in your butt and leg?" I say.

"Holy shit!" He says. "It's gone. I haven't even thought about it since Michael's session."

This is way cool stuff!
I will tell one more story about him…

I was at work and so was Bruce. My mom was watching the kids and dogs. We had a new puppy, Yogi Bear, who was close to a year old.

They were all out playing when Yogi Bear ran down the hillside and yelped. He began limping on his back leg after that. My mom calls me and asks what she should do. She describes Yogi Bear to be in pain and limping, so I ask her to take him to the vet.

She does and they x-ray his leg finding a tear in his knee. They say he needs surgery and give him pain medications until we decide what to do. We are also to keep him contained to not worsen his knee.

I am bummed about this and I put my hand over my heart asking my guides for help with this. When I do, I hear clearly, "Call Michael."

Texting Michael, I ask him if he works on animals and it turns out that he does. I tell him what happened to Yogi Bear and he says that he will work on him and reverse the event.

Sounds great to me, but I am curious and cautious.

When I came home a day and a half later, Yogi Bear is running and jumping. He is playing like nothing ever happened.

I look at him in total amazement.
My mom shows me the x-rays and I can see the tear in his knee.
He seems to be completely healed now!

There are so many other amazing stories I could tell you about Michael. I gradually have a whole new awareness of how we can heal without surgery or medications. I have heard stories of shamans and yogis healing themselves and others almost instantly.

I have much to learn.

One of the biggest things Michael showed me was the power and connection of being in my heart space. It is in our human heart that we possess empathic intelligence. Our brain is merely monitoring what is going on around us and making sure that we are okay.

Our heart center has no distortions and when we connect to it, it empowers all of the other chakras.

The heart space is the great transformer.

The easiest way to connect to your heart space is to simply take a deep breath and put your hand on your heart. Keep it there as you are connecting to your heart which is where you will find Source. You can also say the sound "Ahhh" if you choose as that is the sound of the heart space.

Enter here to go within…

CHAPTER 79
SILVERBANK WHALES

When we contemplate the whole globe as one great dewdrop, striped and dotted with continents and islands, flying through space with other stars all singing and shining together as one, the whole universe appears as an infinite storm of beauty.
~John Muir

It's finally here!

Danny and I are headed for a week to the Dominican Republic to live out on a boat eighty miles off the coast where the humpback whales hang out in a place called Silverbank. This is a place where humpback whales come to mate and birth their young. They make the journey here every year from far north. It is crystal blue waters and not super deep.

We fly in and stay at a resort for a day before we meet up with the group. It's a beautiful day and we play in the resort pool. Danny loves this and he digs the "All you can eat" buffets, too.

The following day, we meet our group who will be going out on the live aboard boat for eight days with us. Everyone is super excited and we leave at night for the long crossing which takes about eight hours to get to Silverbank.

I look up before leaving the dock and the star, Arcturus, is right above us.

Hmmm…

I wonder if the Arcturians will be joining us out in the ocean.
They are so present in my world these days.
These off-world beings have so much to teach me.

Our first morning out, we learn about the smaller boats which will take us around to find whales. Each boat will have about eight people on them. We head out on our little boat with a guide and captain. Everyone is looking for the whales and we find some right away.

It's a mom and baby whale.

We all get in slowly with our guide and slowly approach the whales. Mom is down deep and we watch the baby come up and down for air.

The baby whale is just so incredible and you can feel how aware he is.
You can feel the sweetness and wisdom of this amazing being.
I am in awe.

The baby whale comes close to Danny and they look directly at each other. There are just no words for this interaction. Then, the mother whale comes up and we feel her incredible presence. We stay with them for a long time before they decide to move off.

In the water, on the way back to the boat, I ask Danny what that was like for him.

"Mom, my life will never be the same," he replies.

I can feel the magnitude in my body of what just took place between them and how I feel being with them as well. I breathe deeply into it all. There is something indescribable about being with the whales.

The space they hold.
Their presence.
Their wisdom.
A knowing that I know them.

We go out mornings and afternoons with the whales for days. They are long and incredible days. Sometimes, we have lots of whales and other days, few whales.

One morning, we found a "singer" whale. This is a whale who is singing whale song in the ocean. Typically, they are male. We are with him for hours and the vibration moving through our bodies is outta this world. The feeling of the sound throughout my body feels as if it is rearranging our DNA with every note.

I love sound and I am so happy to be here listening and feeling this whale song.

Another day, we are out on the water and suddenly, there are dolphins! All of us are so excited that we can't wait to get in the water. They are jumping and leaping. Danny and I get in the water and we swim with these joyful dolphins. They are a different energy than the wise whales. They are just so playful and you can feel their bliss.

We are diving and swimming with the dolphins when suddenly, three huge whales come right in front of Danny and I. They are playing with the dolphins and I stop to watch. I have to back up so I don't run into them and I know they are so aware of exactly where I am in the water.

It is a mom, baby, and an escort (auntie usually, or sometimes uncle) whale.

They are massive and they look at Danny and I.
They swim slowly and I can feel love coming from them.
I send them love and appreciation back.

I am just in awe once again and I feel honored to be in their presence.

It's a fascinating group of people who came to be with the whales, too. Many are from all over the world and they just love whales. Even more fascinating to me is that many of them are remembering past lives as whales while being on the boat.

The leader of the group, Joan, teaches us about the whales and she begins to tell a story about how when she brought a group last year, a spaceship showed up one night. She goes on to say that everyone was sleeping in their cabins and one guy from the crew saw the spaceship. He went around yelling and telling everyone to wake up because there was a big spaceship hovering over a bunch of whales.

Everyone was half asleep and in shock coming out of their rooms. They looked up and saw the spaceship. Joan telepathed with the spaceship and they said that they were downloading new information for the whales to sing into the Earth.

Fascinating.

So, is that why whales and other animals sing into the Earth?
Perhaps one of many reasons.
Who really are "the whales?"
Extraterrestrials, for sure!

She goes on to say that one of the guests on the boat was a man who was very intellectual and was an engineer. He just kept saying how he couldn't believe his eyes and that it didn't make sense. It didn't fit with his beliefs.

I found this story to be riveting. I thought about how many people don't believe in life from other planets or galaxies. It's just not in their belief system.

Fascinating, right?

And yet, proof of extraterrestrials is all around us even though the government hides much of it. All of our indigenous cultures knew and communicated with them.

Going back to the Arcturians in the beginning of this chapter, I found them to be quite present on the whale trip. Arcturus is in the Bootes constellation and is easy to find off the Big Dipper handle. I wondered if the Arcturians did lots of work with the whales or other creatures on our planet.

Expressing this to a friend on the trip, she laughed and then said she brought a book on this trip called *How the Arcturians Are Healing Our Planet* by Wayne Brewer. She was almost done with it and would give it to me to read.

I read most of it on the boat in a day as it was a quick read. The author talked about how he was working with the Arcturians to heal planet Earth by removing dense energies like reptilians and demons. He would work with the Archangels, Christed beings, and the Arcturians to remove these dark beings from our planet taking them to the light.

Finding this fascinating, I decided that I would try to do this with these beings as he taught you how to do this in his book. We were leaving and at the airport in the Dominican Republic when I decided I would try because we had some time waiting for our flight. My son and three friends from the seminar were all waiting for the same flight to leave for Miami.

Getting quiet and breathing, I tuned into the energies of the airport. I wondered if there were really these dark energies below us in the Earth. I went through his protocol, or so I thought from my memory, when suddenly a huge storm began to gust outside. The energies became dark and chaotic. I wondered what was happening.

It became so bad that they shut down the airport cancelling our flight and all other flights. It was really crazy and my son became upset. We would all have to stay another night and leave the next day. We had to pick up our luggage and while we waited, I began to wonder if what I was doing energetically had an effect on this shut down.

Nah.
Couldn't be.
Not that powerful.

Yet, something inside me could feel that I had awakened a hornets nest down below the airport. As I was doing this clearing, I felt they were pissed off and letting me know they weren't happy by causing a storm which shut down the airport.

Still I was skeptical.

Later that night, once we all found hotels, I re-read the part of the book on clearing again. It verified what I had felt. Turns out I missed some important steps of calling in the "good" beings and awakened the dark ones in the wrong order.

This was really a fascinating experience and opened me more to energies on other levels. I began to use his techniques all over the place and it worked well when I did it in the right order!

So, who are these Arcturians and why are they helping?
Perhaps they are ready to help us move into the next paradigm?
Maybe they are here to help us evolve and remind us of who we are?

CHAPTER 80
YOUR TIME TOGETHER IS DONE

Don't take anything personally. Nothing others do is because of you. What others say and do is a projection of their own reality, their own dream. When you are immune to the opinions of others, you won't be the victim of needless suffering.
~Don Miguel Ruiz

It is really interesting to me how what we experience in childhood follows us around in adulthood. It's like that energy is all around us and follows us. Watching my parents and their craziness of how they lived their lives, influenced me to never get married. As I mentioned before, I also decided that if I did get married, I would never have kids or get divorced.

These were my "vows" to myself.
I had a lot to live up to.
Funny the things we decide when we are young.

Then, life happens and throws you curve balls, fast balls, high balls, low balls, and even ones that have no names.

Yep.
All of it.

Basically, I realize that I am not in control even though I would like to be.
Talk about trust issues with the universe!

Anyways, Bruce and I were on the same page with staying married and doing whatever we could to work things out. Both of us came from divorced families and we both knew how horrible our experiences were. We wanted to keep our family together as I feel we were both reliving our childhoods as wanting a family that stayed together.

We were trying to do this for our kids.
I questioned my logic.
Can I make this marriage work?

Is this really the best decision though?

We loved each other, but at this point, it was more a brother/sisterly love.
We were good roommates and played house well together.

Something just wasn't right.
You shouldn't be married to your sibling.
Yeh, I said it!

Anyways, as mentioned before, we separated for a year in 2013 to 2014. We still lived together, but in separate rooms. We both worked as firefighters, so there weren't that many days that we were actually home together. It seemed to give us what we needed and the kids got both of us.

We were good to each other mostly.
Friends.
Or really just roommates.
Roommates with benefits sometimes.

Talk about a hard time of pulling the plug and letting go.

We decided to give it another try and I was going to do my best to come from love with him all the time. He had stopped drinking, but his anger was still over the top. Bruce tried to get me to fight with him, but I just found this pointless.

I decide that I need to make this marriage work until the kids were eighteen.

I can do this!
Why though?

I wanted to stay together because I am scared he will start drinking again and the kids won't be safe. I will sacrifice myself and my happiness for the kids.

Wow.
Really, Hydee?
Now, I am a martyr?
Yuck.
Aren't you past that yet?
Guess not.

Wondering if this is really the right thing to do for the kids, I realize that I am also not showing them a healthy, loving relationship. My gut is screaming that my soul wants to move on. Not long after we got back together, a friend of mine asked if I wanted to visit a medium that she loves in Beverly Hills.

"Sure!" I said.

I love mediums and all things out of this world as you know by now.

When I go in for my session with this medium, Kellee, I find her to be amusing, funny, and very outgoing. She is also a licensed psychotherapist. I ask her when her gifts of seeing the other side came in. She said she hit her head on a car, ended up with a traumatic brain injury, and was in the hospital for about a year. When she started to come back around, she was seeing and hearing spirits from the other side.

Cool!
I love this stuff.

Kellee is also an astrologer and does numerology. She had also asked for my husband's birthday as well as my kids.

I had no idea what to expect.

She starts off telling me all about me and my soul.
My journey here and why I came in.
My past lives and off planet lives.

I am blown away. I have never had a reading like this and it feels so spot on. I am getting goose bumps on and off. I get this when I hear or feel truth. My grandmother on my mom's side is in the room, too. She knows all about her and is right on with all of it.

Then, she drops a bomb on me.

"You aren't supposed to be married to Bruce anymore," Kellee states matter-of-fact.

Whuutttt?!

I am looking at her dumbfounded.
I need to make this marriage work for the kids.
I promised myself that I wouldn't get divorced.
My head is spinning.

She does say this in a very nice way and she is just so sweet. To hear someone tell you what you already know but don't want to acknowledge, felt like a nuclear bomb going off. It is like knowing there is an elephant in the room, but not acknowledging it.

And don't shoot the messenger!
I needed to hear this message.

Kellee goes on to tell me that she has looked at both of our charts and our relationship is complete. We came in to help each other heal and have kids together. She continues saying that our time together is done.

I don't like hearing this and no one can tell me what to do! I am in charge of my relationship not this astrology! My stubbornness comes out bigtime.

I ask her, "What if we want to stay together?"

She says, "You can, of course, as you both have free will. I am just telling you what your charts say and what your guides are saying. If you do decide to stay together, it will take a lot of work from you and you will be bringing in all the love as he is not capable."

I take this whole session in. She shared so much about my kids as well and it makes me feel honored that they picked me to be their mom. She shared about my soul path and where I am going. It was powerful. I knew I was in for some major changes ahead and I was trying to just keep going in my daily life as a wife, mother, and firefighter while keeping any type of change out.

"Well, good luck with that," I told myself as I realized that change is the only thing constant in this universe. I've never liked change as I had too much of it growing up.

I decide to just flow with whatever is coming my way.
I can feel divorce coming and even retiring from the fire department.
I really want to move to Hawaii and swim every day.
I just don't know how it will all happen especially with kids.

Kellee also saw different spiritual trips I would go on and said that I might be interested in a book called *Fractals of God* by Kathy Forti. It resonated with me and it was about Kathy's transformation from a near death experience. She was a therapist and when she came back from her near death experience, she began to bring in information from beings who were teaching her about new healing technology needed for this planet.

It was called *Trinfinity 8* and it was ancient Atlantean technology working with the subtle energies of our body system.

I went to Kathy and experienced *Trinfinity 8* directly from her. It was a powerful session and I kept seeing these three tall beings with purple capes and collars working with the energy of the machine and me. They were so loving and I felt like they were the Andromedeans. I wondered if I could bring this machine into the fire department to help the guys heal as you just needed an intention to heal and to hold onto two quartz crystals in your hands. I decided that I would experiment with more sessions and see how this could work.

The Andromedean beings felt so loving and healing to me. Each time I worked with *Trifinity 8*, I would feel and see these beings. Their presence is powerful. I have heard that our galaxy and the Andromedean galaxy are coming closer and closer together. Are they helping us now so it is easier when our galaxies come together? Are they healing us so that we can join the galactic community?

Sure feels that way!
Anyways, back to Bruce and I…

Bruce also decided to have a session with Kellee. She told him the same thing. Kellee said that we finished what we came in together to do and we should celebrate this instead of resisting it.

I hadn't thought about celebrating our marriage and all that came with it even if it ended in divorce. We accomplished our agreements together in this life. This is something to be proud of especially since we still got along so well and respected each other.

Celebrate completing our path together?!
What a fantastic idea!
I love this perspective!

Not long after all this, Bruce and I are separated again in early 2016. Our divorce was easy and final in 2017.

I feel free.
So free.
I had no idea how free.
It's like the chains binding me were finally removed.

Thank you, Bruce.

I am honored to have been your wife, lover, friend, and partner.
I am sorry for any hurts I caused you.
I forgive you for any hurts you caused me.
I love you from a deep soul level…always.
But our time together is done.

CHAPTER 81
MOTHER OCEAN

However, when you take a walk in the woods and fields, or go into the oceans, you will see other life forms around you that are much more aware of who you are. They change their response, and their DNA changes because yours is changing. Though you, all of nature becomes more available as the Living Library.
~Barbara Marciniak

I deeply love the ocean and all of her inhabitants.
There is something about it that draws me to her.
I have loved her since I was a kid.

We went to the beach often with my dad in Orange County, California. These were some of my favorite memories growing up and being in the water with him was so fun.

My brother and I were little and my dad would hold us up with his arms as the waves came. My dad would yell, "Wamera!" I never knew what it meant, but he would say it when there was a big wave. We would all laugh and just miss the big wave.

As I got a little older, my dad taught me to body surf and I loved this. Flying through the ocean then tossed and tumbled by her as the wave crashed on top of me. Sometimes, the waves were so big that I didn't know which way was up or down to catch my breath, but I always made it back on top.

Reminds me of how I went on many drowning calls over the years. Sparrow City had lots of beaches, so many people came to swim and surf. Sometimes, the rip current pulled people out and they became exhausted swimming against it instead of going parallel to it. Lifeguards were always busy and we got called when people drown. Many times, we were able to revive them.

A few times, I went on a "tombstone." This is where a surfboard is inverted in the water and sticking up. It is not good as there is a surfer attached to the other end under the water. It was pretty unusual though for a surfer to drown.

I can remember this feeling as a young adult of never wanting to die by drowning.

What is that?
Past life memory?

I have a vague memory of struggling in the water some lifetime ago. Thank goddess this memory eventually shifted and passed. It makes me wonder though if we get to choose how we die? Do we decide if it is it quick? Traumatic? Peaceful? Drawn out?

Well, if we pick all the other circumstances of our life, then we certainly choose our death as well!

One of my favorite things about being in the ocean is just allowing myself to float. Salt water keeps us buoyant and it is so freeing to float. Often, after swimming with the dolphins, I lay back in the water, look up to the sky, and just float on my back.

I am being held by the ocean.
Letting go into mother's arms.
Feeling loved and held.
Feeling freedom and oneness.
Trusting I am always taken care of.

Mother ocean is so vast and it is fun to float in the deep ocean. I can remember a friend saying to me when she saw me do this, "Aren't you afraid sharks will come up to get you?"

"No," I replied as it wasn't even in my consciousness.

It's really fascinating though because I feel that in our collective consciousness, there is a fear of sharks or a fear of the unknown. The movie *Jaws* was put out there in the 1970's and still makes people afraid of sharks.

I have swam with many sharks and I find them incredible. There is something about their electrical energy that intrigues me. Ancient Hawaiians revere the sharks and swam with them. What is it that we are forgetting about them?

Oh, and sharks remind me of dogs.
It's the way they are so curious and come right up to you sometimes.
Perhaps that is why the Hawaiians sometimes called sharks their pets?
I want them to teach me more about them.

When I was in my first "dolphin seminar" with Joan, we went out far off shore and found pilot whales. I had never swam with them and I was excited. Before getting in, Lisa mentioned to the group that sometimes pilot whales swim with Oceanic sharks and to just be aware.

I was curious about this and asked Lisa what does she do when she sees the Oceanic sharks. She replied, "I just make my energy big."

This made so much sense to me.
Make my energy "BIG!"
My energy body!

So, the sharks sense that your energy is bigger than theirs and leave you alone. Wow. It made me realize that I can do this in other situations with people or animals, too.

It gave me something to play with.
Fun!

Swimming with pilot whales was incredible and I heard their high-pitched sonar sounds. It sounded almost like a laser. They swam so beautifully in the deep blue ocean. People call them pilot whales because they often helped guide ships to shore in the fog.

I didn't see any sharks on that swim, but I felt them around.

Anyways, back to Mother Ocean…

I ask the ocean before getting in if it is okay for me to come in. Almost always, it is a "yes." Only a few times has there been a "no" and I feel it is when it is stormy or unsafe. I do this out of respect for her and myself.

One time, I was sitting on the beach and went into a tide pool. I stood watching the ocean and the waves coming in. It was so mesmerizing and I just looked at the ocean asking for a sign if she could hear me. Then, I waited for a reply.

My eyes looked down at the tide pool and I see a symbol again and again.

The vesica pisces.
I smile.
I love this symbol.
It is the beginning of the flower of life and to me, it represents the goddess.
Thank you, Mother Ocean.

Everything is always listening to us.

I remember a story a friend of mine named Dave who told me about a native American guy who was doing ceremony on the beach. The tide was coming in and getting close to his things, so the native American said a chant to the water.

Dave continued to tell me the story and said that the tide kept coming up, but where his ceremony was, the water never came close. The ocean went around it.

Amazing.

So cool, really.

Everything has consciousness and an intelligence within itself, even inanimate objects. Humans aren't the only intelligent species on the planet. In fact, I feel we are often the most ignorant of all the species on the planet because of our ego and competitive ways. We have forgotten how to work together like nature does.

Mother Nature listens to us and as we develop our relationship with her again, she will respond.

I was meditating one time and I saw myself as a twelve-foot beautiful, blue being coming from out of the ocean to land. I went to meet with a group of indigenous people there, and then I went back into the water.

Who am I?
What am I doing?
I love this memory and would love to understand it more.

I love the water.
Rivers, lakes, waterfalls, etc…
Mother Ocean.
We came from the ocean.

Remember?

CHAPTER 82
SASQUATCH LIVES

Go inside and listen to your body, because your body will never lie to you. Your mind will play tricks, but the way you feel in your heart, in your guts, is the truth.
~Don Miguel Ruiz

I don't know about you, but it seems that everyone has heard of Sasquatch, Bigfoot, or Yeti sometime in their life. There are sightings and stories of a big Chewbaccas roaming the forests and mountains from all over the world.

For me, I knew there were ETs (or extraterrestrial life) on other planets.
I just knew it.
I felt it.

And yet, for some reason, I didn't believe in the Sasquatch.

I don't know why either.
Well, shit was about to get real.

Anyways, I was on my first dolphin seminar in Hawaii. After the lecture part, I went and laid down outside while staring at the stars. It felt good and I was sinking into the land just feeling.

I was feeling grateful.

Feeling the ETs, I decided to ask for some contact from loving light beings. I breathed deeply and close my eyes. I just kept breathing and going deeper. Not sure know how long this was, but all of a sudden, I was wide awake.

I felt beings all around me.
Very large and loving.
I could see them.
Sasquatch!

My mind couldn't quite believe that they were real and yet, my whole body was basking in their love that they were radiating. I felt as if they came and were giggling, telling me, "Yep, we do exist."

Their presence was so powerful.
Ancient.
Loving.

The Ancient Ones…

This was my first encounter with them and I didn't realize that this would be the first of many. They would come in energetically and I felt as if they were guardians of Mother Earth.

I would call them Chewbacca from *Star Wars*.
I always loved Chewbacca.
Pure Bigfoot.

Speaking of powerful, loving beings, there is a group of extraterrestrials that are called the Hathors. I heard about them from Tom Kenyon and also from Egyptian times. There is something about them that is so familiar to me and I just love them like I do the Pleiadians.

It warms my heart to feel them.
I just love their ears.
Look up a picture of them and you will see what I mean.

From what I understand, the Hathors worked with the Goddess Hator in Egypt. The Goddess Hator was their sky goddess and cosmic force. Later on in Egyptian times, she became the fertility goddess of love, ecstasy, and bliss.

The Hathors apparently came through Sirius to Venus and then to Earth. They are about twelve to fifteen feet tall and in perfect balance. Hathors specialize in sound and frequency and are back on Earth to help us evolve by raising our consciousness. They can also move up and down the energy spectrum, disappearing from a space where a conflict may occur.

Just like the Sasquatch!

There is something to be said about the Hathors and the Sasquatch for not fighting or going against someone or something. They don't engage in conflict and it is not because they are scared. Instead, they raise their vibration using their consciousness in other ways. I now understand this as when you fight or go against something, typically you lower your vibration and strengthen what you went against. You signal the universe to keep bringing you more to fight against.

What you resist, persists.

When you keep your vibration up, you raise your consciousness staying in alignment with Source. This doesn't mean that you never stand your ground, but you hold the vibration of pure stillness. Anything that is not of this vibration will be transformed and transmuted. You are purely in the moment of what is occurring as pure presence is powerful.

There is a power in stillness.
You access your power becoming aligned with Source in pure presence.
You also hold space for the other to join you in a higher vibration.

Anyways, time passed and I forgot about the encounter with the Sasquatch. I got into other things spiritually and so many things were opening up for me. I would take hikes a lot and there was one hike that I frequented into the woods by my house. Sometimes, I brought my kids who were little and my dogs. Sometimes, it was just me with my dogs.

It gave me such peace to be in the woods.
To feel the trees and climb them.
To connect with the hawks above circling and screeching.
So magnificent.

There was a place off the path that went deeper into the woods and I always felt called to go into it. I would cross a fallen tree and go into a place I called the "Fairy forest." I always asked permission to enter as it felt like their domain. The trees held such a presence and it was pure Mother Nature.

I would sit back in this area and just be.
Sometimes I would meditate.

It felt like a portal where I could teleport to and from. I began to bring crystals there and burying them amongst the trees. I would bring offerings of food as well to thank all of them.

My daughter liked to come with me into the "fairy forest" and we would play. We would talk to them and sing. We would leave fruit for the fairies and trees when we left. One day, I said let's leave some fruit for the Sasquatch. My daughter got excited.

A few weeks passed and one day, I had gone to work at the fire station. After workout, I decided to take a walk around the fire station which was about a mile loop. It was close enough to run back if we got an emergency call.

As I walked, I saw a persimmons tree. It was in a neighbor's yard, but half of its fruit was hanging over the wall close to the street. So, I decided to pick one and eat it on my walk. I did this on and off for a few weeks. I would walk during work out and pick persimmons while they were in season. Then, one day, while eating the fruit, I felt a presence.

It was a large loving presence and I recognized it.

Sasquatch!
What?!
Here in Sparrow City?
How?

My mind wondered and my body felt.
They were coming to me.
I just stopped and felt them.
I asked them what they needed.

I didn't get an answer, but just felt their presence as if to say that they are around me sometimes. Their ancient presence held a very powerful energy signature. I telepathically told them that I would love to have more contact with them and to work with them.

About a week later while I am hiking back by my house, I am walking past some enormous Eucalyptus trees and I stop suddenly.

No way.
Really?

There is a persimmon sitting right next to a tree along the path. It is totally out of place and there aren't even any persimmons trees around here.

Feeling honored, I know it is the Sasquatch leaving me a gift and telling me they are here. I have the biggest grin on my face and I thank them telepathically. It is exciting to feel them here and I ask them how they get around. I see them showing me portals that they go in and out of.

Cool.
Makes total sense.

I wonder what portals are around my station that they came through. They must have brought the persimmons through with them. I somehow know they can make themselves invisible and visible as they desire by raising and lowering their frequency. This must be how there are so many sightings of them and then they just disappear.

We leave fruit for each other in this fairy forest and I am enjoying connecting with them. I know that I want to get into more environmental work helping the Earth. I wonder if this is why they are coming to me to teach me.

A few months go by and I am working at the fire station again. It is after dinner and I decided to go into my room to read. Laying down on my bed, I suddenly feel some energy in my room. I hear the sound of monkeys in my head and can see, in my mind's eye, Sasquatch!

Feels different to me and I sit with it.
It feels like they are outside my window now.
I wonder if they have some messages for me.
Hmmm…Sasquatch now in the fire station?!

The energy leaves and I read. It gets to be later and I decide to go to bed. Not long after, I am awakened for an emergency call coming over the speakers. It's 11 pm. I get my turnouts on and go out to the engine. I get in, see where we are going, and the type of call. This is part of my job as the fire captain.

My firefighter jumps into his seat and we are waiting for my engineer to get in as he is the one that drives us to the calls. He jumps in and says that his wife just stopped by late from a party and needed her tire filled since it was low. She will leave after we take off.

We are off with lights and sirens to our emergency and turn left out of our station. Off we go!

It is a normal routine call for us and we come back to the station and go to bed. The next morning at about 5 am, we have another emergency call come over the loud speaker.

My crew and I all come out of our rooms and onto the engine. It's a traffic collision and we head off. As we come back from the call, my engineer, Denny, says to Dan and I through our headsets, "I gotta tell you guys something strange."

He knows I love strange things and I can't wait to hear what it is.

He begins, "So, you know my wife, Nichole, came to the station last night to get her tire filled. Then, she left and got in her car right after we got the call."

"Yes," I answer.

He goes on to say, "Well, she watched us turn left out of the station. Then, she turned right on to the street to head home."

Denny says, "This is where it gets weird. As she passes the fire station, she turned on her headlights and to her right, a large creature that was crouched down, stands up in a ditch."

I am just so excited and can't wait to hear more.

He continues with his story, "She floors the accelerator and looks back in her rearview mirror. She says it looks like a ten-foot Bigfoot and it crossed the street going into some trees!"

"Holy shit!" I exclaim with a huge smile on my face! I was feeling Sasquatch last night

341

and this was them telling me that it's not my imagination.

They are very real!

Denny says to us that Nichole doesn't make this stuff up and she doesn't even believe in this stuff. He says she was really freaked out and worried for our safety. She called him last night right after we got back from our call.

I am all smiles.
I know they are here and any disbelief that was there at all is now completely gone.

Where the Sasquatch crossed the road was not far from my bedroom. I went out that morning and felt the portal they come in and out of. I had no idea and I had passed by it for years on my walks.

Portals.
Sasquatch.
I just fucking love this stuff.

CHAPTER 83
THE WORLD OF EXPECTATIONS

Actually, you invite all the players in your life, and you, as director, cast the parts and run the show. If you are now finally tired of your script, remember, you write it! Blame and victimhood are the ultimate traps to insure a state of disempowerment.
~Barbara Marciniak

I find expectations fascinating.

Often, when you expect something, you are let down. Yet, if you let your expectations go, the universe often surprises you by bringing something even better.

Ever heard that what we put our attention on is what we find in our reality?
This is an interesting concept that I have been contemplating.

I have always loved to just observe what people say. Sometimes, I feel like people don't even have a clue what they are saying, but are really a tape recorder repeating the same thing over and over in a different way.

It's like they are on auto pilot.

Captain Jay always had a lot to say and had opinions about many things. He was quite knowledgeable and could read people as well. Towards the end of his career, I was also a captain and I worked on an opposite shift as him. We would chat in the mornings when we did shift exchange about the calls we went on or about pertinent information we needed.

One thing he would always tell me was that they would go on a call around 2 am every morning. He hated this and wanted his sleep, but like clockwork, he and his crew would get up at 2 am. Another thing that he complained about was that he always had trouble with the computer. It just never seemed to work for him.

I pondered this and wondered if his words and expectations were creating his reality. Is he creating this call at 2 am and creating the problems with the computer?

Yes.
Yes, he is.
He expects this and the universe responds.

My step-mother Priscilla used to tell me in high school that what we think about is what we create. Our words are even more powerful than our thoughts. The vibrations that words hold, bring us the exact frequency back that we just put out into the world.

Remember plasma physics?

Plasma is just a "house of fields" that responds directly to our consciousness!
Mehran Keshe said that.
Plasma carries the electrical currents which create a magnetic field.
It collects as we put our attention on it.
Then, it becomes physical in the third dimension!

Everything is alive and listening!
Can you imagine that?!

We are gated by time, so we don't typically see these instant results, but the universe is already responding to our expectations and requests.

Or is time just an illusion?

I love this question, as depending on your point of attraction, things can manifest instantly or can "take time."

Mind-bender, right?!

It is like what Abraham-Hicks (or as I like to call her, "Esterham," since Esther is channeling a being named Abraham or Source), says how our positive or negative thoughts or words are bringing us what we said. The universe doesn't judge, but just follows the vibration.

The universe is simply following what we put our attention on and brings it to us for us to experience.

If we don't like it, we can create again!
And yes, we are really that powerful.

Wouldn't it have been nice to get a handbook of rules on how this universe works when you arrived?

Ummm…duh!?

Funny how we walk around this planet blind trying to figure out how this reality works. Let's take all this one step further…

So, we have all this chaos in the world. We see environmental destruction, overfished oceans, poisoned land, shortages, floodings, poverty, wars, etc…

We created all of this.
Why?
Because of our attention and focus on it!
Whatever we focus on gains power.
And really, because we wanted to experience it!

If we don't like it, let's create something different!

There really is no lack.
Only abundance.

All we need to do is put our attention on what we want. Focus on a healthy, balanced environment with abundant oceans. Focus that everyone is abundant and at peace. Vision all of this in your heart space, not your head.

And, ya know, when you do this, the universe is obligated to respond and give you this!

You got this!
We got this!

CHAPTER 84
TREES

The Earth is alive and contains the knowledge you seek. It is your consciousness that determines what it reveals. How to access this knowledge? And where are the keys to open it and make it yours? The Earth speaks. Love her, honor and respect her and she will reveal her secrets.
~Barbara Marciniak

There is something about trees that I have always loved…

Their strength.
Their wisdom.
Their silence.
Their incredible presence.

As a kid, I felt a kinship with trees. I would climb them as most kids do and swing from their branches. I could hear them calling me to them. I would listen to them giggle.

I love trees.

How could I have forgotten the tree beings and who they are? Why does it happen in this world that we forget our connection to life itself? Why do we project externally instead of more internally as we grow up? We get connected to what is outside of us instead of listening to the small, still voice inside of us!

Well, the majority of us forget our inner voice but, there are still those special people whose internal voice remained connected and powerful instead of falling away.

I want mine back!
I want to hear you and remember more.
Pretty please?!

I can hear the trees again. I can hear the voice of nature when I quiet myself and listen. They have been waiting patiently for me to listen again. As I do this, I remember my favorite tree in Texas when I was a kid. This tree helped me get through these tough years living with my mother and the emotional abuse I endured.

She was a big tree…maybe twenty feet tall and in our neighbor's yard. She had large branches that were easy to climb.

She was my mother…Mother Nature.

I would climb her when I needed to get away. If other kids were around, I would sneak away in the bushes and then climb up in her when they weren't looking. I would go high up in her and lay against her thick branches. I was like a cheetah sprawled out sleeping in the tree.

I could spend hours here. I would talk to my tree and spill my heart out to her. She would hold me and listen. She was powerful, yet gentle.

She loved me and I loved her.
I still feel her today.
I send her my hugs and love.

Maybe that is why the book called *The Giving Tree* is so popular with kids? She gives a boy everything she has as she loves this boy. She gives him everything until she is just a stump for him to sit on as an old man.

Look at what trees do for humanity. We use them for shelter, for furniture, for warmth, for healing, for food, for oxygen, for shade, for beauty, etc…

All trees are connected and I know the giant tree in my yard today feels my love. I talk to her all the time and hug her. I say, "Good morning" and "Good night" to her. I tell her my problems and ask her to help.

I know she talks to my tree in Texas.

The energy you feel when you walk into a forest is incredible. The intelligence of who the trees are and their stillness has no words.

I love to hike and talk to the trees.
I see them.
I put my hands on them.
I put my arms around them and hug them.
Sometimes, I kiss them.

It's fun to see what type of being is in a tree. There are times that I have seen the whales come through or a bear.

Everything is connected.
So many types of trees out there, even rainbow ones.

We must not forget the trees. They love humanity and give so much. They call in the rain and keep nature in balance. The trees can call in the wind or stop the wind. It is the humans who have cut down so many trees without replanting that has caused the imbalance of nature and erratic weather patterns.

Although, some people are planting more trees and making it their mission now. Yay!

I remember hearing a story about a guy that was a logger around 2013. He went to work one day and began cutting down trees. Except this day was different because he could actually hear the trees screaming as he cut them down.

This freaked him out and he quit that same day.
He became an environmentalist.

"Talk to us," the trees say.

Are you ready to remember?
They miss us and want us to talk with them again.
Talk to them whether we are kids or adults.
They are our ancestors.

CHAPTER 85
THE MALE GODDESS

What do I want? I want to accelerate my personal evolution. I want Spirit to assist me in a greater capacity. I want my body to regenerate itself. I want to emanate health. I am willing to give up difficulty so that I can be a living example of what humanity can be.
~Barbara Marciniak

I have learned to follow my heart.
Well, most of the time.

I do listen and follow what feels right. This took some time as I was never taught this and was mostly in my head!

In December 2015, I felt a calling to go to a conference in Estes Park, Colorado. It was going to talk about Native American wisdom, ETs, angels, sasquatch, crop circles, and other fun stuff that I love.

I went by myself as I enjoy meeting new people. It had been over twenty years since I had been back in Denver. The airport was rather strange with weird artwork on the walls depicting the end of the world. I wondered what was going on there.

A shuttle picked me up taking me to the hotel where the conference was and the drive up into the mountains was just so beautiful. Once getting there, I settled in and unpacked. It was late and my roommate hadn't arrived yet, so I went to sleep.

I met my roommate the next day and turns out that she was one of the conference leaders. The conference started and it was being led by native Americans. They opened it with drumming and that was powerful.

The conference had many awesome speakers and you could choose which ones you wanted to listen to. About mid-day, I went out to get water during one of the breaks. Standing by the water was this gorgeous man in his thirties wearing a dress. I had this immediate love/hate feeling that came over me. I was shocked by the intensity of emotions.

He was smiling and looking at me.

He then said, "Hi. I'm Grant."
I said, "Hi Grant. I'm Hydee."
I then spun on my heels and left!

I don't know what that was, but I decided to stay curiously open to see what my feelings were about.

There were many amazing people there and I got to know many of the presenters as we all ate together. I met a couple people there who I felt like I knew, but couldn't remember how.

Perhaps past lives?

The next day, I came down into my room during a break and I found my roommate there with Grant!

Ummm....
Yeh.

He was giving her some type of energy healing. Grant was also wearing a red and yellow patterned hat that was the same color as my backpack. This surprised me. He was once again sweet and kind to me. Grant was also quite funny. We engaged in some conversation for a minute and I left.

I thought this whole thing was strange.
And I like strange.
But, who is this guy?

I went to listen to a couple more speakers and during the last one, Grant sat next to me. He sat close and was being a goof ball. I was opening up to him.

After the speaker finished, Grant asked if I wanted to go down the hall to meet this other energy healer and I agreed. We walked out of the room and down the hall where there was a line of about five people waiting to see this energy healer. We stood in line as well.

Grant had gentle, yet powerful energy and I was still curious about my first initial reaction to him. He turned around and looked me in the eyes. I looked deeply into his eyes and suddenly, I started seeing visions of us together in Egypt.

I said, "I know you. Oh fuck, I know you!"
He says, "Go on. What do you see?"

I start crying as I see that he was a goddess and I was a god. We were lovers. I tell him what I see and he continues, "Keep going."

"You were the cat goddess, Bast. You were from the Lyra constellation. I was from Sirius and you left me! You all left me here!"

Suddenly, I realize this is why I had the initial love/hate response when I saw him!

Grant says that the dog people from Sirius protected the cat people from Lyra. He continues telling me things that I am seeing and that the cat people had to leave because the Earth's energy was shifting, becoming too dense.

Now, I am still learning about all these extraterrestrials out in the cosmos. Apparently, there are lots of galactic races like the Pleiadians, Hathors, Arcturians, Sirians, Grays, Orions, Andromedeans, Lyrans, insectoid type races, feline type races, and on and on it goes. Some of these races appear to be humanoid looking.

This makes me wonder…

What if galactic races came to Earth and colonized parts of it? What if we are the most recent humanoids that live here now? There were giants and those with elongated skulls here before us.

So, are galactic races really any different than someone from another country or race here on our planet? What if the current races on Earth were seeded from other places in the galaxy?

What if humans are intergalactic royalty?
So many questions!

When I first learned and had confirmation about ETs, I began to realize that we humans are powerful, too. I tended to think that the extraterrestrials knew everything since most had a higher perspective than us. Really though, we have been manipulated and our eyes veiled so that we don't see the richness of our universe or how powerful we are. Our hearts and minds haven not been connected to the galactic races.

And just saying…

Don't worship ETs.
You are sovereign.
Stand in your power.
Benevolent ETs will NEVER tell you what to do.

What if most of our human gifts haven't been unfolded yet because we haven't raised our vibration enough and instead stay at a lower, more dense frequency? Our superpowers are dormant just waiting to be awakened, but we need to stop killing each other first.

Where does our pineal gland fit into all this? It is our antennae that connects us with

353

the universe. It looks like a pine cone and many religions show symbology of a pine cone. Coincidence? I don't think so. Those in power have kept the masses from awakening to their power instead monopolizing it for their own power and profit.

Science has even found crystals in our pineal glands. Quartz crystals are used in computers for communication. Perhaps that is why we are using them too!? We don't need to go outside ourselves for information. All we need to do is to ask within ourselves.

Earth is really an amazing reality system.
Ask to be shown the beauty of this Earth.
The more we love ourselves, the more we can open.
Love is the most powerful force in the universe.

Our planet is going through a radical paradigm shift as I write this. Focus on yourself as when you make a major change in your personal reality, it affects the collective. When enough of us do this, we have a revolution of consciousness creating greater freedom. Radical shifts in the paradigm also cause spiritual emergencies giving way to spiritual emergences.

A sudden shift in your view of reality emerges and expands your perception!

It is our journey back to Source discovering our divine nature. As we do this, we let go of judgments, beliefs, and manipulations. Fear and drama dissolve as we realize that we don't need the game of victim/perpetrator any longer.

Well, I guess I will get off my soapbox now!
Back to Grant...

He is crying and remembering, too. We are hugging and crying in the hallway as we have found each other again in this lifetime. I have an overwhelming feeling of wanting to make love with him that feels like it came out of nowhere.

So, what do we do with this?
Did the universe bring us back together to release that old energy?
Where do we go from here?

We have dinner that night with everyone and we share lots of stories. I am still amazed to remember our life together.

Grant, this powerful, man goddess is here, Now!
Right in front of me.
He is very male.
He chose a beautiful male body.
And he loves to wear beautiful women's clothes.
He is totally sexy.

I take a deep breath and just remember who we were together. I wonder how many other people that we have lived lives with on this planet from different times and don't realize it.

Grant tells me about how he grew up in Texas and had to hide who he was until he was older. He is bisexual and knows he is a goddess. He came here to shift paradigms at this time, but it has been extremely hard on him. His family has disowned him.

Grant picked one hell of a mission this time around!
Haven't we all?!

I head to bed smiling that I met someone that I deeply loved in Egypt.
I have always loved Egypt.
Someday, I will go there again.
Thank you for the remembering.

CHAPTER 86
A NEW PHILOSOPHY

There are three ways to ultimate success. First way is to be kind. Second way is to be kind. Third way is to be kind.
~Mr. Rogers

Be kind.

Is this really a new philosophy or one that we have just forgotten? To treat people with kindness seems to have been forgotten by many. You feel the lack of kindness in the big cities where there are so many people rushing around and then you notice kindness when you go to small towns.

People in small towns wave to you as you are driving down the street. They acknowledge you even if they don't know you. They tend to be kinder and more talkative.

What happens to humans when we move to big cities?
Do we forget about being kind to others?
Does competition take over instead of helping each other?

I often think of a fire captain, Adam, whom I first worked with who was so kind and loving to everyone. When I first met him, he gave me a big welcoming hug and reminded me of Mr. Rogers. He had such a presence about him.

He had a great laugh that just kept on once he got started. I have to admit, I loved this guy, but I wondered how he ever made it through the fire department. Adam had been on the department for over twenty-five years by the time I got hired, and it was rough back then. Most guys were from the military and were hard on each other, especially if you were different, like Adam was.

There were stories of how Adam got picked on by gnarly captains when he was a firefighter. He wasn't the typical "man's man." Adam was very intelligent and witty. I realized this is how he got through those years as well as with a great sense of humor.

Now, I know that I have told you this in an earlier chapter, but I feel it bears repeating as it shows you just how Adam gets the bigger picture and doesn't just follow along like a sheep. He is a rebel, an agent of change, in his own way showing how the fire department could change if it wanted to. We are always evolving, but is society ready for that change?

Something to ponder.
Anyways…

Adam told me one time, "Don't be surprised if I tell you not to go into a building on fire."

"What?!" I said, as I was a new, gung-ho, rookie firefighter that wanted to fight fire.

He goes on, "Well, you see, if there is no one inside the building, it makes no sense to put us at risk. Most of the buildings that burn are all knocked down. We could fight the fire from the outside and just keep it from spreading."

I knew he was right, but I had never heard a firefighter talk this way about fire.

New thought and new ideas.
Evolution of consciousness.
Are we ready?

Adam loved to be kind and help others. He loved kids and had a fire education program for young ones where he used puppets. Adam even had a remote controlled fire hydrant for his programs! Kids and teachers loved him. He was the fire education captain for many years and schools would call to schedule him for his puppet programs all the time.

One time, when he was my captain, the battalion chief came over to talk to Adam. They went into the front office and we could hear the chief yelling at Adam. Then, he was screaming at Adam! This went on for about an hour and even into dinnertime. We called Adam on the intercom a few times telling him dinner was ready.

Finally, Adam and the chief came out of the room. Adam looked super happy and cheery. The chief looked stressed out and angry. When the chief walked out of the station, Adam just said with a total straight face, "Thanks, Jack, for stopping by!"

I couldn't believe he said that. We laughed out loud once the chief was gone. He taught me a valuable lesson as to never lose your cool and to always be kind no matter what.

Adam really did have a philosophy of peace and being kind.
He was full of love and acceptance.
He loved to help others.
He really was the Mr. Rogers of the fire department.

I know people make fun of Mr. Rogers, but he was really a trendsetter in his time. He went out to make a show for kids where kids could love and accept themselves no matter what was going on in their lives. He respected kids and they could feel it.

Their opinion mattered.
By accepting them, the kids feel good about themselves.

So much of today's television programming doesn't make you feel good about yourself. Mr. Rogers set out to change that. I was one who watched his program as a kid. Thank you, Mr. Rogers!

I asked Adam about a lot of things over the years. When I was pregnant with my first child, I asked him if he had any advice about raising kids since he had four of his own.

He told me that his mother gave him the best advice ever and she had six kids. It was...

Do for.
Do with.
Stand by.
Let go.

I was confused. He continued, "You do everything for the child in the first years. Then, you do everything with the child until they are about twelve. In their teenage years, you stand by them and help as they ask. Finally, when they are an adult, you let go and trust they will find their way from all you have taught them."

Wow.
So simple and so perfect.
If only more parents could follow this.

I am grateful for Adam and all he taught me and for Mr. Rogers, too. Thank you to both of them for reminding me to always...

Be kind.

You just never know what others are going through.

CHAPTER 87
ONENESS

Love is a state of Being. Your love is not outside; it is deep within you. You can never lose it, and it cannot leave you. It is not dependent on some other body, some external form. In the stillness of your presence, you can feel your own formless and timeless reality as the unmanifested life that animates your physical form. You can then feel the same life deep within every other human and every other creature. You look beyond the veil of form and separation. This is the realization of oneness. This is love.
~Eckhart Tolle

I have had this feeling with me ever since I was born in this body of being part of the oneness.

It's strong.
Really strong.
And I have yearned for it since I have been in a body.
It's a deep calling.
Calling me "home."

I had been to a few different seminars swimming with whales and dolphins when a good friend of mine asked me to help out in her seminar. She told me that the only way she would do the seminar is if I would help.

"Sure!" I said. "Happy to help."

I had no idea what that meant or why I had to be at her seminar. She wanted me to be a swim guide and help people in the water.

No problem.

The seminar was in February of 2016 and as it got closer, I was questioning why I was going. I knew I needed to be there, but it was a different feeling. It was a peaceful feeling with no expectation and no wants. I would be gone ten days and Bruce and the kids were good with me going, although Piper really wanted to come. When I got to Hawaii, I felt at home. It was a feeling of aliveness and curiosity. I met up with friends that I had met before at prior seminars and went to dinner with them.

Lisa, who was a swim guide from past seminars, was there and we were excited to see each other. She knew my kids and I could feel her kid at heart. I would be working with her on this seminar as she was a swim guide too. Lisa was also an incredible underwater photographer who often captures the soul of the being in the photograph.

After a great night's sleep of listening to the ocean, I met up with my friend, Sheri, who was running this seminar. We had connected the first time both of us swam with dolphins and now she was bringing a group of twenty-five people to the Big Island.

She was stressed and was hoping all would go well. I knew it would and then she told me she needed me to play a bigger role in her seminar besides being a swim guide. She wanted me to lead meditations for the group and do more of the right brain stuff. This would allow her to teach the left brain type stuff that she loved.

I was game and happy to.

The week was great and amazing. I witnessed so many people going from having their walls up to hugging and laughing with each other. I felt their hearts open. The swims with dolphins were awesome and the lectures and meditations were powerful.

I was grateful that I was there to be a part of it all and to witness so much transformation.

One day, while we were out swimming with dolphins and getting the people back on the boat, Lisa and I felt and heard a humpback whale really close. We got really excited and stayed out a little longer to see if we could see the whale. Suddenly, Lisa grabbed my hand and pointed down.

Below us, silently swam a beautiful humpback whale.
Just magnificent.

We had a group dinner the night before it was all over. We laughed and cried with many people in the group getting up to say how grateful they were to have Sheri, Lisa, Celeste, Donald, and myself help out. They spoke from their heart.

I had no idea what was coming next.

We were all in a circle with Sheri in the middle. Sheri had her eyes closed and people were saying beautiful things to her. She was crying. It was amazing. Then, someone decided to break the circle and hug Sheri while still holding hands with the group. The group began to spin around in a circle with Sheri in the middle.

We went around and around until everyone was one still holding hands.

I could feel it in my whole body…Oneness.

I thought I had to die to truly feel part of the oneness again, yet here I was…breathing, pulsating as one group with about thirty people. In fact, it reminds me of the scene in the movie, *Avatar*, where the indigenous group was around their tree and moving in sync together. It was a powerful scene for me as it I could feel their oneness.

Back to the oneness of our group with Sheri…

I began to cry.
Tears of joy.
We were one with Source moving in synch with each other.
Oneness.

I realized that I can experience this feeling while still alive. As you can see throughout this book, I have had other experiences with oneness while making love, swimming with dolphins, experiencing past lives, or working with plant medicine. There is still something about this feeling of oneness that I long for and I feel it when I meditate aligning to Source. How do I feel it all the time? I realize that it is a vibration and the more I keep my vibration in one of joy and bliss, I feel this oneness.

Is that what the statement, "You must be like a child to enter the Kingdom of Heaven" (not the exact quote, but close) in *The Bible* means? The "Kingdom of Heaven" is really becoming one with Source? We can enter it now while alive if we live in wonderment, simplicity, and joy?

Be like a child to be in oneness.

On the level of oneness, I am drawn to the subtitle that came in so strong for this book…Awakening the Dragon Within. I feel that there is an embodiment the dragon holds of all of the elements within itself. This book is named Fire and Water which seem to be opposites yet, there is a blending of the two.

Two sides of the same coin.

It reminds me of the fire triangle which is what I learned in the fire academy of needing fuel, heat, and oxygen to have a fire. If you take away one of these sides, the fire will go out. Then, firefighters realized that there is a fourth component for creating fire and called it the fire tetrahedron. The fourth component is a chemical chain reaction and seems to be more unknown as to how this was realized.

This makes me think of the four elements of Earth, fire, water, and air and how there is a fifth element in there. In the Western culture, there are typically four elements recognized and in the Daoist cultures, there are five elements which are wood, Earth, metal, fire, and water. The elements are still teaching me about themselves, but I feel the fifth element is Source.

To me, Source is the dragon energy that comes in with its chemical chain reaction or pure power.

There is a mastery with the four elements and how to work with them as they are all alive with a consciousness of their own. To me, the dragon is mastery with these elements and really, it is mastery of oneself.

It is the mastery of being in one's own power.

I am still learning about this dragon energy as it awakens more inside me every day. It is interesting as Christianity has made dragons bad and many of us are fearful because of this religious belief. Even in the kid's movie, *How to Train Your Dragon*, humans are fearful of dragons and attack them. In the movie, one young man learns about dragons and teaches the village how dragons are just misunderstood. He regains his power as do the dragons.

Perhaps a dragon is a metaphor for your power? Are you scared of your power and being powerful? The elements of nature teach us how to step into our power and perhaps the word "Dragon" is really someone who has fully stepped into their power? You have mastery over yourself and your power?

You have awakened the dragon within.

Kundalini comes to mind as well and I wonder if this is the merging of all the elements within oneself as you awaken with Source? Is kundalini seen as a dragon? I know often it is seen as snake-like energy winding up through our spines merging with the cosmos. Is this energy aligning all the elements within ourself back to Source?

It all goes back to awakening our power within.
Also known as...awakening the dragon within.

I realize that there are many truths and no absolute truths. There are deeper meanings to everything and many multidimensional layers of truth within teachings depending on your perspective.

This fascinates me.

The more we evolve our consciousness and our vibration, the wider the perspective. Power is truly the ability to direct energy for creating, destroying, and regenerating. Everything is looking for power.
There is unlimited power when staying aligned with Source within.
True oneness.

CHAPTER 88
WHAT'S HAPPENING?

To come upon love without seeking it is the only way to find it.
~Krishnamurti

Sometimes life has a way of deciding when certain things are done. You can either flow with it or fight it. Deep down you know what your soul wants even if your mind can't figure things out. I've learned to let go as the universe always has a better plan in mind than I could ever figure out for myself.

I wasn't like this always though.
I used to push against the waterfall of water trying to go upstream.
Maybe as I get older, I finally got wiser?
Sometimes.

So, you know how I said that I just needed to be there at Sheri's seminar? I trusted even though I didn't know why. So many things happened in those ten days that blew my mind and my heart was just so open. I am being incredibly vulnerable here sharing my inner world with all of you in this book and I will share one last experience.

During the ten days of the seminar, Lisa, from the prior chapter, and I hung out a lot together. I remember when I first met her. It was February 2014 and it was my first dolphin seminar. I walked into the seminar and Lisa came bounding up to me.

"Hi! I know you!" Lisa says.
I am surprised by this and I look at her smiling.

"Hi. Why yes, I know you too," I reply.

Somehow, I know her on a cellular level.
I can feel that we have known each other somewhere before.
Something is very familiar with her.
Was this a past life?

I realize that I mention past lives often when I have familiarity with someone. It is interesting to think about as really there is no past or future. All is going on right now as time is just a specific group of frequencies in one location. We are multidimensional beings having many experiences right now!

So, fast forward to 2016 when we are at dinner the first night before the seminar. Lisa tells me she is dating someone and he is in the next town over from where I live in California. She will be coming a week after the seminar to California. We plan to meet up and she can see the kids again.

We carpool during the seminar and talk a lot about our lives, sharing deeply throughout. We have lots of fun.

About mid-week, I notice something is happening.
What's happening?!
There is this energy between Lisa and I.
It's powerful and I hadn't felt it so strong before.

I know her.
I really know her.

I notice during the seminar that we are both always close to each other and drawn together no matter where we are.

What's happening?!

I still can't wrap my mind around this feeling. I wonder if she is feeling what I feel. I finally ask her on the second to last day of the seminar as we drive back from the boat.

"There is this energy between us that I feel," I say. "Do you feel it?"

She is driving and puts it back on me.

"Yeh, I feel it. What does it feel like to you?" She says.

Oh goddess.
Damn.
She put me "on the spot."
What do I say?

I take a deep breath and reply, "Well, it feels all encompassing. It feels sisterly, friendly, motherly, childlike, and…like lovers."

I can't believe I just said this.
We are close and I don't want to mess up a friendship.
Help!

"Oh, I feel all of that," she says very matter-of-fact.

Thank goddess she met me there.
My mind is racing.
Now what?
I said all that and what do we do with this energy?

As she drove, I began to see in my mind's eye the energy that had been there all along in our relationship, but I never was really ready to see it.

Had she?

We don't talk anymore about this energy, but we can't stop being drawn together. We laugh, play, and I am sad as I am only here for another two days before heading home to California.

Fuck.
What's happening?!

The group in the seminar parts ways which is always sad. We watched Lisa's video that she made of everyone swimming with dolphins and do one last group share. It's powerful.

It's time to part ways from Lisa.
My heart screams, "NO!!!"

She doesn't want to leave me either. We will see each other again in a week in California when she comes to visit. Somehow, this gives me some peace.

I go back to California and it is harder and harder to be there when my heart longs to be in Hawaii. It is especially harder this time. So strange for me as I have always loved California, but something is telling me that Hawaii is calling me there.

I am so happy to see my kids and Bruce. I have missed them and yet, they are always with me. How do I keep Hawaii always with me?

What am I doing back in California?
I can't get my grounding.
I am in tears for two days on and off.
Something isn't right.

Finally, I ask myself while sitting in my car in the parking lot of a bank.

"What is going on?" I ask myself inside.
"Why can't I get ahold of myself?"
"What do I need to do?"

I am sobbing and listening...

"Speak your truth, Hydee. Speak your truth," I hear from inside myself.

Speak my truth?
What is my truth?
Oh goddess...
I know my truth!

I have to tell her how I truly feel about her...

To be continued in the next book, Sacred Union.

GLOSSARY

Alarms: These are designations to call more resources. More alarms is more resources.

Ambu bag: A bag used to help a person breathe.

Battalion Chief: A chief who is in charge of a battalion which is typically five or six station captains and crews. Their rank is above a captain and below an assistant chief.

Captain: The firefighter who is in charge of the station, crew, their safety, and emergency calls. Their rank is above an engineer and below a battalion chief.

Chief: The head of the fire department.

Code 3: Driving lights and sirens while not having to obey typical driving laws.

Coded: A term to describe a person who has died. They are not breathing and have no pulse.

Engine: A vehicle with lifesaving equipment, hose, and water.

Engineer: The firefighter who drives the fire engine and is in charge of taking care of the fire engine. Their rank is above a firefighter and below a captain.

Firefighter: The firefighter who has the least sonority and does most of the "grunt" work.

Firefighter/Paramedic: Same as the firefighter, but is also a paramedic.

Fire hydrant key: A tool used to shut off a water valve. It is about seven feet tall and looks like a "T".

Flashover: Conditions when a fire heats up all of its contents inside a building to ignition temperature and spontaneously bursts into flames.

Incident commander: The person in charge of an incident.

On air: When firefighters put their masks on and connect to the air in their SCBA bottles to typically go into a building on fire or some other unsafe respiratory hazardous environment.

RIC: Abbreviation for rapid intervention crew which is dedicated for rescuing firefighters.

Rookie (Probationary firefighter): A new firefighter on probation for a year having to pass tests and show that they can do the job.

Salvage and overhaul: A process once the fire is out of saving things that are okay and removing things that are burned. Firefighters also make sure anything smoldering is completely extinguished.

Salvage cover: A large tarp to protect important things from damage.

SCBA: A bottle full of air and a mask that firefighters use to breathe in fires and other hazardous environments.

Sector: An area that a fire station/engine covers in a city or county for emergency calls.

Stage: To stay somewhere safe (usually a block away) before going into an emergency call that is unsafe.

Tactical front: The front of the building on fire.

Take command: Take over as incident commander of an incident.

Triage: To put patients into categories from least to most critical.

Truck: A vehicle with lifesaving equipment, ladders, and extrication equipment.

Turnouts: Protective clothing that firefighters wear into fires.

Ventilating/Ventilation: To cut a hole in the roof to release hot smoke and gases.

Ventricular Fibrillation: Where the heart has no rhythm except to quiver before going flatline.

Resources Cited

Andy Basiago: Chrononaut, speaker, lawyer, writer, visionary, and whistleblower
Projectpegasus.net

Jean-Luc Bozzoli: Visionary, shamanic artist, and filmmaker
Eyewithin.com

Wayne Brewer: Author, healer, and investigator
Waynebrewer.net

Michael Dake: Master Alchemist, Reiki Master/Teacher, long distance healing facilitator, and soul flow
regeneration master
Dakeiteasy.com

Lisa Denning: Author, ocean guide, photographer, and producer
Lisadenning.com

Karen Glass: Medium, energy healer, and spirit guide
Karenglassmedium.com

Kathy Forti: Ph.D., licensed psychotherapist, author, and Trinfinity 8 designer
Trifinity8.com

Bruce Lipton: Ph.D., scientist, author, and speaker
Brucelipton.com

Penny Kelly: Author, counselor, naturopath, researcher, and consciousness
explorer
Consciousnessonfire.com
Patreon.com/pennykelly

Tom Kenyon: Author, teacher, channel, and sound healer
Tomkenyon.com

Barbara Marciniak: Channel, speaker, and author
Pleiadians.com

Joan Ocean: Psychologist, author, shaman, and scientist
Joanocean.com
Etfriends.com

Don Miguel Ruiz: Spiritual teacher and author
Miguelruiz.com

Mary Soliel: Speaker, author, visionary, channel, and gazer
Marysoliel.com

Jill Bolte Taylor: Neuroanatomist, author, and speaker
Mystrokeofinsight.com

Eckhart Tolle: Spiritual teacher and author
Eckharttolle.com

Brian Weiss: Psychiatrist, past life hypnotist/teacher, and author
Brianweiss.com

Kellee White: Medium and licensed psychotherapist
Kelleewhite.com

Movie: What the bleep do we know?
Whatthebleep.com

Bibliography

Bradley, Marion. *The Mists of Avalon*. Ballantine Books. 1983.

Brewer, Wayne. *How Arcturians are Healing Planet Earth*. Wayne Brewer and Associates, Inc. 2012.

Fomenko, Anatoly. *History: Fiction or Science Volumes 1-8*. Mithec. 2004-2015.

Forti, Kathy. *Fractals of God*. Rinnovo. 2014.

Kelly, Penny. *Consciousness and Energy Volume 1-4*. Lawton: Lily Hill Publishing. 2006-2019.

Kelly, Penny. *The Evolving Human*. Lawton: Lily Hill Publishing. 2006.

Kelly, Penny. *"Plasma, Consciousness, and the Nature of Reality: Part 1-3."* April 14, 2020. Patreon Website: patreon.com/pennykelly

Kenyon, Tom and Kennedy, Wendy. *The Great Human Potential: Walking in One's Own Light*. Ariane Editions. 2013.

Kenyon, Tom. *The Hathor Material*. Orcas: ORB communications. 1996.

Kenyon, Tom and Sion, Judy. *The Magdalen Manuscript: The Alchemies of Horus and the Sex Magic of Isis*. Orcas: ORB Communications. 2002.

Lipton, Bruce. *The Biology of Belief*. Carlsbad: Hay House. 2008.

Marciniak, Barbara. *Earth*. Santa Fe: Bear and Company Publishing. 1995.

Ocean, Joan. *Dolphins into the Future*. Kailua: Dolphin Connection. 1997.

Ruiz, Don Miguel. *The Four Agreements*. Amber-Allen Publishing. 1997.

Taylor, Jill Bolte. *My Stroke of Insight*. Penguin Group. 2009.

Tolle, Eckhart. *A New Earth: Awakening to Your Life's Purpose*. Penguin Group. 2005.

Weiss, Brian. *Many Lives, Many Masters*. Fireside. 1988.

ABOUT THE AUTHOR

Hydee Tehana is really just a big kid in an adult body who sometimes acts her age while exploring this amazing universe. Her favorite age to be is eight because eight reminds her of being playful and full of wonder. She has had an amazing life with all of the ups and downs. And now, more and more ups!

She remembers the greater meaning of life and what it was like on the other side while taking on a human incarnation this lifetime. Hydee loves adventure and travel along with swimming in the ocean with her ocean friends as much as possible. Time travel and teleportation are close to her heart.

The author loves the fire elemental as well as all the elements. She has a deep connection with all of Mother Nature. Hydee was a Captain/paramedic in the fire department for just over twenty years. She also has her master's degree in psychology and is a licensed psychotherapist. Hydee is currently working on authoring books, producing enlightened movies, and most importantly, expanding her consciousness.

Knowing that we are in a huge transition right now on this planet, Hydee comes from her heart contributing her light and love to the major shift that we are all going through. She knows one day soon, we will all be teleporting, flying, shapeshifting, instantly manifesting, etc.. with our physical bodies. Basically, we will have our super powers once again when we let go of all our baggage and remember who we truly are! We got this!

To contact Hydee Tehana:

Hydeetehana.com
hhtehana888@protonmail.com

Made in the USA
Las Vegas, NV
01 June 2023

72812610R00216